A PASTORA[…] ON *Sacrosanctum Concilium*

THE *Constitution on the Sacred Liturgy* OF THE Second Vatican Council

Joshua Brommer • Joseph DeGrocco • Michael S. Driscoll •
David W. Fagerberg • Mark Francis, CSV • Genevieve Glen, OSB •
J. Philip Horrigan • Steven R. Janco • Corinna Laughlin •
Paul Turner • Mark E. Wedig, OP • Joyce Ann Zimmerman, CPPS

WITH A FOREWORD BY

ARCHBISHOP GREGORY MICHAEL AYMOND

LTP
LITURGY TRAINING PUBLICATIONS

Nihil Obstat
Very Reverend Daniel A. Smilanic, JCD
Vicar for Canonical Services
Archdiocese of Chicago
July 12, 2013

Imprimatur
Most Reverend Francis J. Kane, DD
Vicar General
Archdiocese of Chicago
July 12, 2013

The *Nihil Obstat* and *Imprimatur* are declarations that the material is free from doctrinal or moral error, and thus is granted permission to publish in accordance with c. 827. No legal responsibility is assumed by the grant of this permission. No implication is contained herein that those who have granted the *Nihil Obstat* and *Imprimatur* agree with the content, opinions, or statements expressed.

Printed in the United States of America.

17 16 15 14 13 1 2 3 4 5

Library of Congress Control Number: 2013943772

ISBN: 978-1-61671-134-4

PCSC

The Church earnestly desires that all the faithful be led to that full, conscious, and active participation in liturgical celebrations called for by the very nature of the liturgy. Such participation by the Christian people as 'a chosen race, a royal priesthood, a holy nation, God's own people' (1 Pt 2:9; see 2:4–5) is their right and duty by reason of their baptism.

—*Sacrosanctum Concilium,* 14

Contents

FOREWORD *Archbishop Gregory Michael Aymond* vii

PASTORAL NOTES An Introduction to this Resource
Corinna Laughlin xiv

Introduction: (SC 1–4)
Paul Turner 1

Chapter I: General Principles for the Reform and Promotion of the Sacred Liturgy (SC 5–46)
Joshua Brommer, Michael S. Driscoll, David W. Fagerberg, J. Philip Horrigan, Corinna Laughlin, and Mark E. Wedig, OP 7

Chapter II: The Most Sacred Mystery of the Eucharist (SC 47–58)
Joyce Ann Zimmerman, CPPS 77

Chapter III: The Other Sacraments and the Sacramentals (SC 59–82)
Mark Francis, CSV 97

Chapter IV: Divine Office (SC 83–101)
Genevieve Glen, OSB 115

Chapter V: The Liturgical Year (SC 102–111)
Joseph DeGrocco 143

Chapter VI: Sacred Music (SC 112–121)
Steven R. Janco 155

Chapter VII: Sacred Art and Sacred Furnishings (SC 122–130)
J. Philip Horrigan 173

Appendix: Declaration of the Second Vatican Ecumenical Council on Revision of the Calendar (SC 131)
Corinna Laughlin 187

ADDITIONAL QUESTIONS FOR DISCUSSION AND REFLECTION 192

ABOUT THE AUTHORS 194

INDEX 201

Foreword

Archbishop Gregory Michael Aymond

There are some who claim that it takes a century to fully implement an ecumenical council. Whether this is true or not, fifty years certainly provides ample perspective to consider what happened at the Second Vatican Council and its continued impact today. Fifty years of perspective have much to teach us regarding *Sacrosanctum Concilium* (SC) and the liturgical reform it enabled. This perspective is, perhaps, all the greater because of the diverse voices which have sounded in the years since 1963, when SC was promulgated. Those voices have varied from exhilaration at the changes, to disappointment that there were not more changes, to dismay that there were any changes. Still to this day, there are voices who critique and call for reevaluation, as well as voices who praise and celebrate the reform. This cacophony of voices speaks to the diversity of experiences of the liturgy (good and bad), as well as the diversity of desires within the human heart. Where charity prevails, these contradictory opinions contribute to the deepening perspective we have gained in the years since 1963 as the story of salvation, enacted in the liturgy, continues to bear us onward toward fullness of life in Christ (see Ephesians 3:19).

In the pages that follow, reputable scholars of the liturgy bring their considerable talents to bear in providing commentary on and evaluation of *Sacrosanctum Concilium*. With this brief introduction, I would like to highlight six areas where the liturgical reform flowing from this document has impacted diocesan and parish life, both cleric and lay, professionally and spiritually. These will be reflections that come from a pastor's heart and with an eye toward the effect of the reform in the Christian's ordinary liturgical life.

I. The Vernacular

Perhaps one of the greatest changes called for by SC was the turn to the vernacular, which the generations since have overwhelmingly embraced. It is true that, while the Council Fathers did not call for the complete vernacularization of the liturgy, nevertheless, they did open the door to and welcome the use of the mother tongues of the faithful. Because of this change, the laity not only continue to encounter the risen Lord in the liturgy (something they certainly did in Latin as well), but now they are able to discuss with one another and with the priest how a particular Collect affected them, or how the Preface touched them, or how the words of their own responses in the Gloria or the Creed continue to sink more deeply into their spirituality. The spirituality of priests is similarly affected as they are able to carry with them the words of the Eucharistic Prayer in a more personal way than was possible with Latin. Because of this change, parish ministers in the United States have a wealth of resources readily available to them in English for preparing the liturgy. Using a new language, for example, has required new music to fit the new words. Not all of the music used in the liturgy since 1963 has been of uniform quality, but the increased variety of musical genres and cultural styles of music have been a tremendous enrichment for the Church, plus over the years certain hymns have proven their worth and become Catholic classics in English. This will surely continue to happen. More recently, we see a growing availability of English-language chant, which may be one way of fostering a bridge for pre- and post-Conciliar liturgy.

II. Sacred Scripture

With the monumental expansion of biblical texts in the post-Conciliar liturgies, Catholic biblical literacy has grown tremendously in the past fifty years. The greatest expansion has been in the *Lectionary for Mass*, especially with texts from the Old Testament, but with the advent of a three-year cycle for Sundays and two-year cycle for weekdays, a greater percentage of the New Testament is also proclaimed regularly now. Besides the greater familiarity and study of the Word by Catholics, another indication of the success of the Lectionary is the fact that so many other Christian denominations have followed suit with a "common Lectionary" nearly identical to the Catholic one. More and more pastors from other Christian communities have seen the pastoral benefit of having a rhythm of scheduled weekly readings that do not rely on the whim of the pastor, but take the whole community through much of the Bible over the course of three years.

The rituals of the sacraments are now enriched by a Liturgy of the Word, something that was not previously a regular part of the sacramental rites. This turn to the Word in the liturgy has encouraged Catholic Bible studies in parishes around the country and led to an explosion in resources for such Bible studies. In recent years, renewed attention has been given to the importance of interpreting the Word precisely in its liturgical context, even to the point of saying that the liturgy gave birth to the New Testament in the sense that the apostolic period put the New Testament books together specifically for the liturgical event and under its inspiration, that is, under the inspiration of the Paschal Mystery as a celebrated, ritual event. Certainly, the development of scriptural studies, greatly spurred by Pope Pius XII's 1943 encyclical, *Divino afflante spiritu,* was key in leading the Church toward and through the Second Vatican Council, nevertheless, the *Constitution on the Sacred Liturgy* represents more than a sanctioning of what was already occurring. It also was a tremendous help in promoting Scripture for the Church. The recent decision by the United States bishops to revise the *New American Bible* with a view to having one scriptural translation for liturgical proclamation, catechetical use, and personal prayer illustrates how closely tied together are liturgy and Scripture.

III. The Divine Office

One of the major revisions mandated by SC, but which is unfortunately less well-known by the laity, is the reform of the Divine Office, more commonly known as the Liturgy of the Hours or the Breviary. The Holy Spirit continues to be at work, however, as this prayer of the Church is seeing a resurgence in fidelity to praying it by clerics and a growing interest by many laypeople (perhaps, spurred in part by the availability of electronic "apps" for the Office—albeit currently without official approbation or approval). The Council Fathers desired that the hour known as Matins (now called the Office of Readings) be simplified with "fewer psalms and longer readings."[1] They suppressed the hour of Prime,[2] and perhaps most profoundly, called for the Psalter to be distributed no longer over a single week, but over a four-week cycle.[3] Such changes were made with a view especially for "those who are called to labor in apostolic works."[4] This reduction of the daily

Office—together with the turn to the vernacular—has greatly facilitated the prayerful recitation of the Hours. Clerics are less inclined simply to "recite" the Breviary in order to get through it because of time constraints or mental and spiritual weariness, but are, one hopes, more able "to attune their minds to their voices when praying it."[5] One of the exhortations of SC that could certainly be better fulfilled is the desire "that the chief hours, especially Vespers, are celebrated in common in church on Sundays and the more solemn feasts."[6] It does happen with some frequency, however, that parish councils or staff meetings begin with praying one of the Hours. In such ways, the reform of the Breviary has an ongoing and growing effect on the laity and the whole Church.

IV. The Liturgical Year

Prior to the reform of the Sacred Liturgy, it was not unusual for pastors to celebrate the sanctoral cycle more frequently than Sundays or the high seasons (Advent/Christmas Time and Lent/Triduum/Easter Time) of the liturgical year. The Council Fathers desired, rather, that the Lord's Day or Sunday retake its place as the original feast day. "Other celebrations, unless they be truly of greatest importance, shall not have precedence over the Sunday which is the foundation and kernel of the whole liturgical year."[7] Such a reorientation in our worship has had ecumenical implications as well as internal ecclesiological ones. When the Church is clear regarding the priority that the Paschal Mystery of Christ holds over the participation of the saints in his Paschal Mystery, then this communicates to our separated brothers and sisters, more loudly than words, that Christ is always the center for us.

Sacrosanctum Concilim led to a simplification of the system of feasts and ferias, making the liturgical year more accessible to clergy and faithful alike. It also called for a culling of the number of saint feasts on the universal calendar; something which the Church has done fairly regularly over the centuries. The feast days of saints were reviewed and only those were left on the universal calendar that could be considered "truly of universal significance."[8] The others were left to be celebrated by the diocese or region or religious order where they have developed a cultus of prayer and devotion. The desire was also realized to purge the accounts of the saints of any material that was not reliable historically or in accord with good piety. The encouragement to local churches to develop their own particular calendar with local saints has led dioceses in the United States in recent years to add native saints both to our diocesan and national calendars (examples of the more recent additions would be St. Kateri Tekakwitha and St. Katharine Drexel). This balance between universal and local feasts highlights the diversity of the Church and the principle of subsidiarity in action.

V. A Simplification of Rubrics

Article 34 of SC provided the rationale for a great simplification of rubrics that came to fruition later with the ritual editions that were promulgated for Mass and the other sacraments:

> The rites should be marked by a noble simplicity; they should be short, clear, and unencumbered by useless repetitions; they should be within the people's powers of comprehension and as a rule not require much explanation.

This brief paragraph was the inspiration for the subsequent instructions for implementing *Sacrosanctum Concilium* (for example, *Inter oecumenici, Tres abhinc annos,* and *Liturgicae instaurationes),* which called for the simplification of rubrics, especially *Tres abhinc annos.* One can argue regarding when repetition becomes "useless," but many priests experienced this simplification in a very positive way. In the pre-Conciliar rite, it was all too easy to become fixated on the rubrics, "evaluating" the Mass on the basis of rubrical fidelity more than interior engagement or devotion. The experience has been similar for some priests who have attempted to learn (or relearn) the Extraordinary Form in recent years, namely, they find the detailed rubrics more a distraction than a help. Of course, this has not been the experience of all, and some easily become comfortable with the rhythm of the Extraordinary Form and find it edifying in its own way, but for many, if not most, this simplification has been welcomed.

The "noble simplicity," to which SC refers, is best grasped in relation to the various Eastern Rites, beautiful and majestic in their own way. The sheer length of the orations for the Eastern Rites, combined with their many tropes and hymns—profound and ancient—can make the description of "noble simplicity" for the Roman Rite seem a great understatement! On the other hand, SC did not intend for the liturgy or the liturgical environment to be severe or devoid of beauty or splendor. The simplification of the rubrics was intended to enable a greater focus on beauty both interior and exterior; in other words, to express "mystery" not as something confusing, but as something transcendent.

VI. Reverence

One of the criticisms of the reformed rites has been a perceived loss of reverence, and it is certainly possible that there were pastors and communities who were less reverent in the years following the implementation of the post-Conciliar reform. At the same time, however, human nature is not apt to change and one may wonder to what extent there was universal reverence before the Council. It is possible, however, that some of the changes—the use of English, proclaiming the Mass aloud and in dialogue with the assembly, and the priest facing the assembly—did not so much lead to a loss of reverence as much as make the lack of reverence in some individuals more apparent. In recent years, there has been a definite desire among many in the Church to show that reverence and mystery and splendor are not only possible in the reformed rites, but positively fostered by them. What we have learned, though, is that such qualities arise from a spirituality rather than from a ritual text.

I firmly believe that a liturgical spirituality, nurtured by the reformed rites, is alive and growing in the Church today. This celebration of the fiftieth anniversary of the promulgation of *Sacrosanctum Concilium* is a wonderful opportunity to reflect on the activity of the Holy Spirit in the ministers and assembly through the reformed rites of our Church. In his *motu proprio, Summorum Pontificum,* Pope Benedict XVI stated that the pre-Conciliar rites were "a spur to the spiritual life of many saints." I believe that the examples of holiness fostered and nourished by the reformed rites are just beginning and will continue to nourish and prepare the Church for the fullness of the kingdom, when signs and symbols will give way to seeing face to face! May the following articles on *Sacrosanctum Concilium* be one more contribution toward the unity and renewal of the pilgrim Church!

NOTES

1. *Sacrosanctum Concilium* (SC), 89c.
2. See ibid., 89d.
3. See ibid., 91.
4. Ibid., 88.
5. Ibid., 90.
6. Ibid., 100.
7. Ibid., 106.
8. Ibid., 111.

Pastoral Notes: An Introduction to this Resource

Corinna Laughlin

The Second Vatican Council and the Liturgy

When the bishops of the world gathered in Rome for the Second Vatican Council, their deliberations began with the liturgy. Liturgy came first in part because the renewal of the liturgy was already well underway by October of 1962. From the late nineteenth century, there had been strong currents of interest in the history of liturgy, and a growing sense that the faithful, so long passive, needed to take a more active part in the Church's worship. Scholars, pastors, religious, and lay voices contributed to what came to be called the "Liturgical Movement." Pope Pius XII's encyclical *Mediator Dei* (1948) embraced some aspects of this push for renewal and bore fruit in the reforms of the Holy Week liturgies from 1951 to 1955.

Thus, it made sense to begin the Council with the discussion of liturgy, since the work of renewal had already begun. But there was another reason as well: to begin with the liturgy was to signal its importance. In the words which would be famously enshrined in *Sacrosanctum Concilium*, "the liturgy is the summit toward which the activity of the Church is directed; at the same time it is the fount from which all [her] power flows."[1] The liturgy was the right place to begin.

The debates on the liturgy began on October 22, 1962. The Council Fathers (as the participating bishops were called) had been presented with a draft document, called a *schema*. During the debates, the Fathers were free to propose amendments, additions, deletions, and wholesale revisions to the text. They debated everything from the use of Latin, to concelebration, to Holy Communion under both kinds. The debates continued until November 13, 1962. During the months that followed—months of change during which Pope John XXIII died and Pope Paul VI was elected—the liturgy *schema* was revised. It was resubmitted to the Council Fathers in the second session of the council in the fall of 1963. Again, they discussed and voted on each section of the *schema*. On December 4, 1963, the revised text was placed before the Council Fathers for the last time. Pope Paul VI was present, and began the proceedings by intoning the hymn, *Veni Creator Spiritus*. The beginning of each chapter of *Sacrosanctum Concilium* was read aloud, and the votes were collected: *Placet* or *non placet*—yes or no.[2] As the ballots were counted (using an early computer), prayers were sung: *Ave Maria, Magnificat, Salve Regina*.[3] And then the astonishing results were presented to Pope Paul VI: 2,147 in favor; only four opposed. Pope Paul VI stood, and formally promulgated the document, the first to be produced by the Second Vatican Council. And thus the renewal of the liturgy, with the virtually unanimous approval of the world's bishops, became Church law.

The Council would produce sixteen documents in all. The types of documents are "Constitutions," "Decrees," and "Declarations." The four Constitutions—on the Sacred Liturgy (*Sacrosanctum Concilium*), on the nature of the Church (*Lumen gentium*), on the Church in the modern world (*Gaudium et spes*), and on divine revelation (*Dei Verbum*) are the most important of these documents.

It is worth observing that the Council Fathers did not put liturgy "back on the shelf," so to speak, when *Sacrosanctum Concilium* was complete. Liturgy came up again and again in the other documents of the Council, particularly in *Dei Verbum*, on the link between the "one table of the word of God and the Body of Christ",[4] and in *Ad gentes divinitus*, which recognized liturgy as an essential part of the missionary activity of the Church.[5] In *Gaudium et spes*, the notion that "religion were nothing more than the fulfilment of acts of worship and the observance of a few moral obligations" is described as "one of the gravest errors of our time."[6] This link between liturgy and justice, between acts of worship and acts of mercy, is not specifically articulated in *Sacrosanctum Concilium*, but when we read the liturgy constitution in light of these other documents, we recognize this as one of the key teachings of the Second Vatican Council on the liturgy.[7]

Implementation of *Sacrosanctum Concilium*

With the promulgation of *Sacrosanctum Concilium* on December 4, 1963, the Church entered a new phase: implementation. That process began with the establishment of a Consilium on January 25, 1964 This group of bishops, aided by scholars with a wide range of expertise, was charged with the vast task of bringing the Council's vision to life for the Church. Their work included the renewal not only of the Mass, but also of the Liturgy of the Hours as well as the Church's other rites and sacraments, the revision of the liturgical calendar and the development of a new Lectionary.

It would be five years before the work of the Consilium was largely complete, but in the meantime, there was no going back to business as usual. Some elements of *Sacrosanctum Concilium*, including concelebration and the use of the vernacular for some parts of the Mass, were implemented almost immediately. By the time the revised Order of Mass appeared in 1969, most American Catholics had been praying parts of the Mass in the vernacular for more than four years.

In the decade following the Council, there was tremendous enthusiasm and excitement, as well as well as confusion and resistance. But by and large, the Catholic faithful embraced the reforms the Council brought: "according to the best data available, within five years of the closing of the Council, between 85 percent and 87 percent of practicing Catholics in the United States stated that they preferred the 'new Mass' of Vatican II to that embodied in the post-Tridentine *Missale Romanum*."[8] Now, more than fifty years after the opening of the Council, the "new" liturgy is no longer new. In fact, the vast majority of the people who worship in our parishes today never experienced the Mass before the Second Vatican Council. For them, the renewed liturgy is simply the way the Church prays.

Why *Sacrosanctum Concilium* Still Matters

Does *Sacrosanctum Concilium* still matter today? Has its significance diminished in light of the hundreds of documents that have appeared since 1963—everything from clarifications and notices to instructions, *motu proprio*, and encyclicals? While these later documents are certainly important, *Sacrosanctum Concilium* remains our most important document on the liturgy. Rev. Michael S. Driscoll has called it the "touchstone document," in light of which all other liturgical pronouncements need to be read.[9] That is why, even after half a century, the liturgy constitution matters for parishes, cathedrals, religious communities, diocesan worship offices, schools, and campus ministry centers. It matters for bishops, priests, chaplains, religious, and every layperson who is involved in the liturgy (and that includes every person who goes to Mass!). *Sacrosanctum Concilium* does not tell us *how* to celebrate the liturgy—it does not explain the order for the entrance procession, or the color of vestments, or the number of candles to be used. Those questions are important, of course (and the answers to all of them are found in the *General Instruction of the Roman Missal*). Rather, *Sacrosanctum Concilium* gives the bigger picture. It sets out the priorities for the Church not only in the reform of the liturgy, but in its celebration. It is not a guide to liturgy preparation: it is a reminder of why we celebrate liturgy in the first place.

In his general audience for October 10, 2012—the eve of the fiftieth anniversary of the opening of the Council—Pope Benedict XVI compared the constitutions of the Second Vatican Council to "the four cardinal points of the compass that can direct us. The Constitution on the Sacred Liturgy *Sacrosanctum Concilium* points out to us that in the Church at the beginning there is worship, there is God, there is the centrality of the mystery of Christ's presence."[10] A compass is not a map—but you can't use a map effectively without one. *Sacrosanctum Concilium* is our compass. When we are unsure about our direction, it gets us back on track. And so, while it is not the kind of document we need to consult every day, it is one that we should revisit at least every year, to be reminded of why we do what we do, and to weigh, balance, and correct our own priorities in light of the Church's generous vision.

How to Use This Book

For the introduction and each of the seven chapters of *Sacrosanctum Concilium*, a respected scholar with pastoral experience has provided a general introduction, which gives an overview of the chapter. Then, you will find the full text of *Sacrosanctum Concilium* with detailed commentary on each article of the document, including background about how the liturgy was celebrated before the Council. For those who never experienced the liturgy before Vatican II, this context is invaluable in understanding the reforms. The commentary also includes reflections on how the various directives in *Sacrosanctum Concilium* were implemented, as well as reflecting on what remains to be done. Thus, you can use this resource both to find and cite passages from *Sacrosanctum Concilium* itself, and to explore more deeply the meaning, purpose, and impact of any given passage in the liturgy constitution. At the end of each chapter, each author has provided questions for discussion and reflection which are intended to help you discover the relevance of this document in your own life and community.

Sacrosanctum Concilium is a wide-ranging document, taking us from the nature of the liturgy itself, through the Mass and the sacraments, the Divine Office, the liturgical year, as well as music, sacred art, and church art and architecture. Thus, parishes will find the text and commentary useful in a wide variety of contexts. Liturgy committees can reflect on chapters I and II as they map out priorities for the year. Chapter VI will be helpful for church musicians, especially read in conjunction with documents like *Sing to the Lord: Music in Divine Worship.* Renovation or building committees should read and reflect on the entire text, especially Chapter VII, in addition to spending time with *Built of Living Stones: Art, Architecture, and Worship. Sacrosanctum Concilium* is invaluable for the parish at large, not only for understanding the liturgy, but for understanding the Second Vatican Council. Just as the Council Fathers began their deliberations with the liturgy, so reflection on the liturgy provides the perfect beginning to a study of the Second Vatican Council for the whole parish.

The Council Fathers saw that education was an important, indeed an essential component in the reform of the liturgy. And that is no less true today than it was fifty years ago. "Zeal and patience" [11] are still needed to help every Catholic understand and experience the riches of grace to be found in the liturgy. As Joyce Ann Zimmerman observes in her introduction to the second chapter of *Sacrosanctum Concilium* in this resource, "Liturgical education is never 'finished' because we are dealing with a mystery that has so much richness and depth that no matter how much we pray it, think it, learn about it, we will never exhaust what liturgy can continually teach us."[12] *Sacrosanctum Concilium* is not a thing of the past. To study the liturgy constitution, and to bring its values and priorities to life in our parishes and communities, is to participate in a very real way in the renewal of the liturgy.

NOTES

1. SC, 10. Church documents are typically referred to by their first two or three words in Latin. *Sacrosanctum Concilium* comes from the words with which this document begins—"This Sacred Council."

2. Xavier Rynne, *The Second Session*. New York: Farrar, Straus and Giroux, 1963, 1964), p. 296.

3. Yves Congar, *My Journal of the Council*. Collegeville, Minnesota: The Liturgical Press, 2012, p. 466.

4. *Dei Verbum* (DV), 21.

5. *Ad gentes divinitus* (AG), 16, 19.

6. *Gaudium et spes* (GS), 43.

7. For an exploration of *Sacrosanctum Concilium* in the context of the entire Council, see Massimo Faggioli, *True Reform: Liturgy and Ecclesiology in Sacrosanctum Concilium*. Collegeville, Minnesota: The Liturgical Press, 2012.

8. Mark Massa, "Frederick R. McManus, *Worship*, and the Reception of Vatican II in the United States." *Worship* 81 (2007), p. 122.

9. Michael S. Driscoll, "General Introduction," *The Liturgy Documents: Volume One, Fifth Edition*. Chicago, Illinois: Liturgy Training Publications, 2012, p. xvi.

10. Pope Benedict XVI, General Audience for October 10, 2012; available from http://www.vatican.va/holy_father/benedict_xvi/audiences/2012/documents/hf_ben-xvi_aud_20121010_en.html; accessed June 22, 2013.

11. SC, 19.

12. See page 82 in this resource.

Introduction

Sacrosanctum Concilium 1–4

Paul Turner

Voting 2,147 to four, the bishops probably even surprised themselves at the margin of victory. On December 4, 1963, *Sacrosanctum Concilium*, the *Constitution on the Sacred Liturgy*, became the first document passed at the Second Vatican Council.

When Pope John XXIII announced his intentions to convene the Council, his words stirred great excitement. He wanted to promote "the enlightenment, edification, and joy of the entire Christian people," and to extend "a renewed cordial invitation to the faithful of the separated communities to participate with us in this quest for unity and grace, for which so many souls long in all parts of the world."[1] From these first broad statements, the goals and themes of the Council gradually coalesced to renew the liturgy, ecclesiology, and ecumenical activity of the Church. The strong vote on the liturgy constitution demonstrated collegiality in action on a topic that widened the participation of the people in the life, prayer, and mission of the Church.

Sacrosanctum Concilium (SC) passed through three different drafts before the final version won approval. The drafts actually underwent little significant change, signaling great unanimity from the beginning. The bishops realized they were affirming something historic, yet they were adding to a trajectory of liturgical renewal advanced by Pope Pius X in his 1903 *motu proprio Tra le sollecitudini*, and by Pope Pius XII in his 1947 encyclical *Mediator Dei*. The excitement from those days can still be felt in reading the Council's documents.

Bishops had gathered from around the world, including some from Eastern Rite Churches. Other Christian leaders were also present. A microcosm of earth's nations had gathered in Rome, so the bishops could easily envision the mission of the Church to all humanity. Even when dealing with the liturgy, something that may have seemed an internal matter, its global purpose kept resounding.

The introductory chapters to SC serve as a prelude to all the subsequent documents because they show the aim the bishops had adopted. It elucidated the visionary invitation of "Good Pope John."

1. This Sacred Council has several aims in view: it desires to impart an ever increasing vigor to the Christian life of the faithful; to adapt more suitably to the needs of our own times those institutions that are subject to change; to foster whatever can promote union among all who believe in Christ; to strengthen whatever can help to call the whole of humanity into the household of the Church. The Council therefore sees particularly cogent reasons for undertaking the reform and promotion of the liturgy.

The opening paragraph expresses the aims of the Council—not just those of SC. However, the aims of SC are subordinate to those of the whole Council. The entire paragraph is one sentence in Latin, making this subordination even clearer.

The goals are fourfold, and the subject of each new one grows wider than the previous. The first aim concerns individual members of the faithful, the second the institutions of the Church, the third the entire Christian family, and finally all of humankind.

The first goal borrows from Pope John XXIII's announcement of the Council. His hope that the Council would promote "enlightenment, edification and joy" is enshrined in the hope for "increasing vigor" to the Christian life.[2] Within the liturgy, this goal is achieved through the "full, conscious, and active participation"[3] of the people. Yet ultimately the liturgical life of the faithful should influence their moral life.

Second, the Council aims to adapt institutions subject to change. The liturgy is one of those institutions because it has some elements that have changed over history. This goal more broadly opened the path for the bishops to address other matters in other documents, such as ecclesiology and ecumenism.

The desire for more ecumenical progress rings out in the third aim. The bishops recognized the foundational unity that exists among all the baptized, and they wanted to advance the desire of Jesus Christ that all his followers would be one.[4]

Finally, the Council aimed at evangelization—calling the whole of humanity into the household of the Church. The Church cannot consider her internal matters without also accepting her mission to all nations.

Against this backdrop of the Council's ecclesial goals, the goals of the liturgy are considered. The reform and the promotion of the liturgy should accomplish everything already stated: a vigorous Christian life, an adapted institution, unity among Christians, and an invitation to all people into the Church.

After the Council's embrace of these goals wholeheartedly came the unfolding renewal of the rites. Individual Catholics experienced a renewed participation in and appreciation of the liturgy. The rites were enriched through an expanded repertoire of prayers and occasions, and through a general refocusing of their purpose. Greater unity in worship among all Christians came about. And a more clearly expressive liturgy issued a more frank invitation to the world.

The liturgy, the Mass in particular, is extremely important to Catholics. When something changes, or when ceremonies take place in ways that one finds personally disturbing, it is tempting to focus on the words and actions themselves, without remembering the complete mission of the Church. The opening of SC invites the faithful to take a step back and absorb the full implications of worship.

The title of each document from the Second Vatican Council is also opening words of the document in Latin. This is true of virtually every major statement from the Vatican—whether an encyclical, a *motu proprio*, or some other instrument of communication. In this case, the opening words in Latin refer to the Council itself: *Sacrosanctum Concilium* ("This Sacred Council"). These words serve as a reminder that the liturgy is one expression of the Church's mission, which the Council—the greatest event in the history of modern Christianity—so boldly promoted and embraced.

---

2. For the liturgy, "making the work of our redemption a present actuality,"[1] most of all in the divine sacrifice of the eucharist, is the outstanding means whereby the faithful may express in their lives and manifest to others the mystery of Christ and the real nature of the true Church. It is of the essence of the Church to be both human and divine, visible yet endowed with invisible resources, eager to act yet intent on contemplation, present in this world yet not at home in it; and the Church is all these things in such wise that in it the human is directed and subordinated to the divine, the visible likewise to the invisible, action to contemplation, and this present world to that city yet to come which we seek.[2] While the

liturgy daily builds up those who are within into a holy temple of the Lord, into a dwelling place for God in the Spirit,[3] to the mature measure of the fullness of Christ,[4] at the same time it marvelously strengthens their power to preach Christ and thus shows forth the Church to those who are outside as a sign lifted up among the nations,[5] under which the scattered children of God may be gathered together,[6] until there is one sheepfold and one shepherd.[7]

1. RomM, prayer over the gifts, Holy Thursday and 2d Sunday in Ordinary Time.
2. See Heb 13:14.
3. See Eph 2:21– 22.
4. See Eph 4:13.
5. See Is 11:12.
6. See Jn 11:52.
7. See Jn 10:16.

SC 2 explores the nature of the Church that celebrates the liturgy. The Church is a collection of contrasting qualities: human, visible, active, and present in the world; yet also divine, invisibly equipped, contemplative, and not at home in the world. The first list of qualities is subordinate to the second. In the liturgy, human words and actions are subordinate to the spiritual realities they proclaim.

The liturgy holds all these features in tension. It is the means through which redemption is accomplished, and it strengthens the faithful to manifest Christ and the Church to the world.

The very first footnote comes from a liturgical prayer. At the time the *Constitution* was written, the prayer in question was known as the secret for the Ninth Sunday after Pentecost. St. Thomas Aquinas had quoted it in *Summa Theologica* 3.83.1 to argue that the Mass is truly the sacrament of the sacrifice of Christ. When the calendar was revised in 1969, this prayer became the Prayer over the Offerings for the Evening Mass of the Lord's Supper on Holy Thursday. It was also given a spot earlier in the liturgical year—the Second Sunday in Ordinary Time, where it helps launch the long period in which the Church meditates on the life of Christ and the contributions of the Scriptures, Sunday by Sunday.

Other footnotes in SC 2 all come from the Bible. They show how the Sacred Liturgy relies on the Sacred Scriptures.

In the years after the Council, the liturgy manifested Christ at its center, and it capably equipped the faithful to speak more competently and with more complexity about the mysteries of the faith.

More work can be done to evangelize non-Christians, but the liturgy provides the ultimate source for this activity, and a rewarding place for new Christians to find the work of their redemption accomplished. SC 2 neatly unfolds the tight relationship among Christ, the Church, and the liturgy.

---

3. Wherefore the Council judges that the following principles concerning the promotion and reform of the liturgy should be called to mind and practical norms established.

Among these principles and norms there are some that can and should be applied both to the Roman Rite and also to all the other rites. The practical norms that follow, however, should be taken as applying only to the Roman Rite, except for those that, in the very nature of things, affect other rites as well.

Still introducing the path ahead, SC 3 states that principles and practical norms will follow. As SC 2 explored the various tensions that coexist in the nature of the Church, so SC 3 embraces the tension between theory and practice.

The principles aim to promote and reform the liturgy. They will promote it as central to the spiritual life, and they will reform it to help people pray the liturgy.

Although the subsequent articles will outline some practical considerations, the details developed after the close of the Council. Even the practical norms are somewhat theoretical by comparison with what followed.

The Council carefully distinguished the Roman Rite from other bodies. The Catholic Church embraces some non-Roman Rites in the West (such as the Ambrosian and the Mozarabic), and various Eastern Rites (such as the Maronite, Armenian, and Ruthenian Catholic Churches). The norms will focus on the Roman Rite, while acknowledging that the Church is something bigger.

---

4. Lastly, in faithful obedience to tradition, the Council declares that the Church holds all lawfully acknowledged rites to be of equal right and dignity and wishes to preserve them in the future and to foster them in every way. The Council also desires that, where necessary, the rites be revised carefully in the light of sound tradition and that they be given new vigor to meet the circumstances and needs of modern times.

Over the centuries, the Roman Rite exercised influence over the theology and liturgy of other rites. In some cases, this strained the relationships among the rites. The Council desired to strengthen these friendships. The fourth and last introductory article of the *Constitution* shows respect to the other rites. Such respect does not diminish the Catholic Church, but rather is "in faithful obedience to tradition."

At the same time, the Council hoped that its efforts would set an example for other rites to follow. Their own reforms should also be made "in the light of sound tradition," with the goal of invigorating the Church in modern times. In fact, many of these rites did reform their liturgies in subsequent years.

Hence, the opening of SC lays out the broad goals of the Council, places the Roman liturgy within that context, and invites others to follow. The bishops had prepared themselves to address specific liturgical needs in the subsequent chapters. The liturgical renewal was born.

Questions for Discussion and Reflection

1. In your personal Christian life, does the liturgy "impart an ever increasing vigor" (SC, 1)?

2. Have you noticed that the liturgy adapts to your culture? How?

3. In what ways do you "promote union among all who believe in Christ" (SC, 1)? Do they include worship with other Christians? How?

4. The liturgy should "strengthen whatever can help to call the whole of humanity into the household of the Church" (SC, 1). Have you ever invited someone to church with you? In what other ways have you evangelized your neighbors, coworkers, or family members?

5. Describe any experience you have with Eastern Rite Churches.

NOTES

1. John W. O'Malley, *What Happened at Vatican II.* Cambridge: The Balkans Press of Harvard University Press, 2008, p. 17 [citing *Acta et Documenta Concilio Oecumenico Vaticano II Apparando Series prima (Antepraeparatoria).* Vatican City: Typis Polyglottis Vaticanis, 1960–1961] I, 3–6, at 6i.

2. Ibid.

3. SC, 14.

4. See John 17:20–21.

✣ CHAPTER I

General Principles for the Reform and Promotion of the Sacred Liturgy

Sacrosanctum Concilium 5–46

Joshua Brommer
Michael S. Driscoll
David W. Fagerberg
J. Philip Horrigan
Corinna Laughlin
Mark E. Wedig, OP

An Overview of Chapter I

The title of the first chapter of *Sacrosanctum Concilium* (SC) aptly describes its intentions: it will be concerned with general principles, and those general principles will be directed toward two ends, namely the reform and the promotion of the Sacred Liturgy. The subsections of this chapter are therefore grouped around three goals: to define the nature and importance of liturgy in the life of the Church (subsection 1); to give guidelines for specific reforms (subsection 3); and to promote liturgical activity by a variety of strategies (subsection 2, 4, and 5). With this ambitious agenda, it is no wonder that the first chapter is the longest in the document—almost forty percent of the whole, and roughly four times the length of any other chapter. We will follow those three divisions here, and speak about the nature, reform, and promotion of liturgy.

I. The Nature of Liturgy and Its Importance in the Church's Life (SC 5–13)

God willed that all should be saved, therefore he sent his Son in the flesh to give the fullness of divine worship to us. The Old Testament was a prelude to this, leading to the emergence of the Church from the side of Christ on the Cross. This was not an end, but a beginning. As Christ was sent by the Father, so he sent the Apostles to proclaim his Death and Resurrection, which are brought into effect through sacrifice and sacrament. Christ is always present in his Church, associating it with himself, which makes the Church's liturgy a sacred action surpassing all others. The liturgy awakens our thirst for beatitude, giving us a foretaste of the heavenly liturgy even now, in our earthly liturgy.

Since liturgy is the activity of Christ, it is no surprise that article 10 calls liturgy "summit" and "fount"—the summit toward which the activity of the Church is directed, and the fount from which all the Church's power flows. Nevertheless, this affirmation about the liturgy is not cut off from the whole life of the Church. The article before reminds us that liturgy does not exhaust the entire activity of the Church; and the paragraph after reminds us that unbelievers must be called to faith and to conversion, and believers must be prepared for the sacraments, and taught to observe all that Christ commanded. In order for liturgy to reach its full effectiveness, the faithful must come to it with proper dispositions and cooperate with divine grace. Prayer is needed, both private and in the form of popular devotions.

II. The Reform of the Sacred Liturgy (SC 21–40)

Sacrosanctum Concilium is not a blueprint for how to celebrate a liturgy; if an anthropologist from Mars found this document, it is unlikely he could deduce from it what a Christian liturgy looks like. Rather, SC is a blueprint for drawing future blueprints, and in this subsection, SC identifies four sets of norms to apply in making future reforms. We are warned that there are immutable elements in the liturgy (unchangeable because divinely instituted), but we are also told that there are elements subject to change, and the purpose of any reform to them is to express clearly the holy things they signify.

First, this section considers general norms, that is, norms that apply in every case. The regulation of the liturgy depends solely on the authority of the Church, even if guided by theological, historical, and pastoral investigations. There must be no innovations unless the good of the Church genuinely and certainly requires them. All reforms should promote a love for Scripture, and the Council here gives the mandate that liturgical books are to be revised as soon as possible, employing experts and bishops from around the world.

Second, this section considers norms that arise from the hierarchical and communal nature of liturgy. This is essential because liturgies are not private functions: they belong to the whole Church. The hierarchical structure of the Church means that the liturgy has many offices filled by various ministers, including the faithful who are given an obligation for participation in their Baptism. This should be reflected in the revised rubrics.

Third, the liturgy has a teaching and pastoral character that should guide its reform. Although the liturgy is primarily the worship of the divine majesty, this does not mean the liturgy is not full of rich instruction for the faithful. God speaks and we answer; there are prayers and signs; the rite has a noble simplicity that will not require much explanation if the connection between word and rite stands out clearly. SC urges more Scripture, more preaching, explicit liturgical catechesis, and offers the opportunity for more extended use of the vernacular, though use of the Latin language is to be preserved.

Fourth, the Second Vatican Council came to increased awareness of the culture and traditions of other peoples, so this is given as a guiding norm. Rather than imposing uniformity, reforms will respect the genius and talents of races and peoples. Legitimate variations and adaptations can be prudently made by the territorial ecclesiastical authority.

We notice again that SC is not here legislating particular reforms, it is giving us a point on the horizon from which to take our bearings in future reforms.

III. Promotion of the Liturgy (SC 14–20, 41–46)

It is well understood that simply changing the books will not accomplish the desired effect, so three subsections of this chapter are devoted to describing how to promote participation, liturgical life, and pastoral liturgical action.

Subsection II directs our attention to promoting liturgical instruction and active participation. In perhaps one of SC's most famous phrases we read: "In the reform and promotion of the liturgy, this full and active participation by all the people is the aim to be considered before all else."[1] How can this goal he accomplished? The liturgical formation of clergy is required, professors should be appointed in seminaries where the study of liturgy should be made compulsory, liturgical formation should infuse a cleric's spiritual life, and pastors should promote with zeal the liturgical instruction of the faithful.

Subsection IV directs our attention to promoting liturgical life in the diocese and parish. The bishop is the high priest of his flock, and the faithful's life in Christ derives from and depends on him. Cathedral liturgies are the preeminent manifestation of the Church, and therefore held in great esteem, but since the bishop cannot be everywhere he establishes groupings of the faithful under the care of a pastor.

And subsection V directs our attention to promoting pastoral liturgical action. Zeal for the restoration of the liturgy is a gift from God, and in order to respond to it SC judges it advisable to set up liturgical commissions to promote the liturgical apostolate. Such commissions could be aided by experts in liturgical science, music, art, and pastoral practice. And in addition, in so far as possible, dioceses should have commissions for music and art.

Conclusion

Sacrosanctum Concilium does not fall in the genre of rubrics: it does not direct the actual celebration of a liturgy. Rather, the Church recollected her mind at the Second Vatican Council in order to assure that it was in full accord with the mind of Christ, and that she was carrying out her mission to the world in ways as fruitful and robust as possible. So she turned first to the liturgy, the "summit" and "fount"[2] of her interior life, and which feeds her exterior ministry. She committed herself to reforms that would roll out over the next few decades, but would take much longer to fully penetrate our lives. This chapter identifies the general principles for such reforms.

I. Nature of the Liturgy and Its Importance in the Church's Life

Too often, in the study of *Sacrosanctum Concilium*, the introductory chapter and this chapter on the general principles are glossed over to get to those articles which enunciate clearer indications of specific liturgical reform. Yet, it is precisely in these general principles that the Fathers of the Council illuminate the very essence of the Sacred Liturgy which is the foundation for all of the practical adjustments. The general principles derive from the theological reflection of the Church which reached a renewed intensity during the Liturgical Movement of the late nineteenth and first half of the twentieth century. Combined with the *ressourcement,* theology's critical return to the ancient ritual texts and the reflections of the Church Fathers, the Liturgical Movement of the twentieth century reached a high point with the theology expressed in this dogmatic constitution, which is the first Conciliar document in the history of the Church devoted to the doctrine of the Sacred Liturgy.[3]

Among the doctrinal insights which fashion a line of continuity with the ancient tradition, several find pride of place in the formation of the text of *Sacrosanctum Concilium*: the principle place of Christ the Mediator in the celebration of the liturgy, the centrality of the Paschal Mystery and the Christian's active participation in that mystery initiated by the Sacrament of Baptism, the renewed sense of the key principle of sacramentality in relationship to the liturgy, and the inseparable interior connection between what is celebrated in ritual and what is lived out in everyday life.

Since the Sacred Liturgy, in every word and action, proclaims, celebrates, and makes present the Paschal Mystery of Christ, which has its origins in the universal saving will of God the Father and is made present through the activity of the Holy Spirit, this chapter rightly begins with the Triune God who fashions the Church from the wounded side of the Savior and invites all humanity to "draw water from the wells of salvation."[4] Starting here, with God, the subsequent discussion of the Sacred Liturgy finds itself on the right path avoiding the risk of reducing ritual actions to mere human invention. The liturgy, as the "work of the Holy Trinity,"[5] is infused with divine power and grace that renders human action in the liturgy *sacred* and grace-filled. The Church celebrates the Sacred Liturgy when she is united to Christ in the power of the Holy Spirit as an act of worship to God the Father.

This basic theological concept sews together articles 5–13 of *Sacrosanctum Concilium*. In fact, this foundational notion of sacramental theology is woven throughout the documents of the Council, particularly in the teaching on the nature of the Church as sacrament (*Lumen gentium*) and the mission of the Church in the modern world (*Gaudium et spes*). Reforming the human dimension of the Sacred Liturgy, those "institutions"[6] which are subject to change and adjustment, is never done at the cost of undermining the centrality of divine agency upon which the sacramental and ecclesial life of the Church depend. Without the initiation and ongoing activity of God in the life of the humanity, there would be neither sacraments nor the Church itself.

The articles contained in chapter I represent a rich and dense doctrinal expression of the Church's understanding of the Sacred Liturgy, the fruit of the intense period of reflection, study, and prayer which immediately preceded the Second Vatican Council and the culmination of almost two thousand years of living, celebrating, and contemplating the Sacred Liturgy which continues today in the ongoing return to the treasure which is *Sacrosanctum Concilium*.

---

5. God who "wills that all be saved and come to the knowledge of the truth" (1 Tm 2:4), "who in many and various ways spoke in times past to the fathers by the prophets" (Heb 1:1), when the fullness of time had come sent his Son, the Word made flesh, anointed by the Holy Spirit, to preach the Gospel to the poor, to heal the contrite of heart;[1] he is "the physician, being both flesh and of the Spirit,"[2] the mediator between God and us.[3] For his humanity, united with the person of the Word, was the instrument of our salvation. Therefore in Christ "the perfect achievement of our reconciliation came forth and the fullness of divine worship was given to us.[4]

The wonderful works of God among the people of the Old Testament were a prelude to the work of Christ the Lord. He achieved his task of redeeming humanity and giving perfect glory to God, principally by the paschal mystery of his blessed passion, resurrection from the dead, and glorious ascension, whereby "dying, he destroyed our death and, rising, he restored our life."[5] For it was from the side of Christ as he slept the sleep of death upon the cross that there came forth the sublime sacrament of the whole Church.[6]

1. See Is 61:1; Lk 4:18.
2. Ignatius of Antioch, *To the Ephesians* 7, 2
3. See 1 Tm 2:5.

4. *Sacramentarium Veronense* (ed. Mohlberg), no. 1265.
5. RomM, preface I of Easter.
6. RomM, prayer after the seventh reading, Easter Vigil.

The Council Fathers begin this chapter with a clear declaration that God wants all of humanity to be saved, as revealed in Scripture,[7] and the entire movement of salvation history includes this truth. The means by which this is revealed to humanity is gradual, since the divine economy grows from the events of creation and the fall, through the divine interventions of the Old Testament and the preaching of the prophets, to Jesus Christ who is the fullness of God's revelation (anticipating the teaching of *Dei Verbum* 2). Christ is the divine physician who remedies the bodily and spiritual ailments of humanity, the sole mediator between God and humanity. This mediation, founded in the hypostatic union of divinity and humanity, touches the human race through instrumental agency of the sacred humanity assumed by the Second Person of the Blessed Trinity. Here, there is no break from the traditional soteriological motive of the Incarnation, evidenced by the quote from the late sixth-century *Sacramentarium Veronese*: the unity of divinity and humanity in Christ perfectly achieves the reconciliation of the human race.

At the same time, the result of this reconciliation between God and humankind in Christ is the "fullness of divine worship." As Edward Schillebeeckx, OP, popularized in the years before the Council: "Christ is the Sacrament of the encounter with God."[8] In his text, Schillebeeckx develops the thesis that "Christ is the chief sacrament, the primordial sacrament from whom flow his sacramental prolongations, the Church and the sacraments."[9] The eternal Word joins humanity to himself in the Incarnation, not merely to bridge the gap between fallen humanity and God, but to raise up humanity with a renewed purpose and destiny as the Church which offers a continual sacrifice of praise and glorifies God perfectly in her union with Christ. The idea of worship being more than a ritual performance, but as Christian life and existence itself, derives from the Church Fathers.[10] The Sacraments of the Church were seen as the "prolongation of the great works of God."[11] Calling to mind the other "wonderful works" of God in the Old Testament does not discount them, but puts them in their proper context as the "prelude" to the redeeming work of Christ in the Paschal Mystery. *Sacrosanctum Concilium* situates Christ at the center, as the fullness of what God calls humanity to become in grace. And this comes at the cost the Cross upon which hung the Savior of the world and from whose side was born "the sublime sacrament of the whole Church." This quote from *The Roman Missal* places this theological insight deep into the ancient tradition, alluding to St. Augustine[12] from whom the Church derives the foundations of her sacramental theology that touches not only the reform of the Sacred Liturgy in the Second Vatican Council, but also impacts the Council's ecclesiological expression of the sacramentality of the Church.[13]

Following the Council, these ideas would become even more intensely developed as the Church reflected on her very nature as a sign of the union between God and humanity as well as the instrument which effects that union. In a similar way, a greater awareness of the centrality of the Paschal Mystery and the sacramental economy by which Christians share in its fruits would develop into part II of the *Catechism of the Catholic Church* (CCC) which treats directly "The Celebration of the Christian Mystery." Yet, despite its clear indication in the CCC and in other sources which recovered the spirit of the ancient Fathers, there still lacks a deep practical awareness of the integral unity of worship and Christian existence.[14] This integral unity is found in Christ himself and effected through the participation in the Sacred Liturgy. As Jean Corbon puts it, "The real question is not 'celebration and life' but 'liturgy and life'"[15] in which we drink deeply of the living water from the river of life. For, "If we let the river of life permeate us, we become trees of life, for the mystery that the river symbolizes takes hold of us."[16] This profound indication from article 5 invites such a transformation to take hold. Such is the nature of the Sacred Liturgy as the outward activity bringing about the saving will of the Father.

---

6. As Christ was sent by the Father, he himself also sent the apostles, filled with the Holy Spirit. Their mission was, first, by preaching the Gospel to every creature,[7] to proclaim that by his death and resurrection Christ has freed us from Satan's grip[8] and brought us into the Father's kingdom. But the work they preached they were also to bring into effect through the sacrifice and the sacraments, the center of the whole liturgical life. Thus by baptism all are plunged into the paschal mystery of Christ: they die with him, are buried with him, and rise

with him;[9] they receive the spirit of adoption as children "in which we cry: Abba, Father" (Rom 8:15), and thus become true adorers whom the Father seeks.[10] In like manner, as often as they eat the supper of the Lord they proclaim the death of the Lord until he comes.[11] For that reason, on the very day of Pentecost when the Church appeared before the world, "those who received the word" of Peter "were baptized." And "they continued steadfastly in the teaching of the apostles and in the communion of the breaking of bread and in prayers . . . praising God and being in favor with all the people" (Acts 2:41– 47). From that time onward the Church has never failed to come together to celebrate the paschal mystery: reading those things "which were in all the Scriptures concerning him" (Lk 24:27); celebrating the eucharist, in which "the victory and triumph of his death are again made present";[12] and at the same time giving thanks "to God for his inexpressible gift" (2 Cor 9:15) in Christ Jesus, "in praise of his glory" (Eph 1:12), through the power of the Holy Spirit.

7. See Mk 16:15.
8. See Acts 26:18.
9. See Rom 6:4; Eph 2:6; Col 3:1.
10. See Jn 4:23.
11. See 1 Cor 11:26.
12. Council of Trent, sess. 13, 11 Oct 1551, *Decree on the Holy Eucharist*, chap. 5.

The mission and ministry of the Church is not her own, it is Christ's. This is understood in three senses in article 6: first, the Apostles were sent out by Christ; second, they were sent out in imitation of the Son's mission from the Father; and, third, they were sent out with grace of the Holy Spirit to accomplish this work. The two instruments given to the apostolic mission of the Church are preaching the Gospel and the dispensation of the sacraments. These two instruments constitute the means by which the Church continues the work of Christ, proclaiming and celebrating the Paschal Mystery since the time of the Apostles. In this way, the Apostles and their successors respond to the mandate of the Lord, "go and bear fruit, fruit that will last."[17]

The lasting fruit of this mission is the extension of the effects of the Paschal Mystery to every human person through the Sacrament of Baptism and joining them to the continual share in that mystery through the celebration of the Holy Eucharist. Once adopted into divine sonship through Baptism, Christians become "true adorers." That is, in Christ the Christian assumes the posture and orientation of the only-begotten Son who John's account of the Gospel describes as *pros Theos*—eternally before God—in a continuous act of worship, adoration, and love. The ongoing share and renewal of this orientation comes when the Christian joins himself or herself to the Church in Christ in the perfect act of thanksgiving and praise, the Eucharistic offering. There is expressed here a beautiful dynamism by which the movement of the eternal Son from the intimacy of the Triune Godhead binds himself to the Church and sends out the Church by the power of the Holy Spirit only to return with humanity redeemed to Christ, and in Christ, returns to worship the Father.

The impact of this evangelical teaching would influence the Second Vatican Council's teaching on the missionary aspect of the Church. Even in the context of a broader ecumenical and interreligious sensitivity, the Council Fathers never deny the fundamental mission of the Church is to "gather up all things in him, things in heaven and things on earth."[18] In the time after the Council, there were some attempts by theologians or pastoral leaders to temper the fundamental place of Christ in the mystery of salvation in order to exhibit sensitivity and tolerance. Yet, these misplaced attempts not only undermine the fundamental Christian faith in Christ, but also the meaning and purpose of the Sacred Liturgy which operates under divine power to redeem and raise up all of humanity in Christ.

---

7. To accomplish so great a work, Christ is always present in his Church, especially in its liturgical celebrations. He is present in the sacrifice of the Mass, not only in the person of his minister, "the same now offering, through the ministry of priests, who formerly offered himself on the cross,"[13] but especially under the eucharistic elements. By his power he is present in the sacraments, so that when a man baptizes it is really Christ himself who baptizes.[14] He is present in his word, since it is he himself who speaks when the holy Scriptures are read in the Church. He is present, lastly, when the Church prays and sings, for he promised: "Where two or three are gathered together in my name, there am I in the midst of them" (Mt 18:20).

Christ always truly associates the Church with himself in this great work wherein God is perfectly glorified and the recipients made holy. The Church is the Lord's beloved Bride who calls to him and through him offers worship to the eternal Father.

Rightly, then, the liturgy is considered as an exercise of the priestly office of Jesus Christ. In the liturgy, by means of signs perceptible to the senses, human sanctification is signified and brought about in ways proper to each of these signs; in the liturgy the whole public worship is performed by the Mystical Body of Jesus Christ, that is, by the Head and his members.

From this it follows that every liturgical celebration, because it is an action of Christ the Priest and of his Body which is the Church, is a sacred action surpassing all others; no other action of the Church can equal its effectiveness by the same title and to the same degree.

13. Council of Trent, sess. 22, 17 Sept 1562, *Doctrine on the Holy Sacrifice of the Mass*, chap. 2.
14. See Augustine, *In Ioannis Evangelium Tractatus* 6, chap. 1, n. 7.

The ministry and mission of the Church, commissioned by Christ, are accomplished by Christ who unites the Church with himself and acts in the Church. In article 7, the well-known expressions of the presence of Christ working in the Church, "especially in its liturgical celebrations," are listed in a kind of hierarchy: in the person of the sacred and ordained minister, "especially under the eucharistic elements," in the ministerial action of the sacraments, in the liturgical proclamation of the Sacred Scriptures, and in the Church gathered together in prayer and song. While the hierarchy is not entirely clear, except for the supreme presence of Christ in the Eucharist, the thrust of this article is to clearly enunciate the role Christ plays in the entire sacramental and liturgical life of the Church.

The association of Christ with the Church in the Sacred Liturgy is for purposes of glorifying God and sanctifying humanity. This is a priestly activity, an extension of his role as mediator between God and humanity expressed in the cultic terms of priesthood which makes Christ more than a moral intercessor, but the One who offers the sacrifice which effects the sanctification, the reconciliation, the purification of the Church through the celebration of public worship. In scholarly works from the Liturgical Movement, most especially the studies of Josef Jungmann,[19] the implications of the Incarnation and the priestly dimension of the Paschal offering were influences in the articulation of this passage of SC. At the same time, cautionary voices raised the concern that certain theological positions growing in popularity were undermining the priestly and sacrificial dimension of the Sacred Liturgy. This article seeks to give clear evidence that Christ alone, as the great High Priest, stands before the father interceding for humanity. It is only because of Christ, in Christ and through Christ, that the Church's liturgical actions can be properly called priestly, joined to her Head in the eternal sacrifice of praise.

In the time after the Council, these concerns about a diminished understanding of the priestly and sacrificial dimensions of the Sacred Liturgy developed. Building upon sometimes bloated understandings of the common priesthood bestowed in Baptism, the place of the ministerial priesthood risked diminishment. The great threat here was not the undoing of forms of clericalism, which may have been necessary, but the undoing of the sacramental understanding upon which this article is grounded: every priest stands in sacramental representation of Christ himself. In the Sacred Liturgy, there can only be one Christ, one mediator, one priest, who gathers together all who have been joined to Christ in the one sacrifice to the Father. This is most clearly expressed in the third edition of *The Roman Missal*: "Pray, brethren (brothers and sisters), / that my sacrifice and yours / may be acceptable to God, / the almighty Father. / May the Lord accept the sacrifice at your hands. . . ." In the priest, standing as Christ the Head, the offering of Christ and the personal sacrifices of the entire assembly are united.

---

8. In the earthly liturgy we take part in a foretaste of that heavenly liturgy celebrated in the holy city of Jerusalem toward which we journey as pilgrims, where Christ is sitting at the right hand of God, a minister of the holies and of the true tabernacle;[15] we sing a hymn to the Lord's glory with the whole company of heaven; venerating the memory of the saints, we hope for some part and fellowship with them; we eagerly await the Savior, our Lord Jesus Christ, until he, our life, shall appear and we too will appear with him in glory.[16]

15. See Rv. 21:2; Col 3:1; Heb 8:2.
16. See Phil 3:20; Col 3:4.

Article 8 introduces the eschatological dimension of the Sacred Liturgy drawing principally upon the scriptural tradition and liturgical imagery inherited from Christian liturgy's Jewish ancestry. Jerusalem with its Temple, "called a house of prayer,"[20] the house of the Father, is the center of all worship and the visible sign that God has chosen to make his dwelling among the human race.[21] Throughout the liturgical year, the imagery of Jerusalem and the temple repeats like a mantra, a constant reminder that the true citizenship of every Christian is the heavenly Jerusalem.[22] The inscription into this celestial kingdom comes through the work of the Sacred

Liturgy.[23] In ancient times, the temple symbolized the Garden of Eden and worship effects a return to paradise.[24] Thus, there is begotten a communion between heaven and earth in the celebration of the Sacred Liturgy, whereby the eternal communion of heaven is anticipated and touched.

This article manifests that the traditional ecclesiology still holds, yet there is a linguistic shift as the earthly Church is not described as the Church militant but with the more explicitly biblical term of "pilgrim." Anticipating the development of the theme of the pilgrim Church in *Lumen gentium* (LG), SC subtly introduces the term which engendered debate and discussion at the Council. Chapter VII of LG seems to be seminally present in article 8, particularly in the preoccupation of linking the pilgrim Church on earth to the saints in heaven. The Council Fathers struggled to articulate and preserve the place of the cult of saints.[25] The proper context assigned later by LG is already present in this article of SC where all worship points toward heaven, the communion of angels and saints, and the spirit of hope in which the Church continues to pray, *Maranatha*!, "Come, Lord Jesus."[26] It should be noted that such an interplay of eschatological themes finds its origin in Sacred Scripture, particularly in the final book of the New Testament which contains the great Seer of Patmos's vision of the heavenly liturgy.

Despite attempts to preserve the proper cult of the saints in the Church's liturgical life, the years following the Council saw a marked decrease in devotions to the saints. Partly a purification of excessive expressions of saintly devotion and partly a misplaced prejudice against seemingly lower forms of Christian piety, the lack of a lively devotion to the saints continues to some extent today. This unfortunate loss, more than removing the popular novenas and sanctoral festivities from Catholic life, severely disconnected the earthly celebration of the Sacred Liturgy with its intrinsic eschatological tones. Such a loss negatively affects the deeper spiritual experience of the liturgy which is unlocked by the awareness of the participation in a more-than-earthly ritual. As Jean Corbon beautifully states it, "The liturgy is therefore not a component of the mystery of the Church; rather, the Church is the liturgy as this presently exists in our mortal humanity. The Church is as it were the human face of the heavenly liturgy, the radiant and transforming presence of the heavenly liturgy in our present time."[27]

---

9. The liturgy does not exhaust the entire activity of the Church. Before people can come to the liturgy they must be called to faith and to conversion: "How then are they to call upon him in whom they have not yet believed? But how are they to believe him whom they have not heard? And how are they to hear if no one preaches? And how are men to preach unless they be sent?" (Rom 10:14 –15).

Therefore the Church announces the good tidings of salvation to those who do not believe, so that all may know the true God and Jesus Christ whom he has sent and may be converted from their ways, doing penance.[17] To believers, also, the Church must ever preach faith and penance, prepare them for the sacraments, teach them to observe all that Christ has commanded,[18] and invite them to all the works of charity, worship, and the apostolate. For all these works make it clear that Christ's faithful, though not of this world, are to be the light of the world and to glorify the Father in the eyes of all.

17. See Jn 17:3; Lk 24:47; Acts 2:38.
18. See Mt 28:20.

The Sacred Liturgy presupposes faith, a faith that has the power of repentance and conversion, because through the Sacred Liturgy humanity encounters and enters into relationship with the Triune God. Faith disposes the individual to this relationship which is never isolated but always mediated through the community of the Church. This is the greatest activity of the Church, to invite men and women to turn away from sin and to turn to God. In this way, Christ's faithful illuminate the world with the light of Christ and continue the mission of Christ. Engaging fully the ministry of the Lord, the Church is called to avoid any semblance of ritualism and elitism which reduces her ministry to only what happens within the walls of the Church. Such an erroneous perspective not only ignores the full commandment of Christ to "Go into all the world and proclaim the good news to the whole creation,"[28] but it also contradicts the very nature of the Sacred Liturgy in whose supreme action the assembly is sent forth into the world hearing, "*Ite, missa est.*"

Thus, this cautionary statement of fact in turn acknowledges a much more fundamental connection between the celebration of the Sacred Liturgy and its effects on its participants, shaping and forming them to accomplish the mission of Christ in the world through teaching the faith, performing acts of charity and service, and engaging the various ministries and apostolic endeavors to which the Church summons all of her members. Perhaps the expression attributed to a European cardinal from the twentieth century sums up the essence of this article best, "Liturgy without mission is ritualism. Mission without liturgical foundation is mere religious ideology."[29]

The marriage of mission and the Sacred Liturgy was not always a happy one in the years that followed the Council. Ideological divides and uneven approaches to social justice did not always take into account the necessity of grace for engaging the apostolic work of the Church. To some, the liturgical life of the Church before the Council was seen as an impediment to the practical call of service. Unfortunately, few had the incomparable insight of the great Dorothy Day who saw the Sacred Liturgy as the source of her strength to serve, particularly in the regular participation in the Holy Eucharist and the Divine Office.

Yet, as much as the initial decades after the Council swayed to one side of this issue, it can be observed that in recent times the other side of the issue has taken hold as well. One cannot help but notice a marked decline in the attention toward the charitable and apostolic work of the Church while the recent decade has seen a dramatic rise in the renovation of sacred space for divine worship and the rediscovery of a highly stylized celebration of the rites of the Church. Perhaps what is needed more than ever is a return to the symbiotic and integrated vision proposed by SC which indicates not the "either/or" mentality, but the "both/and" principle, since the Church, born from her share in Christ's Paschal Mystery in the Sacred Liturgy, is created to go forth into the world in loving service of humanity.

---

10. Still, the liturgy is the summit toward which the activity of the Church is directed; at the same time it is the fount from which all the Church's power flows. For the aim and object of apostolic works is that all who are made children of God by faith and baptism should come together to praise God in the midst of his Church, to take part in the sacrifice, and to eat the Lord's Supper.

The liturgy in its turn moves the faithful, filled with "the paschal sacraments," to be "one in holiness";[19] it prays that "they may hold fast in their lives to what they have grasped by their faith";[20] the renewal in the eucharist of the covenant between the Lord and his people draws the faithful into the compelling love of Christ and sets them on fire. From the liturgy, therefore, particularly the eucharist, grace is poured forth upon us as from a fountain; the liturgy is the source for achieving in the most effective way possible human sanctification and God's glorification, the end to which all the Church's other activities are directed.

19. RomM, prayer after communion, Easter Vigil.
20. RomM, opening prayer, Mass for Monday of Easter Week.

Article 10 introduces the ubiquitous catchphrase of SC and the liturgical reform of the Second Vatican Council: source (or "fount") and "summit." In her spiritual commentary on SC, Pamela Jackson notes the origin of these phrases come from Church documents inspired by the Liturgical Movement: "Leo XIII's *Mirae caritatis* (1902) spoke of the eucharistic liturgy as the 'font and most important gift' of all Gods gifts; later, Pius XII would refer to it as the 'font an center of Christian piety,' the 'chief action of divine worship.'"[30] Pius X wrote in 1903 that "active participation in the most sacred mysteries and in the public and solemn prayer of the Church" was the "first and indispensable source" of the "true Christian spirit."[31] These papal documents and the teaching of Pius XII, particularly his encyclical *Mediator Dei* (1947), provide the immediate authoritative doctrinal origin of this essential teaching of the Second Vatican Council.

As "fount" the Fathers of the Council recapitulate the unique and indispensable source of grace effected by the celebration of the Sacred Liturgy, especially the sacraments. Without this grace, the Church would be a human institution fueled by human ingenuity alone. But this cannot be so, since the Church is born from the Paschal sacraments.[32] In Baptism, fallen men and women are elected as God's adopted children in Christ. In this sacrament they enter into a "covenant" with God that is renewed and strengthened by the Holy Eucharist which binds them ever more closely to Christ in the bonds of charity, and enkindles the flame of the Holy Spirit within them. This fundamental change sacramentally caused in humanity orients the work of the Church toward the worship of the Triune God, which is the ultimate purpose of all endeavors, but finds its "summit" in the public worship of the Church gathered for the Sacred Liturgy.

In the time since this Council, through a return to the mystical understanding of the Sacred Liturgy[33] and the development of liturgical theology in its own right,[34] a more integrated notion of "fount" and "summit" reveals the place of the Sacred Liturgy in the lives of believers as more than moments which interrupt the ordinary course of life. Instead, the circularity of "fount" and "summit" recapitulate the truth that the Sacred Liturgy is reality. As Jean Corbon writes, "When we celebrate the liturgy, we participate in an intense and unique way in the totality of our life. . . . We truly 'live' during the celebration. . . . None of us is ever so much himself or herself, nor is the Church so much herself, nor are the universe and history so exalted in hope of glory, as when the liturgy is being celebrated."[35] It is this fundamental belief that compels the Church to celebrate the Sacred Liturgy, and to engage in the apostolic drive of evangelization which draws all of humanity into reality itself which makes them holy and glorifies God.

---

11. But in order that the liturgy may possess its full effectiveness, it is necessary that the faithful come to it with proper dispositions, that their minds be attuned to their voices, and that they cooperate with divine grace, lest they receive it in vain.[21] Pastors must therefore realize that when the liturgy is celebrated something more is required than the mere observance of the laws governing valid and lawful celebration; it is also their duty to ensure that the faithful take part fully aware of what they are doing, actively engaged in the rite, and enriched by its effects.

21. See 2 Cor 6:1.

Anticipating the theme of full, active, and conscious participation, article 11 indicates the traditional doctrine of the state of grace, the notion of intentionality, and the effects of cooperating grace. Carefully avoiding the scholastic distinctions of grace, the article clearly presumes the scholastic categories of *gratia praeveniens, gratia sacramentalis*, and *gratia cooperans*. Grace is at work preparing men and women to share in divine life. Grace is at work transforming men and women by the sacraments. And grace is at work when these transformed, adopted sons and daughters allow themselves to be drawn into the mysteries celebrated through a total cooperation of their minds and hearts, bodies and souls.

Overcoming a passive participation in the Sacred Liturgy was a constant preoccupation of the Liturgical Movement and Pope Pius XII carried the discussion further by promoting a deep and interior devotion in his teachings. In *Mediator Dei* (MD) Pope Pius XII writes,

"[T]he chief element of divine worship must be interior. For we must always live in Christ and give ourselves to Him completely, so that in Him, with Him and through Him the heavenly Father may be duly glorified."[36] Article 11 clearly draws its inspiration from *Mediator Dei*, particularly in the injunction given to pastors to assist the faithful in their full participation in the celebrations.

Zeal for reform in the years after the Council provided for quick and sometimes unprepared-for implementation of liturgical adjustments. Lack of preparation among clergy regarding the theological foundations and the full signification of the reforms impeded, in many places, the proper preparation of the lay faithful. All too often, the call for interior participation sounded in article 11 was drowned out by an enthusiasm for the exterior participation promoted in later articles of SC, such as vernacular changes, the use of dialogues, and the expanded liturgical role of the laity as liturgical ministers. The grace-filled participation of the mind and heart, as envisioned by this passage of SC, has yet to reach its full fruition despite attempts by some recent clarifications of Pope Benedict XVI to stress it. As Pamela Jackson asks, "How many of those at Mass each week could describe what 'proper dispositions' are, or what they are doing in order to 'co-operate with grace'?"[37] The renewal of the Sacred Liturgy envisioned by the Liturgical Movement and called for by the Second Vatican Council saw these fundamental questions being answered, if not before, then at the same time as the promotion of a wider exterior sharing in liturgical ministers, since the faithful cannot "[l]ift up [their] hearts to the Lord" without first handing over their hearts to the action.

12. The spiritual life, however, is not limited solely to participation in the liturgy. Christians are indeed called to pray in union with each other, but they must also enter into their chamber to pray to the Father in secret;[22] further, according to the teaching of the Apostle, they should pray without ceasing.[23] We learn from the same Apostle that we must always bear about in our body the dying of Jesus, so that the life also of Jesus may be made manifest in our bodily frame.[24] This is why we ask the Lord in the sacrifice of the Mass that "receiving the offering of the spiritual victim," he may fashion us for himself "as an eternal gift."[25]

22. See Mt 6:6.

23. See 1 Thes 5:17.
24. See 2 Cor 4:10 –11.
25. RomM, prayer over the gifts, Saturday after the 2d, 4th, and 6th Sundays of Easter.

Articles 11 and 12 form a continuum whose underlying motif is an integral engagement of Christian life and spirituality. As the work of the Church is not limited exclusively to the Sacred Liturgy, so the spiritual work of each Christian is not limited to liturgical participation. However, it should be noted in the same vein that such liturgical participation remains the "fount" and "summit" of every Christian spirituality. Two expressions of a broader Christian spirituality are named: personal, continuous prayer and bodily mortification. These are certainly the staples of traditional Christian spirituality because they form the intimate union with Christ through perfect imitation of him in prayer and bodily penance.[38]

At first glance, this article may appear to be superfluous. Yet, it reflects a certain suspicion of the Liturgical Movement and its spirituality by those who held to the more traditional paths of spiritual life.[39] As early as the source of the Liturgical Movement, Benedictine Abbott Prosper Guéranger (1805–1875) in the mid-nineteenth century, a fear of the liturgy supplanting centuries of spiritual tradition held strong. Dom Guéranger made his position known, "By asserting the immense superiority of liturgical over individual prayer, we do not say that the individual methods should be suppressed; we would only wish them to be kept in their proper place."[40] Guéranger was absolutely convinced that the revival of Catholic life in France and the renewal of the Catholic spirit in Europe were directly linked to the reform of the Sacred Liturgy as the center and core of Christian life.[41] Some extreme positions, or perceived positions, derived from the Liturgical Movement threatened expressions of Catholic piety and devotional life as well as minimized the place of personal prayer and mortification. To that end, this article claims the place of these practices as integral (and not incidental or conflictual) to the spiritual life of Christians.

Although the liturgical reform movement following the Council did possess some of the tendencies to minimize the place of personal prayer and mortification in some circles, one of the greatest gifts from the Council helped to ensure that such would never be lost: the promotion of lay reading of the Sacred Scripture. In many circles, the prayerful study of Scripture and the revival of forms of *lectio divina* have helped to integrate personal and liturgical prayer, using the Lectionary cycle of readings as a starting point for prayer. Perhaps more serious than a threat to personal prayer has been the loss of a sense of penance and the place of mortification in everyday Catholic life. Many factors have contributed to this diminution: the excesses ushered into society by the sexual revolution and consumerism; the loss of a collective sense of penance on Fridays during the entire year; and, the rightful concern expressed against sometimes harmful or excessive penance employed by overly zealous individuals. Continuing the good progress made in uniting personal prayer and liturgical life, hope ushers in a certain confidence that the place of mortification will once again return to the collective sense of Christian spirituality with the advice derived from St. Benedict's axiom: "all things are to be done with moderation."[42]

---

13. Popular devotions of the Christian people are to be highly endorsed, provided they accord with the laws and norms of the Church, above all when they are ordered by the Apostolic See.

Devotions proper to particular Churches also have a special dignity if they are undertaken by mandate of the bishops according to customs or books lawfully approved.

But these devotions should be so fashioned that they harmonize with the liturgical seasons, accord with the sacred liturgy, are in some way derived from it, and lead the people to it, since, in fact, the liturgy, by its very nature far surpasses any of them.

Like the preceding article, article 13 responds definitively to the fear that the Liturgical Movement will remove the traces of popular devotion and piety from Catholic life. The statement that they are to be "highly endorsed" goes beyond permission to promotion. In many places, especially in Europe, local shrines and communities have particular expressions of devotion that form not only the backbone of their Christian life but also of their ethnic identity. The loss of devotional life in the Church would impede not only the spirituality of the faithful but also risks cultural repercussions. With the ease of a compromise statement, article 13 acknowledges firmly the place of these devotions while at the same time ordering them to the rhythm of the liturgical life of the Church. In no way does the liturgical reform of SC give indication that expressions of popular piety or devotional expressions are to be eradicated from the life of the Church. In some ways, this article repeats themes introduced above in articles 8 and 12.

In the time since the Council, great attention has been paid by liturgical ministers to the issue of integrating the traditional devotions of the Church into the liturgical seasons and sanctoral cycle. Any initial hesitation to do this has given way to a broader scope of the recitation of the Rosary in most parishes during the months of May (traditionally dedicated to the Blessed Mother) and October (the Month of the Holy Rosary). At the invitation of both Pope John Paul II and Pope Benedict XVI, Eucharistic processions and Eucharistic adoration have seen a great resurgence. While the work of implementing the Council's vision is still not complete, signs such as these, as well as the careful attention to respecting the manner in which these devotions relate to the liturgy give indication that the devotional life of the Church has not disappeared.

II. Promotion of Liturgical Instruction and Active Participation

---

14. The Church earnestly desires that all the faithful be led to that full, conscious, and active participation in liturgical celebrations called for by the very nature of the liturgy. Such participation by the Christian people as "a chosen race, a royal priesthood, a holy nation, God's own people" (1 Pt 2:9; see 2:4–5) is their right and duty by reason of their baptism.

In the reform and promotion of the liturgy, this full and active participation by all the people is the aim to be considered before all else. For it is the primary and indispensable source from which the faithful are to derive the true Christian spirit and therefore pastors must zealously strive in all their pastoral work to achieve such participation by means of the necessary instruction.

Yet it would be futile to entertain any hopes of realizing this unless, in the first place, the pastors themselves become thoroughly imbued with the spirit and power of the liturgy and make themselves its teachers. A prime need, therefore, is that attention be directed, first of all, to the liturgical formation of the clergy. Wherefore the Council has decided to enact what follows.

Article 14 lies at the very heart of the liturgical reforms mandated at the first session of the Second Vatican Council. The call for full participation is the cornerstone of the liturgical reforms and has been called the "refrain" of *Sacrosanctum Concilum*—appearing sixteen times throughout the document.[43] The sentence—"this full and active participation by all the people is the aim to be considered before all else"—has caused much ink to flow in recent decades as authors have debated the meaning of the Latin expression *actuosa participatio.* Nevertheless, the expression *participatio actuosa* is classic. Pope Pius X called for active participation in his *motu proprio, Tra le sollecitudini* (1903).[44] Again in his apostolic constitution, *Divini cultus sanctitatem,* he wrote in 1928 that the restoration of Gregorian chant for the use of the people would provide the means whereby they "may more actively participate in divine worship."[45] However, in this document emphasis was also laid upon an appreciation of the beauty of the liturgy that is capable of stirring the heart of the worshipper, who thereby enters into the realm of the sacred mysteries. Pius XII in his encyclicals *Mystici Corporis Christi* (1943) and *Mediator Dei* (1947) also used the term, but insisted that true participation was not merely external. *De Musica sacra et sacra Liturgia,* an instruction issued in 1958 by the Sacred Congregation for Rites, distinguished between the various levels of participation, indicating thereby that the possibility of profound interior participation was linked to high standards of execution.

What then is meant by full and active participation? What did the Council Fathers intend by using the expression *plena et actuosa participatio?* Mark Searle, in his posthumously published work *Called to Participate,* delineates three levels of participation: participation in ritual behavior, participation in the liturgy of the Church, and participation in the life of God. In this manner, he avoids the false dichotomy between outward and inward participation. Both inward and outward participation are sought in the reforms and they complement one another. Therefore, participation should not be limited to the outer forms, but these should help the faithful enter the deeper interior dimension of praying "in spirit and truth."[46]

The theological reason for the liturgical demands of participation flows directly from the waters of Baptism: "Such participation by the Christian people as 'a chosen race, a royal priesthood, a holy nation, God's own people' (1 Pet. 2:9; see 2:4–5) is their right and duty by reason of their baptism."[47] The Council sought to lead the baptized not simply to a more active engagement in the exterior ritual action of the liturgy but to bring about a fuller participation in the Paschal Mystery of Christ celebrated in the Eucharist as the source and summit of the Christian life. Two (or perhaps three[48]) qualifiers are found in the various citations from SC modifying participation, namely fully "conscious" and "active." In order to ensure that the participation of all the baptized faithful is fully conscious, that is, knowing, responsive, informed, and fully understanding the meaning of the rites and gestures of each celebration, SC recognized the necessity for liturgical formation. Thus, the five articles that follow (SC 15–19) deal specifically with the need for liturgical education and formation. In order to ensure that the participation of all the baptized faithful is "active," all the rites beginning with the Eucharist were reformed in order that the baptized faithful "take part by means of acclamations, responses, psalmody, antiphons, and songs, as well as by actions, gestures, and bearing. And at the proper times all should observe a reverent silence."[49]

But the mention of the importance of Baptism had consequences on the subsequent sessions of the Council and on the development of the document, *Lumen gentium*. Massimo Faggioli has written extensively on how the ideas of SC bore fruit in the overall ecclesiology that emerged from the Council.[50] Twenty years after the Second Vatican Council, a Synod of Bishops met in Rome to discuss the role of the laity. Out of this came the post-synodal apostolic exhortation of John Paul II, *Christifidelis laici*, in which the pope declared that "In the wake of the Second Vatican Council, at the beginning of my pastoral ministry, my aim was to emphasize forcefully the priestly, prophetic and kingly dignity of the entire People of God."[51] A new appreciation of Baptism was shaped at the Council—an appreciation which continues to shape the Church and her ecclesiology.

In *Christifidelis laici*, the Holy Father continues:

> Life according to the Spirit, whose fruit is holiness (cf. *Rom* 6:22; *Gal* 5:22), stirs up every baptized person and requires each to *follow and imitate Jesus Christ,* in embracing the Beatitudes, in listening and meditating on the Word of God, *in conscious and active participation in the liturgical and sacramental life of the Church,* in personal prayer, in family or in community, in the hunger and thirst for justice, in the

> practice of the commandment of love in all circumstances of life and service to the brethren, especially the least, the poor and the suffering.[52]

The link between participation in the liturgy and the sacraments logically leads to engagement with the world and social justice. This theme was in the forefront of the Liturgical Movement well before the Council and the connection between liturgy and social justice, between Eucharist and ethics, continues to be made.

On the fiftieth anniversary of the promulgation of *Sacrosanctum Concilium*, after five decades of experience of the reformed liturgy, it is timely to consider again what the Council meant by *participatio actuosa*. After the Synod of Bishops of 2006 dealing with the Eucharist, Pope Benedict XVI reflected upon this in his post-synodal papal exhortation, *Sacramentum caritatis*: "It should be made clear that the word 'participation' does not refer to mere external activity during the celebration. In fact, the active participation called for by the Council must be understood in more substantial terms, on the basis of a greater awareness of the mystery being celebrated and its relationship to daily life."[53] But he goes on to say: "In their consideration of the *actuosa participatio* of the faithful in the liturgy, the Synod Fathers also discussed the personal conditions required for fruitful participation on the part of individuals. One of these is certainly the spirit of constant conversion which must mark the lives of all the faithful."[54]

Active participation in the Eucharistic liturgy, therefore, requires that one enters deeply into the mystery requiring an examination of the inner disposition. Purifying one mind and heart makes genuine participation possible. So Benedict concludes: "The faithful need to be reminded that there can be no *actuosa participatio* in the sacred mysteries without an accompanying effort to participate actively in the life of the Church as a whole, including a missionary commitment to bring Christ's love into the life of society."[55]

A word must be said about the use of vernacular languages. *Sacrosanctum Concilium* was very clear that "particular law remaining in force, the use of the Latin language is to be preserved in the Latin rites."[56] But then in the next sentence it goes on to say, "But since the use of the mother tongue, whether in the Mass, the administration of the sacraments, or other parts of the liturgy, frequently may be of great advantage to the people, the limits of its employment may be extended." It seems that this provision had missionary countries in mind where use of Latin would be an impediment to evangelization. The shift from Latin to vernacular languages was one of the most hotly debated topics at the Council.[57] There were some bishops present at the Council who contended that Latin, even if it was not understood by most, was what gave Catholics their identity. The Conciliar debate over language in the liturgy, however, pointed to a much deeper tension that would affect the entire liturgical schema proposed to the bishops in Council. It should not surprise us that debates over liturgical languages ensued and continue today, fifty years after the Council, as evidenced by the translation of third edition of *The Roman Missal* that came into use in November 2011. Rev. Anscar Chupungco, former professor of liturgy at the Pontifical Liturgical Institute at Sant'Anselmo in Rome, emphasized that the vernacular plays an absolute role in assuring the active participation of the faithful in the liturgy. That absolute role demands that liturgical texts be easily understood in order to enable active and prayerful participation. It is little wonder that following the Council the movement to translate the liturgical texts into the vernacular languages took shape so quickly.

15. Professors appointed to teach liturgy in seminaries, religious houses of study, and theological faculties must be thoroughly trained for their work in institutes specializing in this subject.

It is clear that the reforms mandated by the Second Vatican Council did not fall from the sky, like Dorothy's house falling from Kansas into the land of Oz. The foundations for the liturgical reforms of the Council were laid by the Liturgical Movement. Historians mark the beginning of the Liturgical Movement in France when Dom Prosper Guéranger in 1833, along with several priests of the diocese of Le Mans, moved to the Abbey of St. Pierre at Solesmes on the banks of the Sarthe river in order to restore it so that they might live the *Rule of St. Benedict* and celebrate the Divine Office according to the original and most authentic form. As an essential part of the restoration, these priests undertook a comprehensive study of the liturgy in order to restore the French Church to a purer liturgical form that Guéranger believed was found in the Roman Rite. Restoration of Gregorian chant was the keystone to this project. At about the same time the Oxford movement was beginning in England under the leadership of E. B. Pusey. The Liturgical Movement spans roughly one-hundred fifty years, from Guéranger's initial work in the 1830s to the Second Vatican Council and the subsequent reforms of each sacrament up to the 1980s. The movement, which embraces a range of practices and thinkers in both Europe and North America, had three phases: monastic, parish and academic, and official.[58]

Who can say precisely when and where a movement of this kind begins? There are those who have marked the time when the meaning of the Liturgical Movement became clear to them. And there are others to whom it seems to have come as a progressive and continuous experience from childhood. Many scholars mark the beginning of the modern Liturgical Movement to the year 1909, localizing it to the Benedictine Abbey of Mont César in Belgium. There a monk named Lambert Beauduin, recognized both as a liturgical reformer and an ecumenist, brought his interests in liturgy together with his zeal for social justice. Drawn to the *Société des Aumôniers du Travail*,[59] he was ordained to the diocesan clergy but felt drawn to the monastic life. In 1906 he left for the life of a Benedictine monk at Mont César where he prepared to teach dogmatic theology (ecclesiology). It was here that he dreamed about a renewed liturgy both in parishes and monasteries that would renew the Church. In 1909 he attended the general chapter of the Benedictines in Beuron that lead him to the Congress of Catholic Works in Malines, which he declared as the official beginning for his work in liturgical reform and ecumenism. But it was during his years at Rome (1921–1925) while preparing his lectures on ecclesiology that Beauduin became acutely aware of the problem of Christian unity through his contacts with Anglicanism and with the Christian East. He taught university level courses both at Sant'Anselmo in Rome and the *Institut Supérieur de Liturgie* in Paris.

Article 15 of *Sacrosanctum Concilium*, therefore, represents an impetus already underway in three centers of learning in Europe: Trier, Paris, and Rome. The first center developed in Germany in 1946, with the establishment of a chair of liturgy in the theology faculty of the University of Trier. In 1947 the Liturgical Institute of Trier was founded and in 1948 the Herwegen Institute for the Promotion of Liturgical Studies at Maria Laach soon came into being. A decade later in 1956 a French center was created with the establishment of the *Institut Supérieur de Liturgie* in Paris. Dom Bernard Botte[60] tells of the institute's early years and his apprehension at the news of a similar institute that was to be established in Rome at the Benedictine Athenaeum of Sant'Anselmo in the early 1960s. A few years later, in 1966, a doctoral program in liturgy began at the University of Notre Dame, built on the foundations of the Master of Arts summer program begun by Rev. Michael Mathis, CSC, in 1947. Initially it was these schools who produced the professors of liturgy to teach in universities, colleges, and seminaries. Other schools in turn followed suit by adding doctoral programs in liturgical studies, most notably the Graduate Theological Union in Berkeley founded in 1962 representing Catholic, Protestant, Unitarian Universalist, Greek Orthodox, Jewish, Muslim, and Buddhist faith traditions and the Catholic University of America in Washington, DC, which began its graduate program in liturgy in 1970.[61]

There are several Catholic institutions offering graduate degrees other than the PHD in liturgy, which provides an alternate route for those preparing to teach liturgical studies in seminaries and colleges. For example, there is the pontifical degree in theology (STD) with a specialization in liturgy and sacramental theology. This degree is required for pontifical faculties who grant pontifical degrees and is very appropriate for seminary teachers. There is also the Doctorate in Ministry degree (DMIN) that could have a strong liturgical component.[62]

From the beginning the study of liturgy has been very ecumenical.[63] Within the United States, PHD programs with some form of liturgical concentration exist at Duke University, Emory University in the Candler School, Drew University (although this degree has been withdrawn recently), and Garrett-Evangelical Theological Seminary (Evanston, Illinois), just to mention a few.

Suffice it to say that liturgical studies as its own discipline is a relatively new field. The intentional training of professors of liturgy for seminaries is of recent origin. Prior to this time, seminarians were taught how to "say Mass" and perform the sacraments in courses of Canon Law where a rubrical approach dominated the discussion, whereby following the liturgical rules was enough to ensure the sacramental effect.[64] There was more of an interest in the "how" rather than the "why." With the creation of schools with doctorates specializing in liturgical studies, this new field was born. Initially the principle methodology was historical. To this was added a more theological dimension. Finally the human sciences were incorporated with the advent of ritual studies, a method that had been pioneered in theatrical circles under the form of semiotics and later applied to ritual performance.

On the fiftieth anniversary of *Sacrosanctum Concilium*, the Catholic Academy of Liturgy (CAL) at its annual meeting in Albuquerque looked at articles 15 and 16 reflecting on the future of liturgical studies and the mission of CAL in light of the last half century of experience of liturgical reform and teaching. A survey was prepared and administered electronically to all the members of CAL. Although the survey is still in progress, preliminary results show much hopefulness in the group. The largest cohort of respondents are in their sixties, and well over half the respondents see themselves continuing in their present profession for ten years or less. Most respondents (about three-fourths) see their current position continuing after they retire. A minority, but a fairly sizable one, would *not* counsel young people to go into graduate studies in liturgy. But the vast majority of respondents, more than nine out of ten, *would* pursue graduate studies in liturgy if they themselves had it to do over. There was optimism that the quality of liturgical music will improve in most places, that preaching training will improve, that laity will increasingly claim their baptismal dignity and insist on active liturgical participation, that institutional support for academic liturgy will remain strong. But there was concern expressed about training in presiding skills, about whether preaching will improve, about diocesan support for good liturgy, about future rates of Mass attendance, about bishops wanting liturgical experts in their diocese, about bishops' commitment to multicultural issues (questions concerned Asians, African Americans, Native Americans).

---

16. The study of liturgy is to be ranked among the compulsory and major courses in seminaries and religious houses of studies; in theological faculties it is to rank among the

principal courses. It is to be taught under its theological, historical, spiritual, pastoral, and canonical aspects. Moreover, other professors, while striving to expound the mystery of Christ and the history of salvation from the angle proper to each of their own subjects, must nevertheless do so in a way that will clearly bring out the connection between their subjects and the liturgy, as also the underlying unity of all priestly training. This consideration is especially important for professors of dogmatic, spiritual, and pastoral theology and for professors of holy Scripture.

The broad background of this article demonstrates the tremendous development that took place in the study of liturgy over the past century reflecting both scholarly research and widespread pastoral experience. This article then deals with two distinct questions: (1) the formal teaching of the science of liturgy in seminaries, religious houses of study, and theological faculties; and (2) the relation and integration of other ecclesiastical disciplines and the study of liturgy. Since the Second Vatican Council there has been a movement toward the study of liturgy as a field of its own and not simply as a subset of Canon Law. Kathleen Cahalan notes: "There were no dramatic changes in the official theology and practice of the sacraments between the Council of Trent and Vatican II. Sacramental practice was defined according to the moral and legal obligations that were summarized in the third part of moral theology manuals, according to the rubrics of canon law."[65] Bernard Häring used to recount that as a young seminarian he was taught that a priest could sin countless times just by saying Mass if the rubrics (the ritual directions printed in red ink) were not followed to the letter. The preparation of professors must be in accordance with the whole intent and purpose of SC, certainly more than an education in the history of liturgical law. The intent of SC was to promote the pastoral purpose of the liturgy; nevertheless professors of liturgy would need the same scientific background as other seminary professors in the other disciplines therefore necessitating specialized institutes for higher liturgical training.

Following the Council the mandate for liturgical formation had to be interpreted and implemented by each episcopal conference and religious order. In the United States the American bishops drafted and approved the *Program of Priestly Formation* (PPF) now in its fifth edition.[66] Liturgical practice and studies were interwoven among the four pillars of formation: human, spiritual, intellectual, and pastoral. The program provided a way of life permeated by the threefold charge given priests at ordination to teach, to sanctify, and to govern. College-level seminarians were encouraged to begin the study of theology, with undergraduate courses that focus on the fundamental beliefs and practices of the Catholic faith. College-level theology courses should study the themes contained in the *Catechism of the Catholic Church,* including courses on Catholic doctrine, liturgy and sacraments, Catholic morality, Christian prayer, and Sacred Scripture.

At the post-baccalaureate level, the theology studied in preparation for priestly ministry in major seminaries, in a particular way, had to find integration and focus in the liturgy as the celebration of the mystery of Christ. To enter a major seminary a minimum of twelve semester credit hours or their equivalent are required in appropriate courses of undergraduate theology. These courses should study the themes of the Catechism (doctrine, liturgy and sacraments, morality, prayer) as well as Sacred Scripture. In liturgy, the core curriculum included studies in the theological, historical, spiritual, pastoral, and juridical aspects of liturgy.[67] Courses in theology, history, and liturgy, where appropriate, include the role and contribution of the Eastern Churches.[68]

---

17. In seminaries and houses of religious, clerics shall be given a liturgical formation in their spiritual life. The means for this are: proper guidance so that they may be able to understand the sacred rites and take part in them wholeheartedly; the actual celebration of the sacred mysteries and of other, popular devotions imbued with the spirit of the liturgy. In addition they must learn how to observe the liturgical laws, so that life in seminaries and houses of religious may be thoroughly permeated by the spirit of the liturgy.

Liturgical formation goes beyond the classroom. Liturgical formation is regarded as a part of a life of steady prayer first and foremost centered in the sacraments, especially in the Eucharist, the Liturgy of the Hours, and the liturgical cycles, but also in prayer that is personal and devotional. Therefore, either the director of spiritual formation or the director of liturgy provides for the liturgical life and prayer of the seminary community, making provision for the daily celebration of the Eucharist, the Liturgy of the Hours, and opportunities for celebration of the Sacrament of Penance. Liturgical formation includes retreats and days of recollection, making sure they are well planned and carefully executed. Thus good liturgy is taught best by experiencing good liturgies.[69]

An oft-quoted passage about the role of good liturgy is found in the American bishops' document *Sing to the Lord: Music in Divine Worship*: "Faith grows when it is well expressed in celebration. Good celebrations can foster and nourish faith. Poor celebrations may weaken it."[70] This is particularly true in seminary education. Well prepared and celebrated liturgies go a long way in the formation of the seminarian both liturgically and spiritually. Over the past half century, attention has been given to the mystagogical nature of liturgy.[71] The mystagogical method is very experiential. One learns best through experience. But following the experience, there is need for some reflection and sharing. Much like a three-legged stool, if any of these dimensions are missed, the stool falls over.

Reference is also made to the role given to popular devotions. Instances of popular devotions commended by the Apostolic See may be found in the encyclical *Mediator Dei*.[72] The Council clearly provided norms by which existing devotions (such as evening observances, holy hours, novenas, and so on) should be reappraised: (1) harmony with the liturgical seasons (an easily violated rule); (2) conformity to the liturgy itself and certainly not oppositions to its celebrations; (3) derivation from the liturgy, that is, at least a broad observance of the liturgical pattern of common worship, its hierarchical, communal, pastoral, didactic shape; (4) encouragement by the devotional practice of popular participation in liturgy itself, for example, frequent reception of the Holy Eucharist.

The relationship of devotions or popular piety to the official liturgy is more complicated than it first seems.[73] Rather than pitting devotions against the liturgy in binary opposition, it is necessary to plot the gesture of popular piety on a spectrum ranging from liturgical to anti-liturgical with two intermediary points of para-liturgical and quasi-liturgical. For example, there are certain gestures which originated as an expression of popular piety that were later incorporated into the liturgy. The distribution of ashes on Ash Wednesday, for example, is such a case. (Of course, the distinction between liturgical and devotional seems anachronistic for the Middle Ages, since certain elements began as a popular expression and only later were made official. There are many examples of this but certainly the private dispositional prayers that a priest would say before, during, and after Mass is an example. At the Second Vatican Council, many of these private prayers were eliminated but some still remain like the Confiteor ("I confess . . ."). A modern example of how a popular practice is gradually making its way into the liturgy is the lighting of the candles of the Advent wreath during the Introductory Rites of Mass.

There are many examples of quasi-liturgical devotional forms of prayer. Morning and Evening Prayer is often patterned after the Liturgy of the Hours but is not a strict liturgical form *per se*. In this case, it is adapted from and patterned after the Liturgy of the Hours and would constitute what might be called a quasi-liturgical form of prayer. The third category is para-liturgical forms of devotional prayer. Many prayers and practices that correspond in some way to the liturgical year, respecting the various feasts and seasons, but which are not derived from the official liturgy might fall under this category. The lighting of the Advent wreath in the home would constitute but one example of this kind of devotional form of prayer. Finally, there are devotional forms of prayer that can be classified as anti-liturgical. I hesitate to give an example here but one that readily comes to mind is the Novena for Divine Mercy. When Sister Faustina had her visions in the 1930s, the liturgies of Holy Week had not yet been reformed. About twenty years after her life, however, Pius XII mandated the reform of Holy Week with the result that the penitential Novena for Divine Mercy, which begins during the Paschal Triduum comes into direct conflict with the Church's liturgical practice of the feast of all feasts—Easter. It seems inconceivable that the Paschal Triduum would be overshadowed with a penitential practice. So that which began as a fine expression of popular piety eventually came into direct conflict with the Church's liturgical year. Now that this feast has been incorporated into the general liturgical calendar (Second Sunday of Easter), it presents its own set of challenges in harmonizing the feast with the Easter Triduum celebrated a week earlier. Finally, there are other forms of devotional prayer, which seem to have no rapport with the official liturgy but are not harmful to the liturgy. *Sacrosanctum Concilium* provides a helpful principle in judging the value of devotions if they flow from the liturgy and bring the faithful back to the liturgy. Using the aforementioned criteria might be a further way to evaluate the rapport between devotions and liturgy.

Regarding the study of liturgical law, until the Council, Canon Law made provision for the study of liturgy as a subsection of law. Until then, this was felt to refer to the courses in the manner of celebration, that is, the study of liturgical legislation and more especially the rubrics. The challenge was to move liturgical studies into the broader understanding of the "spirit of the liturgy" rather than reducing good liturgy to a matter of blindly and slavishly following rules.

18. Priests, both secular and religious, who are already working in the Lord's vineyard are to be helped by every suitable means to understand ever more fully what it is they are doing in their liturgical functions; they are to be aided to live the liturgical life and to share it with the faithful entrusted to their care.

The retooling of priests already ordained before 1962 was a great challenge in the years following the Council. But the challenge was expanded to include the liturgical formation of religious women and men as well as the laity. At a diocesan level offices of worship were established, in-service programs were developed, and workshops were conducted in order to educate priests who had been trained in the manualist tradition in vogue before the Council. This kind of formation is not done in graduate programs but on the diocesan level. It is fair to say that the implementation of this was fairly spotty with a focus on externals (the "new" rubrics). Also, since this kind of liturgical formation requires development of skills, this means that practical training as opposed to just listening to lectures or reading was imperative. In a similar way, surgeons learn in clinical situations. There was some aversion to this approach, however, since it might put priests in a situation where they might make a mistake and be embarrassed.

At regional and a national levels, Liturgical Weeks were organized, probably the most important one sponsored by the Liturgical Conference. The Liturgical Conference began in 1940, as an annual "liturgical week" under the leadership of the abbots of the Benedictine communities in the United States. In 1943 it was constituted under an independent board of directors. From 1940–1968, the National Liturgical Weeks brought together priests, religious, and laypeople from all over the United States, often attracting several thousand participants. In the years immediately following the promulgation of *Sacrosanctum Concilum*, the Liturgical Weeks brought together close to twenty thousand people.

In the United States much credit in the ongoing liturgical formation of the clergy is due to the Federation of Diocesan Liturgical Commissions (FDLC). As a national organization composed primarily of members of diocesan liturgical commissions and offices of worship, the FDLC serves as an official collaborating agent between the local churches and the United States Conference of Catholic Bishops' Committee on Divine Worship (BCDW). Diocesan liturgical personnel, appointed by their bishops, have responsibility for the promotion of the liturgical life of their dioceses. The stated goal of this federation is to promote the liturgy as the heart of Christian life—especially in the parish community. But as a pastoral and professional organization, the FDLC is committed to assist the Catholic Church in the United States, its hierarchy, the local churches, and the individual bishops in their responsibilities of providing positive leadership in liturgical celebration, education, and development.[74]

In recent decades other societies and associations have come into existence that help in the task of ongoing liturgical formation. Some thrive and grow while others have come and gone. Many could be named, but for the sake of space let me point to one that has special merit: the National Association of Pastoral Musicians (NPM), founded in 1976, gathers pastoral musicians together with the clergy. The genius of this association was the notion of the dual membership–pastoral musicians and pastors both receive the association's magazine and both groups are welcome and encouraged to attend the national and regional conventions. Special sessions for clergy are offered allowing for the ongoing education of the clergy, while sessions aimed at pastoral musicians assist them in their liturgical and musical formation.

For some (but not all) the ongoing formation of priests, religious women and men, and lay ecclesial ministers lie in the domain of summer programs. These programs are numerous and have been successful in educating thousands of people who have worked diligently for liturgical reform within religious communities, parishes and diocesan offices of worship. Some of the summer programs emphasize liturgy and music, while others may have several foci. Summer programs in liturgy have attracted many priests and religious was and were later extended to lay ecclesial ministers. Several summer programs in liturgy distinguished themselves nationally and internationally and attracted thousands of students over the years. The summers-only format initially catered to priests and religious women and men who could take time away from their apostolic activity to study. Later it suited well lay faithful with full-time professional and/or family responsibilities allowing students to implement in their own ministerial settings what they learn as the program unfolds, and then to bring their experience to bear on further study. Three of the oldest summer programs were at the University of Notre Dame (Indiana), St. John's University School of Theology•Seminary (Collegeville, Minnesota), and St. Joseph's College (Rensselaer, Indiana). Rev. Michael Mathis, CSC, founded the liturgical studies program at the University of Notre Dame in 1947. Out of his summer programs in liturgical studies grew the Notre Dame Center for Liturgy (previously the Center for Pastoral Liturgy), established in 1970, and the annual pastoral liturgy conferences, sponsored by the Center since 1971. In 1947, he petitioned university authorities to allow him to hold a summer session in liturgy. It was for undergraduates only and consisted of three courses: History of the Sacred Liturgy in the Latin Rite, Theory and Practice of Gregorian Chant, and a miscellany entitled Important Features of the Liturgy. By 1948, he was given permission to launch a graduate school of liturgy. Thus, he scoured Europe and the United States for the very best of the liturgical scholars. The summer faculty rosters he assembled read like a "Who's Who" of the Liturgical Movement.

Another great center for liturgical studies was at the monastic school of St. John's University in Collegeville, Minnesota, and the monk whose name is recognized as the driving force behind the beginnings of liturgical studies there was Rev. Virgil Michel, OSB. There is perhaps no other single individual to whom more credit is due for the inception and promotion of the Liturgical Movement in America. Those who knew Fr. Virgil well were in admiration of the broad range of his activity, and of its intensity, and of its sureness.

Finally, St. Joseph College in Rensselaer, Indiana has sponsored a summer-only program of Church Music and Liturgy for many years. Grounded solidly in liturgical tradition, the program maintains a pastoral focus on liturgical celebration in local communities. The program prepares students to promote quality liturgy in small rural communities as well as in large, urban, and suburban churches. Liturgy calls for full, conscious, and active participation in every kind of worshiping assembly—in every region and ethnic community.

Normally the Master of Arts in Liturgical Studies theologizes from the liturgies themselves, introducing students to the historical, theological, and pastoral dimensions of the Church's liturgical traditions, the nature of the ritual process, and the relationship between culture and liturgy. Academically specialized, this kind of study presumes a solid background in theology and Scripture and prepares students for service in liturgical formation, liturgical ministries, liturgical leadership, or further academic study. The following are some of the other programs that offer Master's degrees and have played a key role in the ongoing formation of clergy and pastoral liturgists: Santa Clara (California), Yale Divinity School and Yale Institute of Sacred Music (Connecticut), and St. Michael College (Vermont). By and large these programs emphasize the necessity of integrating academic work with practice. Study of the liturgy is always situated in the context of a praying, worshiping community. The most recent program specializing in liturgical studies is the Liturgical Institute of the University of St. Mary of the Lake at Mundelein (Illinois). Since 2000, the Liturgical Institute has focused on training, research, and publication in the fields of sacramental theology and liturgy. The Institute offers a professional Master of Arts in liturgy, an academic Master of Arts (liturgical studies), and a licentiate in sacred theology.

---

19. With zeal and patience pastors must promote the liturgical instruction of the faithful and also their active participation in the liturgy both internally and externally, taking into account their age and condition, their way of life, and their stage of religious development. By doing so, pastors will be fulfilling one of their chief duties as faithful stewards of the mysteries of God; and in this matter they must lead their flock not only by word but also by example.

Later in SC in article 41, mention is made of the bishop as the chief liturgist of a diocese. Thus, he has the responsibility to provide for liturgical instruction of the faithful. But because it is impossible for the bishop always and everywhere to preside over the whole diocese, he depends upon priests and deacons working in parishes. The experience for the past half century is that this responsibility is shared with all the faithful, particularly lay ecclesial ministers, many of whom have received special training and formation in liturgy.[75] In many places, the experience of the Sunday Celebration in the Absence of a Priest (SCAP) has become quite common. Thus, the liturgical life of the parish and its relationship to the bishop must be fostered among the faithful and clergy and efforts made to encourage a sense of community within the parish, above all in the common celebration of the Sunday Mass or the Sunday Communion Service.

In addition to the formational work done in dioceses, there was also the creation of national and diocesan liturgical centers to assist in this process. Various centers for liturgy have emerged over the years to assist in the formation of liturgical ministers. Three are of special note: Notre Dame, Georgetown, and Collegeville. Out of the summer programs in liturgical studies begun in 1947 grew the Notre Dame Center for Liturgy (previously the Center for Pastoral Liturgy), established in 1970, and the annual pastoral liturgy conferences, sponsored by the Center since 1971. The Georgetown Center for Liturgy, founded in 1981 by Georgetown University and Holy Trinity Catholic Church, is an education, research, and consultation center dedicated to transforming American Catholic parishes through the Liturgical renewal initiated by the Second Vatican Council. Finally the Godfrey Diekmann, OSB, Center for Patristics and Liturgical Studies, created in 1997, seeks to deepen contemporary understanding of early Christian theologians of the first through seventh centuries, and to promote the liturgical renewal called for by the Second Vatican Council.

There are a number of liturgical publications that have assisted in the ongoing liturgical formation and education. Some are decidedly academic while others tend to be more popular. Still there are others which straddle the divide. Some are specialized, tending toward the liturgical arts and architecture, while others focus on sacred and liturgical music. A special word should be said about *Worship*. This journal has been in existence since 1926. Formerly known as *Orate Fratres*, it is published by the monks of Collegeville, Minnesota. The first issue appeared on the First Sunday of Advent, 1926. In 1951, twenty-five years after the founding of the journal, its name was changed to *Worship*, an indication of the growing interest in the use of the vernacular in liturgical celebrations.

In terms of other kinds of publications, certainly The Liturgical Press has dominated the scene, particularly with the acquisition of Pueblo Books and Michael Glazier Press. Finally, Liturgy Training Publications bridges the gap of academic and popular publications with a wide variety of products like books, pamphlets, clip art, videos, CDs, magazines, and the like. Founded by the Archdiocese of Chicago, the mission statement summarizes best its *raison d'être*: To promote the liturgical formation "of the faithful and also their active participation in the liturgy both internally and externally, taking into account their age and condition, their way of life, and their stage of religious development"[76] so all the faithful may "become thoroughly imbued with the spirit and power of the liturgy."[77]

---

20. Radio and television broadcasts of sacred rites must be marked by discretion and dignity, under the leadership and direction of a competent person appointed for this office by the bishops. This is especially important when the service to be broadcast is the Mass.

Pastoral situations arise, where the faithful for many reasons, such as hospitalization, being house-bound, imprisonment and the like, are not able to attend Sunday Eucharist. Thus, episcopal conferences around the world have had to address the good use of the media in transmitting liturgical celebrations over radio, television, or other media such as the Internet. In the United States guidelines were approved by the National Conference of Catholic Bishops at its November 1997 Plenary Meeting. These guidelines were offered as a resource for diocesan bishops and communication and liturgy personnel entrusted with the televising of liturgies. Recognizing that being a part of the Sunday worshiping assembly is not always possible many dioceses telecast the Mass and other liturgies as a way of reaching out to those who cannot be physically present for the community's celebration of the Eucharist. The televised Mass is never a substitute for the Church's pastoral care for the sick in the form of visits by parish ministers who share the Scriptures and bring Holy Communion, nor is it ever a substitute for the Sunday Mass celebrated within a parish faith community each week. However, televising the Mass is a ministry by which the Church uses modern technology to bring the Lord's healing and comfort to those who cannot physically participate in the liturgical life of the local Church and who often experience a sense of isolation from the parish and its regular forms of prayer and worship. The televised Mass is also a way to evangelize through the media.

Sacrosanctum Concilium clearly articulated the primary importance of the faithful's "full, conscious, and active participation" which is called for "by the very nature of the liturgy" and which is their "right and duty by reason of their baptism."[78] Thus, participation in the Eucharist involves both internal and external expression including, but not limited to, an attitude of prayer and attention, physical movement, sentiments of praise and adoration, and joining in the sung and recited responses. Telecasts, by their very nature, attempt to connect people and places that are physically separated. While there may be a tendency for the medium of television, with its inherent lack of physical interaction, to lead people to more passive roles as spectators, some elements of the telecasts can engage the viewers as participants. Although the televised Mass is not a substitute for participation in the actual celebration of the Church's liturgy, it does provide an opportunity for those unable to be physically present (1) to identify with a worshiping community; (2) to hear the Word of God; and (3) and to be moved to expressions of praise and thanksgiving.

Diocesan liturgists and communication specialists who work to provide the televising of the Sunday liturgy offer a special service, often under very difficult conditions. It takes special skills and pastoral sensitivity to produce a televised celebration of the Mass that is liturgically sound, given the limits imposed by the medium itself and the difficulties often associated with the availability of air time and the funding of such broadcasts. In many instances, the Church does not have complete control over the televising of the liturgy. The Church is a guest in an environment not its own and constraints (length of air time, time of telecast, setting, and so on) are often imposed that are less than ideal. In addition, dioceses and religious groups are finding it very difficult even to be able to purchase air time for a telecast at an hour that is reasonable for viewers who are sick or elderly.

The first requirement for good telecast liturgies is good liturgical celebration. When the Mass or other liturgies are televised, those responsible for the preparation, production, and celebration must make every effort to respect basic liturgical principles. There are a number of models that may be used when the Mass is televised. Each model will be further enhanced if texts for the liturgy to be celebrated—including Scripture readings and music—are made available to viewers of the televised Mass, and if local parishes arrange for Holy Communion to be taken to the viewers of the televised Mass so that their reception of Communion coincides with the end of the televised Mass.

There are different modes of broadcast, namely live, delayed, or pre-recorded. Ideally, the Mass is telecast "live," in real time, as it is celebrated. Here, the viewer is able to join in the prayer of a worshiping community as the liturgy is celebrated. The liturgical days and seasons are respected and the worship setting as well as an actual praying community help the viewer to participate with an attitude of prayerful attention and internal participation. A second model is that of taping the Sunday Mass as it takes place in a local community and telecasting it at a later time that same day. This model is less than ideal because the telecast is separated from the actual celebration of the liturgy. However, it respects the nature of the liturgy and the liturgical season when it is celebrated (and telecast) on the actual liturgical day and allows those who watch and pray to identify with an actual community in its worship. This form of telecast is more difficult for dioceses and television stations because of the short time between taping and telecast and the limited number of personnel available on the weekend. A third model is that of pre-recording the liturgy for broadcast at a later date. While we understand that some dioceses may not be able to use either of the first two models, using the third model will require greater care to be able to overcome the limitations of this model, when the liturgy that is pre-recorded is celebrated outside the liturgical day or season or the assembly is not a community which regularly gathers for the celebration of the liturgy. Often it is a group of people who gather together specifically for the purpose of televising the liturgy. Time constraints placed on the liturgy can affect the flow of the liturgy (limiting the number of readings, length of Homily, choices of music, and other options) rather than allowing the liturgy to flow at an unhurried pace. Editing the liturgy by cutting out particular elements of the Mass, or by using special effects to enhance the liturgy artificially (for example, superimposing a crucifix on the host during the elevation, the incorporation of outside images), can be very distracting and in bad taste. Finally, the studio format and techniques may be distracting for those gathered to celebrate the Eucharist in that setting and may make the priest and other ministers appear to be actors rather than leaders of public worship.

Nevertheless, given the communal nature of liturgical prayer, it may, at times, be preferable to televise some forms of prayer other than the Eucharist, such as Morning or Evening Prayer, a Liturgy of the Word, or Scripture services. As noted earlier, the telecast of the Sunday Mass offers a unique challenge to liturgists and communication personnel. Limited access to air time, the constraints of time and personnel, and the resources needed for a telecast that is liturgically and technically effective create special difficulties for those who provide this pastoral service.

The media continues to assist both in liturgical formation and transmission of actual liturgies. Already distance learning plays a growing role in forming people who do not have the luxury of attending workshops, programs of study and the like, due to geographical distance and financial constraints. The Internet with its streaming possibilities offers access to liturgies to those who cannot physically attend. YouTube also has become a valuable tool as many rites and liturgical ceremonies are regularly posted. Finally there are the other yet-to-be-invented media which will offer yet again future possibilities. No doubt new rules and principles will need to be developed to keep up with the fast changing media, but it is exciting to witness how all the media can be of service to the Church.

III. The Reform of the Sacred Liturgy

---

21. In order that the Christian people may more surely derive an abundance of graces from the liturgy, the Church desires to undertake with great care a general reform of the liturgy itself. For the liturgy is made up of immutable elements, divinely instituted, and of elements subject to change. These not only may but ought to be changed with the passage

of time if they have suffered from the intrusion of anything out of harmony with the inner nature of the liturgy or have become pointless.

In this reform both texts and rites should be so drawn up that they express more clearly the holy things they signify and that the Christian people, as far as possible, are able to understand them with ease and to take part in the rites fully, actively, and as befits a community.

Wherefore the Council establishes the general norms that follow.

In Josef Jungmann's classic historical study, *The Mass of the Roman Rite: Its Origins and Development*, he likens the liturgy to a venerable, thousand-year-old castle that is both strange but noble, holding heirloom treasures of bygone years. And yet for Jungmann the fundamental structure of the liturgy, like a great castle that has been renovated and changed over the centuries, embodies a plan or architecture that communicates intelligibly to people regardless of its history.[79] One can see analogous insight in article 21 which introduces the overall interpretive framework for the renewal of the liturgy in terms of what is unchangeable and what is subject to modification. For at the foundation of liturgical reform established by *Sacrosanctum Concilium* is the theory that there is a liturgical nucleus or essence that is constant and unalterable and a husk or shell that is variable, elastic, and malleable. The latter is the true subject of renewal and renovation.

This overall principle was at the basis of liturgical reconstruction carried out by the *Consilium*[80] after the close of the Council. Historically there continues a fundamental structure to the liturgical rites that remains unalterable, but there is the casing that interfaces with culture that can be altered and modified. The work of the *Consilium*, and what followed in the task of the Congregation for Divine Worship, would be to bring the texts and rites to more full expression that had become opaque by the vestiges of history and no longer communicated effectively to communities of faith. Liturgical experts who understood the nuances of the historical development of the rites would discern what was unchangeable in relationship to what needed to be refurbished so as to express more clearly the mystery of faith in a contemporary age.

This interpretive framework remains the starting point of all the liturgical changes that were set in motion by the Liturgical Movement and the Council, and that continue today. Undergirding this framework is an ecclesiology that understands the Church and its most sacred expression as both divine and human, as both immutable and subject to change.[81] Theologically this viewpoint moves the Church away from a more legalistic liturgical agenda to one that is more dynamic and symbolic in its expression without eradicating the essential truth of that expression. Such ecclesiology at the basis of liturgy urges the Church to preserve what is atemporal for all ages while modifying, transforming, and restoring its expression in time and space.

A. General Norms

22. § 1. Regulation of the liturgy depends solely on the authority of the Church, that is, on the Apostolic See and, accordingly as the law determines, on the bishop.

§ 2. In virtue of power conceded by the law, the regulation of the liturgy within certain defined limits belongs also to various kinds of competent territorial bodies of bishops lawfully established.

§ 3. Therefore, no other person, not even if he is a priest, may on his own add, remove, or change anything in the liturgy.

Sacrosanctum Concilium clearly establishes that liturgical laws arise from not only the Holy See but also from episcopal conferences and local bishops. It breaks new ground in this matter differing from the Council of Trent that reserved the control of the liturgy solely to the Apostolic See. Similar to Trent, Pius XII taught in *Mediator Dei* that the "the Sovereign Pontiff alone enjoys the right to recognize and establish any practice touching the worship of God, to introduce and approve new rites, as also to modify those he judges to require modification."[82] Differently, article 22 concedes that each bishop has genuine authority and regulatory power over the liturgy. Hence a Copernican Revolution in matters of liturgical authority is established here. R. Kevin Seasoltz, OSB, explains this change: "The presumption is no longer that the bishop lacks authority until it is specifically given to him, but rather that he has authority unless it is reserved to the Pope or Apostolic See."[83]

Article 22 § 2 addresses the jurisdiction of the liturgy by territorial bodies of bishops legitimately established. Here juridical precedence is given to particular churches through collegiality manifest by culture, language, and territory. The Council underlines the authority of such bodies. Again, Seasoltz delineates the jurisdiction in the local ordinary: "The regional exercise of juridical power by bodies of bishops, whether in provincial and plenary councils or in Episcopal conferences, is certainly a manifestation of Episcopal collegiality and of corporate responsibility of all bishops for all the churches."[84]

The authority over liturgical renewal vested in the bishop is representative of a theology of local Church developed at the Council. This ecclesiology becomes reinforced especially in *Lumen gentium* whereby it says: "The bishop, invested with the fullness of the sacrament of Orders, is the 'the steward of the grace of the supreme priesthood,' above all in the Eucharist, which he himself offers, or ensures that it is offered, and by which the church continues to live and grow."[85]

The role of the bishop in liturgical matters has had a tremendous effect on the post-Conciliar Church. This is particularly evident in the developing world where episcopal conferences especially in Africa and Asia have called for innovations in the inculturation of the liturgy. Remarkable undertakings concerning the translations of the liturgy into the native languages of peoples in the developing world have spurred on new efforts in evangelization.

---

23. That sound tradition may be retained and yet the way remain open to legitimate progress, a careful investigation is always to be made into each part of the liturgy to be revised. This investigation should be theological, historical, and pastoral. Also the general laws governing the structure and meaning of the liturgy must be studied in conjunction with the experience derived from recent liturgical reforms and from the indults conceded to various places. Finally, there must be no innovations unless the good of the Church genuinely and certainly requires them; care must be taken that any new forms adopted should in some way grow organically from forms already existing.

As far as possible, marked differences between the rites used in neighboring regions must be carefully avoided.

Article 23 articulates another general norm about the structural revision of the liturgical rites. It underscores that the renovation of the liturgy should happen, but that the liturgical tradition must be retained and respected as an essential part of that renewal. New liturgical forms should grow organically from already-existing forms. It is emphasized here that liturgical renewal should preserve the worthiness of the tradition and reject unworthy rudiments of the new. This project for renewal had been inspired by the twentieth-century Liturgical Movement and already set in motion by Pius XII's *Mediator Dei* (1947), the revision of the Holy Week liturgies in the 1950s, and other revisions prior to the Council.

This norm articulated by article 23 was comprehensively set in motion by the *Consilium* in the years following the Council. The organization of its work, the composition of its members, and the general plan for liturgical reform itself that was set up by the bishops, linguists, liturgists, and theologians of the *Consilium* ensured that new liturgical forms would emanate from the liturgical tradition and in many cases reestablish the tradition that had been set off course by ahistorical consciousness.[86]

In-depth understanding of the relationship between history and tradition, and how that knowledge affects the creation of successful and valuable liturgy for the Church in any age, is a fundamental requirement for liturgical studies and for those who continue to provide leadership for liturgical matters. The Church is challenged by the need to continue to ensure that a truly informed body of bishops and theologians working together for the good of the Church's tradition has the resources of academies and institutes designed to foster this collaborative work.

---

24. Sacred Scripture is of the greatest importance in the celebration of the liturgy. For it is from Scripture that the readings are given and explained in the homily and that psalms are sung; the prayers, collects, and liturgical songs are scriptural in their inspiration; it is from the Scriptures that actions and signs derive their meaning. Thus to achieve the reform, progress, and adaptation of the liturgy, it is essential to promote that warm and living love for Scripture to which the venerable tradition of both Eastern and Western rites gives testimony.

In Article 24 of SC the bishops establish a principle of liturgical reform that can be seen as one of the most groundbreaking standards that affected modern Catholic liturgy. Integrating the Sacred Scriptures into the body of all liturgical celebrations and emphasizing the paramount importance of the Liturgy of the Word for all liturgical rites, was set up by the normative guidance of this article. Moreover the impetus behind this article was that in order for the liturgy to continue the work of Christ, the Scriptures, preaching, and the sign value of the Word of God needed to be given new importance and prominence in the life of the Church.

Catholic biblical scholarship that had been awakened by the modern biblical movement revealed the limited ministry of the Word of God intrinsic to Catholic liturgy prior to the Council. New approaches to biblical texts that would become explicit Catholic teaching in *Dei Verbum* were foreshadowed by *Sacrosanctum Concilium*'s agenda concerning the Scriptures.[87] The Council Fathers set out to expose the faithful to a much greater tapestry of the Bible. Moreover the program for reform emphasized the sacramentality of the Scriptures themselves brought forth through the Liturgy of the Word fundamental to all liturgical rites. These innovations concerning the relationship between Word and sacrament eventually would transform the laity's access to the mystery of salvation in the Scriptures and truly enliven deep hunger for knowledge of the biblical texts. This phenomenon in the life of the Church over the past fifty years cannot be underestimated as one of the most influential aspects of modern liturgical renewal.

---

25. The liturgical books are to be revised as soon as possible; experts are to be employed in this task and bishops from various parts of the world are to be consulted.

Article 25 simply states that the books used in liturgy are to be revised inclusive of the help of experts and bishops from various parts of the world.

B. Norms Drawn from the Hierarchic and Communal Nature of the Liturgy

26. Liturgical services are not private functions, but are celebrations belonging to the Church, which is the "sacrament of unity," namely, the holy people united and ordered under their bishops.[26]

Therefore liturgical services involve the whole Body of the Church; they manifest it and have effects upon it; but they also concern the individual members of the Church in different ways, according to their different orders, offices, and actual participation.

26. Cyprian, *On the Unity of the Catholic Church 7;* see *Letter 66,* n. 8, 3.

27. Whenever rites, according to their specific nature, make provision for communal celebration involving the presence and active participation of the faithful, it is to be stressed that this way of celebrating them is to be preferred, as far as possible, to a celebration that is individual and, so to speak, private.

This applies with special force to the celebration of Mass and the administration of the sacraments, even though every Mass has of itself a public and social character.

28. In liturgical celebrations each one, minister or layperson, who has an office to perform, should do all of, but only, those parts which pertain to that office by the nature of the rite and the principles of liturgy.

29. Servers, readers, commentators, and members of the choir also exercise a genuine liturgical function. They ought to discharge their office, therefore, with the sincere devotion and decorum demanded by so exalted a ministry and rightly expected of them by God's people.

Consequently, they must all be deeply imbued with the spirit of the liturgy, in the measure proper to each one, and they must be trained to perform their functions in a correct and orderly manner.

30. To promote active participation, the people should be encouraged to take part by means of acclamations, responses, psalmody, antiphons, and songs, as well as by actions, gestures, and bearing. And at the proper times all should observe a reverent silence.

31. The revision of the liturgical books must ensure that the rubrics make provision for the parts belonging to the people.

32. The liturgy makes distinctions between persons according to their liturgical function and sacred orders and there are liturgical laws providing for due honors to be given to civil authorities. Apart from these instances, no special honors are to be paid in the liturgy to any private persons or classes of persons, whether in the ceremonies or by external display.

The norms delineated in articles 26–32 can be analyzed as a whole, especially as to understand them in their historical context. While recognizing the hierarchical nature and organization of the liturgy, these articles can be interpreted as a normative critique of the clericalization and privatization of the sacramental rites that occurred in the West beginning in the Middle Ages and which continued to affect the Church up through the twentieth century.[88] The liturgy conceived as the sole possession or jurisdiction of the clergy led to radical misappropriation of sacramental celebrations devoid of true communal action. In the West, practices such as the "private" Mass and the assignment of clerics to altars tucked away in small sanctuaries lacking assemblies had communicated to the laity that their participation was superfluous to the liturgical act. Moreover imbued in the lives of the faithful in the West was a ritual imagination that often followed the alternative structures and participation of popular religion.[89]

In contrast to this history one can see guidelines for liturgical renewal in articles 26–30 which intend to effect a new relationship between liturgy and Church. The liturgy as the fundamental sign which makes the Church manifest to humanity must therefore be both hierarchic and communal so as to reflect the nature of the Church. Nevertheless, private liturgies defy it, especially the Eucharistic liturgy.[90] Various roles pertain to all who worship and each role should be understood as a ministry.[91] The assembly actively responds through its appropriate voice embodied in psalm, hymn, gesture, movement, and intended silence.[92] In this fuller sense the liturgy makes the Church and the Church makes the liturgy. A liturgy devoid of half its essential makeup disregards itself.

One sees here a foreshadowing of theological concepts and pastoral plans later developed in *Lumen gentium*. Rita Ferrone sums up this development as follows: "By asserting that liturgy is a communal action of the Church as a whole, not a private or individual function, firmly grounds the liturgical renewal in the idea of the Church as the people of God."[93] The guidelines for establishing a relationship between liturgy and Church in articles 26–30 purposely intend to supplant an ecclesiology that dominated the landscape of the Church for three centuries following the Council of Trent. They establish the practical framework for the ground plan teaching in article 14 by giving particular strategies for full, conscious, and active participation in the liturgical rites.[94]

Article 31 instructs that the rubrics of revised liturgical books should ensure that the liturgy pertains to the whole People of God and that the roles identified in articles 29 and 30 are integrated into the rites that will be revised. Whereas article 32 clarifies that a Church which identifies itself as the People of God, does not embody its liturgy with private ceremony that discriminates according to social class or prestige. The sacramental life of the Church defies such distinction.

What do these norms in articles 26–32 mean for us today? Clearly debates over their liturgical ecclesiology are alive in our contemporary Church and continue to represent ecclesial paradigms that are representative of pre- and post-Conciliar praxes of liturgical ministry. Massimo Faggioli claims that subverting the liturgical agenda of the Second Vatican Council clearly means undoing the ecclesiology established by the Council.[95] How local Churches and Conferences of Bishops respond to the need to integrate liturgical roles into their regular worship remains a crucial task for our day. Educating ourselves to see the direct relationship between liturgy and Church as enacted in our local assemblies is needed as an essential mystagogy for adult faith formation.

C. Norms Based on the Teaching and Pastoral Character of the Liturgy

33. Although the liturgy is above all things the worship of the divine majesty, it likewise contains rich instruction for the faithful.[27] For in the liturgy God is speaking to his people and Christ is still proclaiming his gospel. And the people are responding to God by both song and prayer.

Moreover, the prayers addressed to God by the priest, who presides over the assembly in the person of Christ, are said in the name of the entire holy people and of all present.

And the visible signs used by the liturgy to signify invisible divine realities have been chosen by Christ or the Church. Thus not only when things are read "that were written for our instruction" (Rom 15:4), but also when the Church prays or sings or acts, the faith of those taking part is nourished and their minds are raised to God, so that they may offer him their worship as intelligent beings and receive his grace more abundantly.

In the reform of the liturgy, therefore, the following general norms are to be observed.

27. See Council of Trent, sess. 22, 17 Sept 1562, *Doctrine on the Holy Sacrifice of the Mass,* chap. 8.

---

34. The rites should be marked by a noble simplicity; they should be short, clear, and unencumbered by useless repetitions; they should be within the people's powers of comprehension and as a rule not require much explanation.

---

35. That the intimate connection between words and rites may stand out clearly in the liturgy:

1. In sacred celebrations there is to be more reading from holy Scripture and it is to be more varied and apposite.

2. Because the spoken word is part of the liturgical service, the best place for it, consistent with the nature of the rite, is to be indicated even in the rubrics; the ministry of preaching is to be fulfilled with exactitude and fidelity. Preaching should draw its content mainly from scriptural and liturgical sources, being a proclamation of God's wonderful works in the history of salvation, the mystery of Christ, ever present and active within us, especially in the celebration of the liturgy.

3. A more explicitly liturgical catechesis should also be given in a variety of ways. Within the rites themselves provision is to be made for brief comments, when needed, by the priest or a qualified minister; they should occur only at the more suitable moments and use a set formula or something similar.

4. Bible services should be encouraged, especially on the vigils of the more solemn feasts, on some weekdays in Advent and Lent, and on Sundays and holy days. They are particularly to be recommended in places where no priest is available; when this is the case, a deacon or some other person authorized by the bishop is to preside over the celebration.

---

36. § 1. Particular law remaining in force, the use of the Latin language is to be preserved in the Latin rites.

§ 2. But since the use of the mother tongue, whether in the Mass, the administration of the sacraments, or other parts of the liturgy, frequently may be of great advantage to the people, the limits of its use may be extended. This will apply in the first place to the readings and instructions and to some prayers and chants, according to the regulations on this matter to be laid down for each case in subsequent chapters.

§ 3. Respecting such norms and also, where applicable, consulting the bishops of nearby territories of the same language, the competent, territorial ecclesiastical authority mentioned in art. 22, §2 is empowered to decide whether and to what extent the vernacular is to be used. The enactments of the competent authority are to be approved, that is, confirmed by the Holy See.

§ 4. Translations from the Latin text into the mother tongue intended for use in the liturgy must be approved by the competent, territorial ecclesiastical authority already mentioned.

This section of chapter I of SC addresses another important foundational liturgical theological teaching. Article 33 serves to establish this theology whereas articles 34–36 give the practical implications of it. This section undertakes the seminal question of the proper ends to which the liturgy is directed. What it investigates is that even though the liturgy is directed primarily to the worship of God, nevertheless, the entire liturgy, by its very essence, is also directed to a pastoral and didactic end. There is a dual purpose to the liturgical act. In praising and loving God in worship the community simultaneously engenders the self-realization of the Christ manifest in the midst of the local Church at prayer. Consequently the principal celebrant, the liturgical ministers, and the entire assembly are disposed to the grace freely offered, especially in the sacraments, when the Church worships God more genuinely and authentically. This formational dimension of the liturgy is not to be overestimated as a type of Pelagian fallacy (merit-based reception of grace), but it is not to be underestimated in just relinquishing the significance of human response to apathy and indifference or an excuse for it.

Articles 33–36 get at the heart of liturgical spirituality. Even though *Sacrosanctum Concilium* can be rightly criticized for its lack of explicit pneumatology,[96] these articles do implicitly reflect the role of the Holy Spirit in the dual ends of liturgical worship mentioned above. The Eastern Churches have taught us much about the educative or formative ends of liturgy and disposing ourselves to the Holy Spirit at work in the Church at prayer. Said simply, the liturgy is our greatest teacher. In disposing ourselves to its riches we are sanctified by its treasury of graces. Therefore we are called to enter into the liturgy with the fullness of our voices, our gestures, and our dispositions.

As stated above, articles 34–36 provide the practical dimensions of modern liturgical formation. Article 34 delineates that the rites should be simple, noble, and unburdened by useless repetitions. Even though some have taken issue with the meaning and intention of the juxtaposed notion of such concepts as rich (noble) and simple,[97] the bottom line of this article is that the rites need be understandable and accessible. Language and symbol can obfuscate meaning especially if it is unadulteratedly foreign, anachronistic, or strange. The bishops at the Council instructed by this norm that the renewal of the rites needs to follow an aesthetic of dignity and intelligibility.

Article 35 appeals to the centrality and importance of the Liturgy of the Word and how the readings from Scripture in the liturgy should be expanded to reflect a greater breadth of the biblical canon. Moreover the article again underlines the importance of preaching in liturgy and that it should not be an optional or occasional part of the rite. The integral role of the Word and the ministry of proclamation of it is presented here as an essential dimension of liturgy. Preaching and presiding are basic to liturgical action. An aspect of the proclaimed Word involves a mystagogy that not only breaks open the Scriptures but also explains the meaning of the liturgical rites themselves to the faithful. *Sacrosanctum Concilium* recognizes that competency in ministering the Word requires a conscientious responsibility for ministers to carry out this daunting task.

Article 36 considers one of the major factors in the educative and pastoral dimension of the liturgy. It is clear that the Council Fathers intended that Latin should be maintained in the Roman Rite, however it is unambiguous from this article that the vernacular languages were also being introduced as a necessary way to overcome the obstacle that the Latin language had created in the evangelization of peoples throughout the world. By the time of its promulgation this article was being interpreted as the widespread introduction of the vernacular languages and an opportunity to make the liturgy accessible to cultures and societies where the Latin language did in fact confuse the meaning of the Christian message.[98] In this sense article 36 is best read in relationship to article 34's appeal to intelligibility. Moreover the debates over Latin in the liturgy at the Council suggest that the article was a compromise between staunch defenders of the language of the tradition and the strong pull of representatives from non-Western churches and the missionary dioceses to implement the vernacular.

These norms deriving from the educational and pastoral nature of the liturgy continue to embody debate within the Church today as they did at the Second Vatican Council. Discussion about the appropriateness and quality of language and symbol that is sacred yet comprehensible, rich yet simple elicits disputes over aesthetic, cultural, and linguistic translation and interpretation in the postmodern world. Many would say that these issues are at the heart of current ecclesiological polemics in particular Church circles. It would be an understatement to say that the subject of preaching has been solved in the Catholic Church, nor that the Catholic peoples of the Latin Rite have achieved a successful liturgical spirituality.

D. Norms for Adapting the Liturgy to the Culture and Traditions of Peoples

Articles 37–40 of *Sacrosanctum Concilium* have been viewed for many years now as the *Magna Carta* of liturgical inculturation. The well-known liturgical theologian Anscar Chupungco writes: "SC 37–40 expresses the church's recognition of its own pluralistic structure, of its being Roman in tradition and international in expression, of its doctrinal unity in cultural diversity."[99] These articles can be seen as fundamental to the principles of ecclesiological renewal of SC. According to Chupungco, articles 37–40 open the door to a much more expansive catholicity that found expression in the Conciliar documents and increasingly developed in the years following the Council. For Chupungco, there is a continuum that runs through liturgical inculturation that begins with adaptation and ends in a creative assimilation.[100]

---

37. Even in the liturgy the Church has no wish to impose a rigid uniformity in matters that do not affect the faith or the good of the whole community; rather, the Church respects and fosters the genius and talents of the various races and peoples. The Church considers with sympathy and, if possible, preserves intact the elements in these peoples' way of life that are not indissolubly bound up with superstition and error. Sometimes in fact the Church

admits such elements into the liturgy itself, provided they are in keeping with the true and authentic spirit of the liturgy.

Article 37 introduces the norms for adaptation. It sets the stage for the Church's affirmation of pluralism in the liturgy when that pluralism does not militate against the unity of faith or the good of the whole Church. This article reinforces that the Church recognizes, respects, and promotes the cultural context of all peoples. It upholds that liturgical adaptation is inclusive of the elements of culture that keep with the authentic and true spirit of the liturgy and that are not tied to superstition or error.

---

38. Provisions shall also be made, even in the revision of liturgical books, for legitimate variations and adaptations to different groups, regions, and peoples, especially in mission lands, provided the substantial unity of the Roman Rite is preserved; this should be borne in mind when rites are drawn up and rubrics devised.

---

39. Within the limits set by the *editio typica* of the liturgical books, it shall be for the competent, territorial ecclesiastical authority mentioned in art. 22, §2 to specify adaptations, especially in the case of the administration of the sacraments, the sacramentals, processions, liturgical language, sacred music, and the arts. This, however, is to be done in accord with the fundamental norms laid down in this Constitution.

---

40. In some places and circumstances, however, an even more radical adaptation of the liturgy is needed and this entails greater difficulties. Wherefore:

1. The competent, territorial ecclesiastical authority mentioned in art. 22, §2, must, in this matter, carefully and prudently weigh what elements from the traditions and culture of individual peoples may be appropriately admitted into divine worship. They are to propose to the Apostolic See adaptations considered useful or necessary that will be introduced with its consent.

2. To ensure that adaptations are made with all the circumspection they demand, the Apostolic See will grant power to this same territorial ecclesiastical authority to permit and to direct, as the case requires, the necessary preliminary experiments within certain groups suited for the purpose and for a fixed time.

3. Because liturgical laws often involve special difficulties with respect to adaptation, particularly in mission lands, experts in these matters must be employed to formulate them.

Three principles are then given for adaptation that are organized by articles 38–40. The first affirms that the revised books should allow for legitimate variations. The second states that within the limits set by the typical editions of the liturgical books, the Conferences of Bishops are to adapt the liturgy to their regions. And the third speaks to places and circumstances in which a more radical liturgical adaptation is needed.

Anscar Chupungco outlines a double-movement of liturgical inculturation which can be defined either from the standpoint of the liturgy or from the standpoint of culture.[101] From the standpoint of the liturgy, inculturation may be defined as: "The process of inserting the texts and rites of the liturgy into the framework of a local culture. As a result, the texts and rites assimilate the people's thought, language, value, ritual, symbolic and artistic pattern."[102] Therefore from the perspective of the liturgy, the goal of inculturation is the grafting of the Church's worship tradition onto "the cultural pattern of the local church."[103] This grafting of rite to culture occurs along a continuum, ranging from mere adaptation to the creation of completely new liturgical forms.[104]

In many ways liturgical inculturation can be viewed as the underlying tow of the Second Vatican Council that has been most resisted. The norms for adaptation of the liturgy in SC represent an ecclesial paradigm shift that de-centers North Atlantic cultural influence.[105] In that respect inculturation uniquely challenges one's traditional understanding of catholicity itself. Modern views of catholicity unfortunately have suffered from some of the same exhaustion as nationalism, totalitarian thinking, and other authoritarian solutions of the post-industrial pluralistic world. The Second Vatican Council hoped to revise traditional views of catholicity that bridged differences and gave credence to both local and universal claims about Church authority. Nevertheless it can be suggested that Chupungco was correct in stating that inculturation remains the least realized of the principles of liturgical renewal. Might not his words spur us on to realize that contemporary challenges to catholicity remain fundamental to the contemporary global Church? Might not Robert Schreiter's words encourage us to retrieve the salience of articles 37–40 with new vigor? Schreiter says:

> It seems to me that a renewed and expanded concept of catholicity may well serve as a theological response to the challenge of globalization. It can provide a theological framework out of which the Church might understand itself and its mission under changed circumstances. Faced with the diversity of cultures and the implications of taking them seriously, and the challenge of maintaining the unity and integrity of the Church worldwide, the eschatological sense of catholicity, so important to the Orthodox and many Protestant churches, takes on new salience at the interface of the global and the local.[106]

Despite resistance to the principles of liturgical inculturation by those who hold fast to Roman ecclesiologies based on monolithic cultural interpretations, there remain those who deeply resonate with local churches that creatively assimilate the Catholic faith through new forms.

IV. Promotion of Liturgical Life in Diocese and Parish

41. The bishop is to be looked on as the high priest of his flock, the faithful's life in Christ in some way deriving from and depending on him.

Therefore all should hold in great esteem the liturgical life of the diocese centered around the bishop, especially in his cathedral church; they must be convinced that the preeminent manifestation of the Church is present in the full, active participation of all God's holy people in these liturgical celebrations, especially in the same eucharist, in a single prayer, at one altar at which the bishop presides, surrounded by his college of priests and by his ministers.[28]

28. See Ignatius of Antioch, *To the Magnesians*, 7; *To the Philadelphians*, 4; *To the Smyrnians*, 8.

Sacrosanctum Concilium addresses the role of the bishop as pastor and liturgist of the diocesan Church. This role is regarded as the primary source and vehicle of the spiritual life of the diocesan Church. The bishop stands in imitation of Christ the high priest whose sacrifice on the altar of the Cross gives life to the whole Church through the Eucharistic celebration in every gathering of the Church.

The liturgical celebrations in the cathedral church, especially when the Church of the diocese is gathered, emphasizes in a particular way the very identity of the Church. Accordingly, great importance is attached also to the preparation of these diocesan liturgies so that the full and active participation of the faithful is the primary concern. This concern echoes the words of article 14 which clearly states that the participation of the faithful in the liturgy is to be considered before all else.

The full and active participation of the whole assembly is not just about engagement; it is of the very nature of the liturgy and the right and duty of the faithful by virtue of their baptism. Surely this is especially true when the diocesan Church gathers with the bishop as the chief liturgist of the diocese. The celebrations of the Mass of Chrism, ordinations, the rites of initiation, and of the patronal feast of the diocese are among the particular liturgies which can clearly express the intent of this paragraph. Cathedral liturgies must offer a worthy model for the liturgical celebrations in the local Churches of the diocese.

The Eucharistic liturgy is understood to be a single prayer; this is a fundamental theology that is referenced in other places in the SC. The unity of the Eucharist is thus held up as an image of the unity that is within the very nature of the Church. What better relationship than that between the integral unity of the whole Church and the communion of the diocesan Church around the bishop, all embodied and celebrated in the diocesan liturgy centered on the one altar of the Lord.

It is hoped that those responsible for diocesan liturgies and those who participate would "be convinced" of the richness of the liturgy in all instances and its power to bring about the unity of the People of God around the table of the Lord.

---

42. But because it is impossible for the bishop always and everywhere to preside over the whole flock in his Church, he cannot do otherwise than establish lesser groupings of the faithful. Among these the parishes, set up locally under a pastor taking the place of the bishop, are the most important: in some manner they represent the visible Church established throughout the world.

And therefore both in attitude and in practice the liturgical life of the parish and its relationship to the bishop must be fostered among the faithful and clergy; efforts must also be made toward a lively sense of community within the parish, above all in the shared celebration of the Sunday Mass.

In this article, SC expresses what might be called a practical theology. First, there is the necessary need for parishes to accommodate the population of the larger diocesan Church. These parish communities also provide for the liturgical life of the faithful in the absence of the bishop who simply cannot preside over the "whole flock in his Church" always and everywhere. Second, the importance of parishes is connected to the liturgical life of the diocese as a primary relationship; perhaps in an even more visible and significant way than through the exercise of governance.

There is an underlying assumption that the liturgies of the cathedral are worthy examples of "full, conscious, and active participation"[107] and it is this model that the liturgical celebrations of the parish should reflect. The obligation rests both on a vibrant liturgical life of the cathedral, as noted above, and that of the parish. What are called for are the same level of participation and the same serious efforts of preparation and concern that bring the Church together under Christ, the high priest both in diocesan liturgies and in the liturgies of the parish.

The responsibility of the parish pastoral and liturgical leadership is centered on the parish being a reflection of the universal Church and not just an isolated community of believers, although it is also that. But its identity is not territorial or a distinct social or ethnic gathering; it is a spiritual entity that is theologically defined and spiritually connected to the universal Church, sharing in her mission and identity as the Body of Christ in the world.

This is never more important than in the celebration of the Sunday Eucharist, an obligation that should give the liturgical leadership and liturgical ministers both a vision and an agenda for their respective ministries. The individual parish can be caught up in its own customs and ways of doing things and lose sight of the greater identity that it shares with both the diocesan Church and the universal Church. The prayers, images, texts, and symbols of the liturgy are larger than the local community; all expressions of the Church's public prayer, her liturgy, are the sum of a great tradition and the source of unity and grace for the universal Body of Christ.

V. Promotion of Pastoral-Liturgical Action

The heading of this section may strike us as a somewhat odd combination of ideas: "Pastoral-Liturgical Action." But it is a phrase which captures the impetus of the Liturgical Movement. From the beginning, the Liturgical Movement was not as much about externals as it was about internals: at its deepest level it was not about styles of vestments or statues or sanctuaries, but about breaking through barriers that could prevent the liturgy from touching people's lives. The assembly surely prayed at Mass—but they prayed separately, in what Pascal Botz described as "the spirit of individualism."[108] The active participation of the people dreamed of by the Liturgical Movement, and enshrined in SC, was not an end in itself. Rather, it was a means to an end: celebrating together at Mass, people would grow in awareness of themselves as parts of a corporate body—as the Church, not acting in isolation, but in unison. And once those walls of isolation were broken down, it was hoped that people would begin to recognize their solidarity not only with the people in the pews next to them, but with all their brothers and sisters throughout the world. Thus, the renewal of the liturgy would go hand in hand with the renewal of the world. "We might seriously consider," said Daniel Cantwell in an address at the Liturgical Week in 1949,[109] "whether it is possible to restore all things in Christ on Sunday until we first show ourselves equally concerned with the necessity of restoring to the working lives of the multitudes their Christian dignity and human rights."[110]

While the relationship between liturgy and justice is not explicitly stated in SC, it is everywhere implied. Liturgical action *is* pastoral action: it is not separate from it, a mere aesthetic consideration different from the weightier matters the Council would go on to discuss. Rather, liturgy is the Church's primary means to connect with the faithful, and thus with the world. Liturgy is the Church's primary instrument for action, for evangelization.

43. Zeal for the promotion and restoration of the liturgy is rightly held to be a sign of the providential dispositions of God in our time, a movement of the Holy Spirit in his Church. Today it is a distinguishing mark of the Church's life, indeed of the whole tenor of contemporary religious thought and action.

So that this pastoral-liturgical action may become even more vigorous in the Church, the Council decrees what follows.

In *Mediator Dei* (1947), Pope Pius XII encouraged some aspects of the Liturgical Movement but was cautious about others. Here, the Council Fathers wholeheartedly embrace the "zeal" of those who have worked for the "promotion" of the liturgy—that is, educating priests and people about the importance and value of the liturgy—and for its "restoration," based on historical exploration and the pastoral needs of modern times. All of this, the Council Fathers say, is the work of the Holy Spirit in the Church. The renewal of the liturgy is, in fact, "a distinguishing mark" of the life of the Church, of the "whole tenor of contemporary religious thought and action." Liturgy is not a separate discipline, but integral to the whole sweep of Catholic thought and action. In other words, the primary values of the liturgical renewal are the primary values of the entire Second Vatican Council.

44. It is advisable that the competent, territorial ecclesiastical authority mentioned in art. 22, §2 set up a liturgical commission, to be assisted by experts in liturgical science, music, art, and pastoral practice. As far as possible the commission should be aided by some kind of institute for pastoral liturgy, consisting of persons eminent in these matters and including the laity as circumstances suggest. Under the direction of the aforementioned territorial ecclesiastical authority, the commission is to regulate pastoral-liturgical action throughout the territory and to promote studies and necessary experiments whenever there is question of adaptations to be proposed to the Apostolic See.

The decrees of this section deal with organizational structures, intended to facilitate the renewal of the liturgy and the continued spread of the "zeal"[111] for liturgical renewal. *Sacrosanctum Concilium* first calls for the establishment of new, large-scale organizations, to be established by the "competent, territorial ecclesiastical authority" (defined as the National Conferences of Bishops in *Sacram liturgiam* in January, 1964[112]). *Sacrosanctum Concilium* envisions groups of bishops working together in much the same way they were working at the Council itself: a liturgical commission (made up of bishops) would be assisted by experts in the areas of music and art but also "liturgical science" and "pastoral practice" (the Latin word used here is *peritis*, the same word used to describe those theologians and scholars who contributed so largely to the work of the Council). This group would in turn be aided by an "Institute for Pastoral Liturgy," which could include members of the laity as well. The task of the liturgical commission, aided by the institute, would be to enact some of the provisions of the Council—regulating and promoting liturgical reform, and also carrying out the needed experiments to determine whether local adaptations should be proposed to the Holy See.

The bishops of the United States had a head start on the implementation of this directive. On November 14, 1957, they had created a "Bishops' Committee on the Liturgical Apostolate."[113] Their purpose was to keep the bishops informed on liturgical directives coming out of the Holy See, providing English translations of these texts as well as analysis. In addition, they would track and advise on legitimate variations as well as abuses in the liturgy in the United States. After the Council, the purpose of the Commission shifted toward the implementation of the liturgical reforms. The group was renamed the Bishops' Committee on the Liturgy, and later the Bishops' Committee on Divine Worship. It is worth noting that even before the Council, the Committee was consultative. From the beginning, they established relationships with other bodies, particularly the North American Liturgical Conference, which hosted the incredibly popular Liturgical Weeks held in various American cities from 1940 to 1968.[114] After the Council, the BCL/BCDW formed the consultative body that grew into the Federation of Diocesan Liturgical Commissions (FDLC), which was established both to provide expertise and to share with the bishops the lived, grassroots experience of the local Churches.

---

45. For the same reason every diocese is to have a commission on the liturgy, under the direction of the bishop, for promoting the liturgical apostolate.

Sometimes it may be advisable for several dioceses to form among themselves one single commission, in order to promote the liturgy by means of shared consultation.

In addition to the large-scale bodies, representing many dioceses, each diocese is to have its own consultative groups, along the same model. These groups are not new: back in 1947, Pope Pius XII had called for the formation of liturgical committees. "It is also Our wish that in each diocese an advisory committee to promote the liturgical apostolate should be established, similar to that which cares for sacred music and art, so that with your watchful guidance everything may be carefully carried out in accordance with the prescriptions of the Apostolic See."[115] Pope Pius XII suggests the creation of these commissions in light of each bishop's responsibility to "supervise and regulate the manner and method in which the people take part in the liturgy, according to the rubrics," "injunctions," and canons, without unauthorized "experiments."[116] While the first task named is "promoting the liturgical apostolate," the overall implication is that the commission's responsibility will be to restrain the fervor of reformers, and to suppress unauthorized innovations. Article 45 borrows the language of *Mediator Dei*, but the mandate of the commission is now simply to "promote"—the word is repeated twice—the "liturgical apostolate." Their role is not so much to enforce or control as to spread the zeal for the renewal of the liturgy as far and wide as possible.

46. Besides the commission on the liturgy, every diocese, as far as possible, should have commissions for music and art.

These three commissions must work in closest collaboration; indeed it will often be best to fuse the three of them into one single commission.

The final decree in this section calls for commissions on sacred music and sacred art, which can be combined with the liturgical commission. In this way, SC promotes what might be called a holistic approach to the liturgy. Music, art, and liturgy are not separate disciplines: rather, the Council Fathers recognize that these are inseparable from each other. And if they are inseparable, they are also indispensable. We will see this more explicitly expressed in the closing chapters of SC, dedicated to sacred music, art, and architecture.

Questions for Discussion and Reflection

1. The first chapter of SC states that "by baptism all are plunged into the paschal mystery of Christ" (SC, 6). What is the Paschal Mystery of Christ? How is it revealed in the liturgy?

2. SC speaks of four presences of Christ in the Mass: in the minister, the Word, the Sacrament of his Body and Blood, and the praying assembly. Where do you experience Christ's presence most powerfully? Are there times when you struggle to find his presence in the liturgy? Why?

3. What does it mean for the liturgy to be both "fount" (source) and "summit" (SC, 10)? Do you find that to be a reality in your parish?

4. How does liturgy lead us outward to evangelization, works of charity, works of justice? Or does it?

5. What are some of your favorite popular devotions, or those that are most popular in your parish or community? How do they relate to the liturgy? Do they nurture participation in the liturgy—or clash with it (see SC, 13)?

6. Reflect on those famous words: "full," "conscious," "active" (SC, 14). Do you think the Council's vision for the full, conscious, and active participation of the assembly has been fully realized? Why or why not?

7. All who take part in the liturgy as liturgical ministers "must all be deeply imbued with the spirit of the liturgy" (SC, 29). What is the spirit of the liturgy? What does it mean to be imbued with it? Are you?

NOTES

1. SC, 14.
2. Ibid., 10.
3. See Massimo Faggioli, *True Reform: Liturgy and Ecclesiology in* Sacrosanctum Concilium Collegeville, MN: The Liturgical Press, 2012, p. 1.
4. Isaiah 12:3.
5. *Catechism of the Catholic Church*, article 1 of chapter 2.

6. SC, 1.

7. See 1 Timothy 2:4.

8. Edward Schillebeeckx, OP, *Christ the Sacrament of the Encounter with God.* Lanham, Maryland: Sheed & Ward, 1963, 1960.

9. Elmer O'Brien, SJ, *Theology in Transition: A Bibliographical Evaluation 1954-1964.* New York: Herder and Herder, 1965, p. 179.

10. See Jean Danielou, *The Bible and the Liturgy.* Notre Dame, Indiana: University of Notre Dame Press, 1956, p. 17.

11. See ibid.

12. *Domino, cum dormiret in cruce, latus eius lancea percussum est (John 19:34), et sacramenta profluxerunt, unde facta est ecclesia. Ecclesia enim coniux Domini facta est de latere, quomodo Eva facta est de latere [Adam].* "The Lord, while asleep upon the Cross, his heart was pierced with a lance, and the sacrament flowed forth, from which was made the Church. The Church was fashioned from the side of the Lord like a bride in the same manner Eve had been fashioned from the side [of Adam]" (Augustine, *In Ps.* 126, n. 7: PL 37, 1672; translation by Joshua Brommer).

13. See *Lumen gentium* (LG), 1: "Since the church, in Christ, is a sacrament—a sign and instrument, that is, of communion with God and of unity of the entire human race . . . ."

14. For the ancient Church, as Danielou (p. 17) points out, this relationship was firm: "The life of ancient Christianity was centered around worship. And worship was not considered to be a collection of rites meant to sanctify secular life. The sacraments were thought of as the essential events of Christian existence, and of existence itself, as being the prolongation of the great works of God in the Old Testament and the New. In them was inaugurated the new creation which introduced the Christian even now into the Kingdom of God."

15. Jean Corbon, *The Wellspring of Worship.* San Francisco, California: Ignatius Press, 2005, p. 25.

16. Ibid., p. 29.

17. John 15:16.

18. Ephesians 1:10.

19. Reference here is made to Jungmann's work, *The Place of Christ in Liturgical Prayer,* Second Revised Edition Australia: Geoffrey Chapman, 1989.

20. Matthew 21:13.

21. See John 1:14; Sirach 24:8, 10; Exodus 25:8; 29:46; Zechariah 2:14; Revelation 21:3.

22. See Philippians 3:20.

23. See Laurence Paul Hemming, *Worship as a Revelation: The Past, Present and Future of Catholic Liturgy.* London: Burns & Oates, 2008, p. 2.

24. See ibid., pp. 2–3.

25. See Gérard Philips, *La Chiesa e Il Suo Mistero: storia, testo e commento della* Lumen Gentium. Milan: Jaca Book, 1975, p. 473.

26. Revelation 22:20.

27. Corbon, p. 77.

28. Mark 16:15.

29. Author's paraphrase.

30. Pamela Jackson, *An Abundance of Graces: Reflections on* Sacrosanctum Concilium. Chicago, Illinois: Hillenbrand Books, 2004, p. 3.

31. Ibid.

32. Corbon (p. 6) expresses this powerfully, "People do not invent the liturgy and therefore do not invent the Church; they come to birth in it and experience it as a reality."

33. This is exhibited by such authors as Otto Casel and Jean Corbon.

34. As was championed by such great liturgical figures as the Alexander Schmemann and continues to make steps forward with David W. Fagerberg.

35. Corbon, p. 202.

36. *Mediator Dei*, 24.

37. Jackson, p. 57.

38. The Gospel accounts recount the frequency with which Christ went off to pray to his Father in private (see Mark 6:46). Also, the Gospel accounts recount the fasting done by Christ (see Luke 4:2, a prefiguring mortification which reaches its zenith with his Passion and Crucifixion).

39. See Jordan Aumann, OP *Christian Spirituality in the Catholic Tradition* San Francisco, California: Ignatius Press, 1985 p. 268.

40. Guéranger's *The Liturgical Year, Volume 1*; quoted in Aumann, p. 268.

41. See Louis Soltner, *Solesmes and Dom Gueranger: 1805–1875.* Orleans, Maassachusetts: Paraclete Press, 1995, pp. 89–95.

42. *Rule of St. Benedict* 48:9. English translation from from the *RB1980.* Collegeville, Minnesota: The Liturgical Press, 1981.

43. See SC, 12, 14, 19, 26, 27, 30, 41, 50, 55, 113, 114, 121, 124.

44. See *Tra le sollecitudini* (TLS), opening paragraph: "It being our ardent desire to see the true Christian spirit restored in every respect and be preserved by all the faithful, we deem it necessary to provide before everything else for the sanctity and dignity of the temple, in which the faithful assembly for the object of acquiring this spirit from its foremost and indispensable fount, which is the active participation in the holy mysteries and in the public and solemn prayer of the Church."

45. *Divini cultus sanctitatem*, 9.

46. John 4:24.

47. SC, 14.

48. See TLS, 5.

49. SC, 30.

50. John Baldovin notes, "A profound theology of the church based on baptism and the common priesthood of the faithful undergirds the whole document [CSL], one that the historian Massimo Faggioli has argues was not adequately embodied in the other constitutions and decrees of the council." See "An Active Presence," *America* 208.18 (May 27, 2013), pp. 11–14.

51. *Christifideles Laici: On the Vocation and the Mission of the Lay Faithful in the Church and in the World*, 14. The term "participation" appears seventy-six times in various contexts. It is clear that this is the continuation of the trajectory established in the very first session of the Second Vatican Council.

52. Ibid., 16. Emphasis mine.

53. *Sacramentum caritatis*, 52.

54. Ibid., 55.

55. Ibid.

56. See SC, 36 §1 and 101 §1.

57. For a more thorough treatment of use of the vernacular and the history of the vernacular movement, see Keith Pecklers, *Dynamic Equivalence: The Living Language of Christian Worship*. Collegeville, Minnesota: The Liturgical Press, 2003. For an appraisal of vernacular usage from an ecumenical perspective, see Maxwell Johnson, "The Loss of a Common Language: The End of Ecumenical-Liturgical Convergence?" *Studia Liturgica* (2007) 37, pp. 55–72.

58. For more detailed information on the Liturgical Movement see J. D. Chrichton, *Lights In the Darkness: Forerunners of the Liturgical Movement* (Collegeville, Minnesota: Liturgical Press, 1996); Keith Pecklers, *The Unread Vision* (Collegeville, Minnesota: Liturgical Press, 1998); *The Liturgy Documents, Volume Three: Foundational Documents on the Origins and Implementation of "Sacrosanctum Concilium"* (Chicago, Illinois: LTP, 2013); Robert Tuzik, *Reynold Hillenbrand: The Reform of the Catholic Liturgy and the Call to Social Action* (Chicago, Illinois: Hillenbrand Books, 2009).

59. See Lambert Beauduin's book, *Liturgy Life of the Church* now published by St Michael's Abbey.

60. See Bernard Botte, *From Silence to Participation: An Insider's View of Liturgical Renewal*. Washington, DC: Pastoral Press, 1988, pp. 104–06.

61. As a social history of the Liturgical Movement in the United States, Keith Pecklers, SJ, in his *The Unread Vision* (op. cit.) introduces readers to the movement's pioneers and promoters and to the issues that emerged from the movement in the United States in the years 1926–1955. *The Unread Vision* explores the foundational years of the movement and its major themes and discusses how the movement, its goals and principles, was received by the broader community of American Catholics. Chapters include "The European Roots: 1833–1925," "The Beginnings of a Movement: Toward Full and Active Participation in the Liturgy," "The Liturgical Movement and Social Justice," "The Liturgical Movement and Education," and "The Liturgical Movement and the Arts." Biographies on leading figures of the Liturgical Movement, as well as histories of related organizations, are also included.

62. For example, the Chicago Theological Union offers a Doctor in Ministry (DMIN) degree with a certificate in liturgical studies.

63. Speaking from my experience I can report that as of 2013 among the eighty-five people who have received doctorates in liturgy at the University of Notre Dame, about half represent Protestant and Orthodox Christian traditions. See Maxwell Johnson, "Liturgy and Ecumenism: Gifts, Challenges, and Hopes for a Renewed Vision," *Worship* 80, 1 (January 2006), pp. 2–29.

64. Frederick McManus, the well-known American canonist, comments: "Our concern is with the existing liturgical law, in particular as this has moved in recent years from its post-Tridentine inflexibility to the norms of a renewed liturgy, one that has now been profoundly reformed and in the process made more flexible and open to creativity." Cited in Anscar Chupungco, ed., "Liturgical Law," *Handbook for Liturgical Studies, Volume I* (Collegeville, Minnesota: The Liturgical Press, 1997), p. 399.

65. Kathleen Cahalan, *Formed in the Image of Christ: The Sacramental-Moral Theology of Bernard Häring, C.Ss.R* Collegeville, Minnesota: Michael Glazier Press, 2004, p. 49.

66. This document builds upon the foundation of previous editions. The principal and new direction of the fifth edition stems from its reliance on the post-synodal apostolic exhortation *Pastores dabo vobis* (*I Will Give You Shepherds: On the Formation of Priests in the Circumstances of the Present Day,* 1992) to organize and integrate the program of priestly formation.

67. See *Program of Priestly Formation*, p. 213.

68. See ibid., p. 223.

69. See ibid., p. 331

70. *Sing to the Lord: Music in Divine Worship* (STL), 5.

71. See Kathleen Hughes, *Saying Amen: A Mystagogy of Sacrament.* Chicago, Illinois: Liturgy Training Publications, 1999.

72. See MD, 172–85.

73. For a more detailed account, see Leonard Boyle, "Popular Piety in the Middle Ages: What is Popular?" *Florilegium* 4 (1982), pp. 184–93.

74. See also page 67 in this resource.

75. Parallel to the Program of Priestly Formation (mentioned above), the American bishops have authored and published a program for the formation of lay ecclesial ministers. See *Co-Workers in the Vineyard of the Lord: A Resource for Guiding the Development of Lay Ecclesial Ministry.*

76. SC, 19.

77. Ibid., 17.

78. SC, 14.

79. See Josef A. Jungmann, SJ, *The Mass of the Roman Rite: Its Origins and Development (Missarum Sollemnia).* New York: Benziger Brothers, 1950, p. 2.

80. Those charged with the task of implementing the reforms called for in *Sacrosanctum Concilium.*

81. See Giuseppe Ruggieri, "Beyond an Ecclesiology of Polemics: The Debate on the Church," in *History of Vatican II, Vol. 2*, ed. Giuseppe Alberigo, English version ed. Joseph A. Komonchak (Maryknoll, New York: Orbis, 1995–2006), pp. 345–46.

82. MD, 58.

83. R. Kevin Seasoltz, *New Liturgy, New Laws.* Collegeville, Minnesota: The Liturgical Press, 1980, p. 200.

84. Ibid.

85. LG, 26.

86. See Annibale Bugnini, *The Reform of the Liturgy 1948-1975*, trans. Matthew J. O'Connell. Collegeville, Minnesota: The Liturgical Press, 1990), pp. 60–95.

87. See Faggioli, pp. 54–55.

88. See Edward J. Kilmartin, SJ, *The Eucharist in the West: History and Theology*, ed. Robert J. Daly, SJ. Collegeville, Minnesota: The Liturgical Press, 1998, pp. 134–45.

89. See Nathan Mitchell, *Cult and Controversy: The Worship of the Eucharist Outside Mass.*New York: Pueblo, 1982, pp. 129–95.

90. See SC, 27.

91. See ibid., 28–29.

92. See ibid., 30.

93. See Rita Ferrone, *Liturgy: Sacrosanctum Concilium.* New York: Paulist Press, 2007, p. 33.

94. See SC, 14.

95. See Faggioli, p. 86.

96. See John F. Baldovin, SJ, *Reforming the Liturgy: A Response to the Critics.* Collegeville, Minnesota: The Liturgical Press, 2008, pp. 65–85.

97. See Aidan Kavanagh, *Elements of Rite: Handbook of Liturgical Style.* New York: Pueblo, 1982, pp. 4–5.

98. See Faggioli, pp. 128–32.

99. See Anscar J. Chupungco, OSB, *Liturgies of the Future: The Process and Methods of Inculturation.* New York: Paulist Press, 1989, p. 11.

100. See ibid., pp. 23–35.

101. See Anscar J. Chupungco, OSB, *Liturgical Inculturation: Sacramentals, Religiosity, and Catechesis.* Collegeville, Minnesota: The Liturgical Press, 1992, p. 30.

102. See ibid.

103. See ibid., p. 37.

104. See ibid., pp. 37–54. Here Chupungco delineates four methods by which the liturgy is grafted to cultural patterns: dynamic equivalence, creative assimilation, organic progression, and liturgical creativity.

105. See Chupungco, *Liturgies of the Future,* pp. 11–23.

106. Robert J. Schreiter. *The New Catholicity: Theology between the Global and the Local.* Maryknoll, New York: Orbis, 1997, pp. 127–28.

107. SC, 14.

108. From *Orate Fratres*, 1936. Quoted in *How Firm a Foundation: Voices of the Early Liturgical Movement*, ed. Kathleen Hughes. Chicago, Illinois: Liturgy Training Publications, 1990, p. 45.

109. The National Liturgical Weeks occurred each year from 1940 to 1968, substantial conferences which attracted thousands of people each year. Sponsored by the Liturgical Conference, a group of liturgical scholars in the United States, the first event was held in 1940 under the authority of a number of Benedictine abbots who sought to promote liturgical reform. In 1943, the Conference was reorganized under an independent board and officers, and members of the first governing board included such important persons as Godfrey Diekmann, Reynold Hillenbrand, H.A. Reinhold, William Busch, and many other national and local leaders of American liturgical reform within the Roman Catholic Church.

110. *Hughes*, p. 63.

111. SC, 43.

112. Ibid., 44. See also *The Liturgy Documents: Volume Three*. Chicago, Illinois: Liturgy Training Publications, 2013, p. 304ff.

113. McManus, Frederick R. *Thirty Years of Liturgical Renewal: Statements of the Bishops' Committee on the Liturgy.* Washington, DC: United States Conference of Catholic Bishops, 1987, p. 3.

114. See the website of the Federation of Diocesan Liturgical Commissions, http://www.fdlc.org/FDLC_History.htm#History; accessed May 2013.

115. MD, 109.

116. Ibid.

CHAPTER II

The Most Sacred Mystery of the Eucharist

Sacrosanctum Concilium 47–58

Joyce Ann Zimmerman, CPPS

All the sacraments are attributed to Christ[1]; however, two sacraments in particular can be traced to a direct command by Jesus in the Gospel accounts: the Holy Eucharist[2] and Baptism.[3] The other outward signs we have come to call sacraments trace to Jesus's life and ministry; for example, healing, forgiving, calling followers, and honoring the union of a woman and man. In the early Church other signs were important means of grace; for example, preaching, fasting, and almsgiving. By the thirteenth century the Church had come to recognize seven special signs of grace we now call sacraments, and these were defined as such at the Council of Trent in the sixteenth century.

Because of their direct dominical connection, Baptism and Eucharist have always been regarded as the two foundational, New Testament, sacraments. These have to do with our identity as the Body of Christ: Baptism incorporates us into that identity, and Eucharist nourishes us and helps us grow in our identity as members of the Body of Christ. Remarkable in the overall structure of *Sacrosanctum Concilium* is that treatment of the Eucharist which comes in chapter II, immediately after the nature of the liturgy and its reform addressed in chapter I. Baptism is treated in Chapter III, "The Other Sacraments and the Sacramentals." Eucharist, then, is the only one of the seven sacraments that has a chapter dedicated to it. This structure clearly points to the centrality and importance of Eucharist for the Christian life. Without minimizing the other sacraments, and particularly Baptism, SC does set off Holy Eucharist in a special way. This is to be expected, because in a document dedicated to laying out the principles of liturgical renewal, the Council Fathers knew that the liturgy that most often touches Catholics is the weekly celebration of the Eucharist. Renewing this rite would necessarily have an impact on all the other rites as well as all of daily Christian living. That the Eucharist is addressed in the very second chapter of SC, right after the general principles laid out in the first chapter, also points to the Eucharist's centrality and unsurpassed importance.

Sacrosanctum Concilium offers no clear definition of Eucharist, other than calling it a "mystery" in the title of chapter II. The first two of the twelve articles in this chapter[4] offer a rich description of this sacrament, lay out principal theological points, and exhort the faithful to appropriately participate.[5] These two paragraphs are as true, life-giving, and visionary today, fifty years after the promulgation of SC, as they were at the time of the Council. Basic principles do not change. Our interpretation and application of them are what need to be renewed.

The next ten articles[6] deal with specific issues of renewal of the Mass, all of which have been implemented over the last five decades. While they are not burning issues for most of us today, they do deserve a fresh consideration if the renewal is to continue to bring richness to the lives of the faithful. These last ten paragraphs specifically refer to renewal of various elements of the Mass or recovering forgotten but meaningful elements of the Eucharistic Rite. This was part of the Council's work of *ressourcement*, that is, returning to the sources of our liturgical rites to learn new meanings, eliminate needless historical accretions, and recover lost but still valuable elements of the rite. Not every element of the renewal of the Eucharistic Rite is mentioned in these ten articles. Notably missing, for example, is any mention of the Sign of Peace, an entirely new element for the faithful.[7]

It would be a mistaken interpretation, furthermore, if we judge this chapter on the Eucharist as only referring to Mass. We can tease out of the text a broader understanding of Eucharist: ourselves as the Body of Christ giving God constant thanks for Christ's saving work through the very way we live.[8] It has been left to catechesis after the renewal of the Eucharistic Rite to help the faithful understand that Eucharist refers to more than Mass or Holy Communion or the reserved

Blessed Sacrament. The baptized are members of the Body of Christ and so are a Eucharistic people.

The title of the chapter is significant. By calling the Eucharist "the Most Sacred Mystery," the Council Fathers were saying something quite significant. First of all, by referring to the Eucharist as a "mystery," they were hinting at the fact that we will never exhaust the Eucharist's meaning, richness, and extension into our daily Christian living. We can never learn enough about the Eucharist; we can never live well enough the Eucharist. As mystery, the Eucharist is inexhaustible in its meaning and call to gospel living. Then, by calling this mystery "most sacred," the Council Fathers are setting the Eucharist at the apex of Jesus's life and saving work which is to be the source and summit of the whole Christian life.[9] In a real way the Eucharist is identified with the very heart of the Jesus's life and ministry, the Paschal Mystery.[10] It is no wonder that scores of documents on the Eucharist have been promulgated by the Vatican as well as by Conferences of Bishops since the close of the Council, which have clarified more fully the most sacred mystery of the Eucharist. Chapter II of SC opens a challenge to delve deeper into this mystery that transforms us into the Body of Christ who continues Jesus's saving work.

47. At the Last Supper, on the night when he was betrayed, our Savior instituted the eucharistic sacrifice of his body and blood. He did this in order to perpetuate the sacrifice of the cross throughout the centuries until he should come again and in this way to entrust to his beloved Bride, the Church, a memorial of his death and resurrection: a sacrament of love, a sign of unity, a bond of charity,[1] a paschal banquet "in which Christ is eaten, the heart is filled with grace, and a pledge of future glory given to us."[2]

1. See Augustine, *In Ioannis Evangelium Tractatus 36,* chap. 6, n. 13.
2. Liturgy of the Hours, antiphon for Canticle of Mary, evening prayer II , feast of Corpus Christi.

A very dense paragraph opens the chapter on the Eucharist, succinctly describing something of what the Eucharist is as well as its fruits (effects). Consistent with the long tradition of the Church, SC links the Eucharist with the Last Supper. It qualifies the Last Supper as "the night when he was betrayed." We are invited to reflect on more than the beauty and gift of the Body and Blood which Jesus gave us as a perpetual "memorial" of his saving deeds. Thus, SC identifies the

Eucharist with Jesus's "sacrifice of the cross," not as a repetition of that historical event but instead as a "memorial" for us of Jesus's continual self-giving, made present here and now in each Eucharistic sacrifice.[11]

The notion of "memorial" here is not simply that of recalling a past event; instead "memorial" intimates that the meaning and fruits of the historical event continue through time "until he should come again."[12] At every Eucharistic celebration, then, Jesus teaches us anew the very meaning of his self-sacrifice. Jesus's "sacrifice of the cross" was not only a handing over of his life for our salvation,[13] but also is a giving over of his Body and Blood for our nourishment now. Jesus's self-giving is the origin of our thanksgiving. It is a call for us to be Church giving ourselves for others as he did.

The Divine Lover embraces "his beloved Bride, the Church" in this perpetual sacrifice. Christ is the Head of the Church who brings forth the fruits of the Eucharistic celebration each time we obey his command to eat and drink his Body and Blood.[14] Eucharist is a "sacrament of love" because it manifests most sublimely Jesus's continuing self-giving love for us.[15] It is a "sign of unity" because when we gather for the Eucharistic celebration the members of the Body are joined to Christ the Head in his act of self-giving[16] and manifest the Body of Christ, the Church made visible. It is a "bond of charity" because, united in the one Body of Christ, we care for each member of the Body as if we were caring for Jesus himself.[17] It is a "paschal banquet" because not only do the bread and wine truly pass over (are changed) into the real Body and Blood of Christ, but we ourselves pass over (are changed) to live more perfectly this "sacred mystery" which we celebrate.[18]

Sacrosanctum Concilium 47 does far more than simply lay the foundational theological principles for the renewal of the Mass. It broadens our perspective beyond attending Mass as an obligation and receiving graces from it to understanding the celebration of Mass as our participation in Christ's "death and resurrection," our participation in Jesus's saving events. The principles laid out in this article will never be outdated or changed. They have not always been self-evident throughout the Eucharistic tradition and times, and practices have changed in such a way as sometimes to obscure how we participate in Christ's saving mystery; nevertheless, these principles informed what Jesus did at the Last Supper and have been more clearly formulated by the Council Fathers so they once again guide not only liturgical renewal but also each liturgical celebration of the Eucharist. Embracing these principles brings us to celebrate with the utmost reverence, unequaled awe, and deepest prayer.

---

48. The Church, therefore, earnestly desires that Christ's faithful, when present at this mystery of faith, should not be there as strangers or silent spectators; on the contrary, through a good understanding of the rites and prayers they should take part in the sacred service conscious of what they are doing, with devotion and full involvement. They should be instructed by God's word and be nourished at the table of the Lord's body; they should give thanks to God; by offering the immaculate Victim, not only through the hands of the priest, but also with him, they should learn to offer themselves as well; through Christ the Mediator,[3] they should be formed day by day into an ever more perfect unity with God and with each other, so that finally God may be all in all.

3. See Cyril of Alexandria, *Commentary on the Gospel of John,* book 11, chap. 11–12.

This article shifts from renewing our understanding of the meaning of the Eucharistic celebration itself to focusing on "Christ's faithful" who must be fully engaged during the Mass and not participate "as strangers or silent spectators." These two descriptions speak to the kind of celebration the Council Fathers were seeking to renew. Prior to the Council, those present at Mass minimally engaged directly with the priest and most often were occupied with their own private, devotional prayers that may or may not have had anything to do with the particular celebration. There was a great disconnect between priest and people, celebration and participation. In one sense, we might say that all of liturgical renewal since the Council has been directed to a significant shift from being merely present at liturgy to being full, conscious, and active liturgical participants. The paragraph specifically notes how the members of the liturgical assembly ought to be engaged during the celebration; in other words, the Council Fathers hint at the broad sense in which they understood participation.

First of all, the liturgical assembly must have a deeper understanding of what is happening during liturgy so that their very participation gives evidence of "a good understanding of the rites" and of being "conscious of what they are doing." When the revised rites were introduced, some explanation and liturgical education was given. But that took place almost fifty years ago. Several generations have been born and grown up in the Church since the renewal of the Second Vatican Council. To some extent, these new generations have not been imparted the original enthusiasm for the implementation of the revised rites and for understanding these revisions. Liturgical education is never finished because it involves a sacred mystery with so much richness and depth that this mystery can never be exhausted—no matter how often we pray it, think it, and learn it.

Article 48 sets a clear agenda for liturgical education. It points to the two main parts of the Mass and for people to be "instructed by God's word and be nourished at the table of the Lord's body." Only by a deeper appreciation for how the table of the Word and table of the Eucharist relate to each other can true thanksgiving well up in the hearts of those in the assembly. God's gift is twofold: we are instructed in a self-giving, gospel way of living, and then nourished and strengthened to faithfully continue Jesus's saving ministry. The article concludes by calling the faithful to "learn to offer themselves" along with Christ in a perpetual sacrifice of self-giving. Only by embracing the visible self-giving of Christ's love can the faithful grow "into an ever more perfect unity with God and each other," a unity that is only possible because of our shared identity as Body of Christ united with Christ our Head.

Essentially SC 48 calls for a Eucharistic participation that leads to a life imbued with liturgical spirituality—a liturgical way of everyday living. One of Pope Benedict XVI's greatest liturgical concerns was that the Eucharistic liturgy should not stay within the walls of the church building. We must take what we have celebrated—"our own transformation by the Holy Spirit into ever more perfect members of the body of Christ"—and live this mystery faithfully. This is why the third edition of *The Roman Missal* includes two new dismissal formulae personally requested by the Holy Father: "Go and announce the Gospel of the Lord" and "Go in peace, glorifying the Lord by your life."[19] Both formulae clearly challenge us to live in a Eucharistic, self-giving, loving way which witnesses to Christ's risen presence within and among us.

49. Thus, mindful of those Masses celebrated with the assistance of the faithful, especially on Sundays and holy days of obligation, the Council makes the following decrees in order that the sacrifice of the Mass, even in its ritual forms, may become pastorally effective to the utmost degree.

Sacrosanctum Concilium 49 transitions from principles of celebrating Eucharist to principles of liturgical renewal. This article specifies that the decrees are largely directed to Masses celebrated with the faithful on "Sundays and holy days of obligation," those times when large numbers would be present at Mass. The desire of the Council Fathers is that Mass "may become pastorally effective to the utmost degree."

Without taking away from the value of daily Mass (when the assembly is naturally much smaller than on Sundays and Holydays of Obligation), this paragraph hints at another important consideration for the Eucharistic celebration. Sunday (and Holydays of Obligation which function in the same celebration style and pastoral requirements as Sundays) is the day of the Resurrection: "Early on the first day of the week, while it was still dark, Mary Magdalene came to the tomb and saw that the stone had been removed from the tomb."[20] Every celebration of Eucharist is a Resurrection festival. Every celebration of Eucharist is a pledge to us that we share in Christ's risen life even now. Every celebration of Eucharist makes present the glory of Easter even as it makes present Jesus's continual self-giving sacrifice.[21]

50. The Order of Mass is to be revised in a way that will bring out more clearly the intrinsic nature and purpose of its several parts, as also the connection between them, and will more readily achieve the devout, active participation of the faithful.

For this purpose the rites are to be simplified, due care being taken to preserve their substance; elements that, with the passage of time, came to be duplicated or were added with but little advantage are now to be discarded; other elements that have suffered injury through accident of history are now, as may seem useful or necessary, to be restored to the vigor they had in the traditions of the Fathers.

Two points are made in SC 50. First, the revision of the Order of Mass is to "bring out more clearly" the various parts of the Mass and how they connect with one another. It was the hope of the Council Fathers that when a unified ritual flow is restored, the "devout, active participation of the faithful" would be increased. So, first and foremost, the renewal of liturgy is about increased participation of the faithful. This point comes up again and again in SC.

Second, "the rites are to be simplified" so that the unity and flow of the Eucharistic ritual is evident. Mass is a seamless whole that flows from beginning to end in one dynamic unfolding of divine presence and our response to that presence. It is not simply a string of various elements that come one after another, although historical accretions have contributed to a somewhat disjointed rite that was being celebrated at the time of the Council. Pursuant to this latter point about historical accretions that distract us from the flow of the rite, SC makes a distinction between the "substance" of the rite that is to be preserved and those elements that, for whatever historical reason, were added but do not contribute to the clarity and flow of the rite.[22]

Unfortunately, SC does not clearly enumerate nor even give examples of the essential and changeable elements of the rite. That was left to the work and decisions of the various committees that worked on the revision of the rites. A cursory comparison of the 1962 Mass of Pope John XXIII and the present Order of Mass makes evident some of the changes made in the renewed Eucharistic Rite, for example, elimination of multiple Signs of the Cross, simplification of the Introductory Rites which no longer take place at the foot of the altar, elimination of the repetition of the *Confiteor* (by the servers) before Communion. Other changes are specifically mentioned in the succeeding paragraphs as well as in other chapters of SC. And still other changes were introduced as a result of the tremendous work of historical study with its theological implications undertaken by the Liturgical Movement, especially in the twentieth century as it was given impetus by Pope Pius X.

---

51. The treasures of the Bible are to be opened up more lavishly, so that a richer share in God's word may be provided for the faithful. In this way a more representative portion of holy Scripture will be read to the people in the course of a prescribed number of years.

This two-sentence paragraph addresses one of the most successful and fruitful endeavors of the renewal of the Mass. At the time of the Council there was a one-year cycle of readings that included a very small part of Sacred Scripture. Except on rare occasions there were no texts from the Old Testament. There were two readings: the first usually taken from one of the New Testament epistles (letters), and the other taken from one of the four Gospel accounts. On Sundays and other select occasions the readings were read by the priest celebrant in Latin at the altar and then repeated in English (or other vernacular language) from the pulpit before the sermon. On weekdays there was no sermon and no readings in the vernacular. *Sacrosanctum Concilium* 51 calls for the "treasures of the Bible are to be opened up more lavishly" and suggests that this occur "in the course of a prescribed number of years."

The Lectionary that developed because of the seriousness of this article now includes a three-year cycle of readings. On Sundays, solemnities, and feasts of the Lord, there are now three readings. The First Reading is usually from the Old Testament (except for during Easter Time), the Second Reading is from one of the New Testament epistles, and the third from a Gospel. On feasts and ferial days there are two readings, the First Reading taken from either the Old Testament or from a New Testament epistle, and the Second Reading from a Gospel account. The Gospel readings are primarily from the synoptic accounts and are semi-continuous proclamations from Matthew (Year A), Mark (Year B), and Luke (Year C). While each Gospel is different and has its own purpose, all three of them begin in Galilee where Jesus inaugurates his public ministry and have Jesus journeying to Jerusalem where his Death, Resurrection, Ascension, and sending of the Holy Spirit occur.

John's Gospel account is very different in structure and tone from the three synoptic Gospel accounts. We might say John's account is a theological commentary on Jesus's life and ministry. For this reason the post-Conciliar committee who revised the Lectionary decided not to have a four-year cycle with one year devoted specifically to John's account. Instead, the committee included selections from John's Gospel at key times during the liturgical year (especially during the festal seasons) precisely to be a commentary on Jesus's life and ministry. Further, John's sixth chapter, the so-called "Bread of Life

Discourse," is so rich in Eucharistic theology that the Lectionary compilers wanted to respect the integrity of that important chapter and so they inserted it in the middle of Year B, from the Seventeenth to Twenty-first Sundays in Ordinary Time.

Even with the expanded use of Scripture in the revised Lectionary, we must remember that the Lectionary is *not* a Bible. The entire revised Lectionary still makes use of a rather small percentage of all of Sacred Scripture. But the intent of the revision of the readings at Mass was not to read the entire Bible—the intent was to present the mystery of salvation over a period of time in greater fullness. The Lectionary is a *liturgical* book that selects *from* the Bible individual readings that accord with the purpose of the Sacred Liturgy, that is, to make present the mystery of Christ.

Proclaiming a revised Lectionary that draws on more of the texts of Sacred Scripture is but one consequence of this small paragraph from SC. With the renewal of the Liturgy of the Word, the Council Fathers were also underscoring the importance of this major part of the Eucharistic liturgy. The proclamation of God's Word is not simply "window dressing," or the addition of solemnity and length to the rite. *Sacrosanctum Concilium* 51 calls us to reflect on and catechize about the importance of God's Word and the relationship of its proclamation to the Liturgy of the Eucharist. In these fifty years of post-Conciliar reform, we are still in the infant stages of uncovering the relationship between these two major parts of the Eucharistic liturgy. Indeed, liturgical renewal and understanding is ongoing.

---

52. By means of the homily the mysteries of the faith and the guiding principles of the Christian life are expounded from the sacred text during the course of the liturgical year; as part of the liturgy itself therefore, the homily is strongly recommended; in fact, at Masses celebrated with the assistance of the people on Sundays and holy days of obligation it is not to be omitted except for a serious reason.

Prior to Vatican II, probably few people had ever heard the term "homily." On Sundays the faithful heard "sermons." *Sacrosanctum Concilium* 52 provides a key as to their distinction: "the mysteries of the faith and the guiding principles of the Christian life are expounded from the sacred text." The key words here are "from the sacred text."

A homily, then, is a preaching event that takes place *within* liturgy whereas a sermon can be preached *outside* liturgy, for example, at a parish Lenten mission. A homily interprets the human situation and the lives of the people through the lens of the proclaimed Scriptures[23] while a sermon might draw its content from a moral virtue or a commandment and not be related to the proclamation of God's Word. A homily may contain catechetical and exhortatory elements; however, its primary genre is an interpretation of Scripture that instills deeper faith in the members of the assembly and challenges them to live the Gospel more perfectly.

Sacrosanctum Concilium 51 strongly recommends a homily during Mass and on Sundays and Holydays of Obligation and "it is not to be omitted except for a serious reason." Since *Sacrosanctum Concilium* has been implemented, the homily is understood to be an important liturgical element that follows the proclamation of Sacred Scripture. In many parishes and other liturgical communities a brief homily is often regularly given at weekday Masses. This is a laudable practice. The homily is the perfect time for some point of the Liturgy of the Word to be directly related to the mystery celebrated in the Liturgy of the Eucharist.[24]

---

53. Especially on Sundays and holy days of obligation there is to be restored, after the gospel and the homily, "the universal prayer" or "the prayer of the faithful." By this prayer, in which the people are to take part, intercession shall be made for holy Church, for the civil authorities, for those oppressed by various needs, for all people, and for the salvation of the entire world.[4]

4. See 1 Tm 2:1– 2.

Mass has always included intercessory prayer in various forms and places within the liturgy. For example, intercessory prayer is a constituent element of the Eucharistic Prayer.[25] At one time, intercessory prayer was associated with the *Kyrie* and in the early Church, the Universal Prayer (or Prayer of the Faithful) included extensive intercessions. The Universal Prayer was restored by the Second Vatican Council and it now follows the recitation (or singing) of the Creed on Sundays, solemnities, and feasts of the Lord and follows the homily during other weekday liturgies.

In order to make clear that this is a "*universal* prayer,"[26] that is, not intended to be a private prayer for the faithful's personal intentions, SC mentions five specific areas for intentions: the Church, civil authorities, those in need, all people, and for "the salvation of the entire world."[27] The makeup of the Universal Prayer or prayer of the faithful is elaborated upon in *The General Instruction of the Roman Missal* (GIRM). The 2010 GIRM notes that the intentions should be for the needs of the Church, public authorities, and the salvation of the whole world, for those burdened with need, and for the local community.[28] Other intentions may be added, especially for occasions such as funerals or weddings, for those who have died, or in the event of tragic or unexpected world events, such as a destructive storm.[29]

By specifying a limited number of categories, SC is suggesting that intercessory prayer is not intended to be inclusive of all our needs. As the title suggests, it is a "universal" or *general* prayer. As such, the prayer reminds us that we gather and pray as a universal Church, not just a small, local community.[30] The Universal Prayer concludes the Liturgy of the Word. This is important for it reminds us of the work of salvation that still needs to be accomplished by our own cooperation with God in this saving task. The Universal Prayer is less about asking God to care for our needs (although it does do that) as it is a prayer reminding us to cooperate with God's graces to make the world in which we live a better place. The Universal Prayer is a call to us to make a difference in our world, to put the self-giving sacrifice of the Eucharist to work in our lives.

---

54. With art. 36 of this Constitution as the norm, in Masses celebrated with the people a suitable place may be allotted to their mother tongue. This is to apply in the first place to the readings and "the universal prayer," but also, as local conditions may warrant, to those parts belonging to the people.

Nevertheless steps should be taken enabling the faithful to say or to sing together in Latin those parts of the Ordinary of the Mass belonging to them.

Wherever a more extended use of the mother tongue within the Mass appears desirable, the regulation laid down in art. 40 of this Constitution is to be observed.

Sacrosanctum Concilium 54 addresses one of the most contentious issues of the reform: the vernacular. This article references SC 36, which specified the general norms and competency for determining the extent of the use of the vernacular in liturgy. This article specifically mentions that "a suitable place" for the vernacular is the readings and Universal Prayer, as well as to "those parts belonging to the people," for example, the responses, Creed, and so on. It is fair to say that the Council Fathers did not really envision a liturgy entirely in the vernacular. In fact, the first steps toward implementing the renewal of the Mass were a hybrid of Latin and the vernacular. But once the door was opened to use the mother tongue, it opened very quickly to allow a completely vernacular liturgy. By the early 1970s, Mass was celebrated in the United States completely in English or other native languages. The vernacular liturgy enabled fuller participation by members of the assembly because they were now able to pray in their first language.

While the vernacular was allowed and encouraged, here and elsewhere SC cautions that Latin is not entirely to be abandoned. Specifically, "steps should be taken enabling the faithful to say or to sing together in Latin those parts of the Ordinary of the Mass belonging to them," for example, the *Kyrie*, *Sanctus*, and *Agnus Dei*. The Vatican, as well as Conferences of Bishops, has consistently promoted this usage of Latin. In many parishes, simple ferial chants for these texts have been memorized and are now sung with great fervor. Latin chants also are effective in multilingual and/or multicultural celebrations where Latin can be a common and inclusive language.[31] It should be noted, moreover, that these chants are liturgical texts that are invariable; singing them is truly singing the liturgy. Preserving at least some modicum of Latin during some times of the liturgical year keeps us in a long tradition in the Western Church of using the Latin, while noting at the same time that Latin was not always the universal language of Western liturgy.

---

55. That more complete form of participation in the Mass by which the faithful, after the priest's communion, receive the Lord's body from the sacrifice, is strongly endorsed.

The dogmatic principles laid down by the Council of Trent remain intact.[5] In instances to be specified by the Apostolic See, however, communion under both kinds may be granted both to clerics and religious and to the laity at the discretion of the bishops, for example, to the ordained at the Mass of their ordination, to the professed at the Mass of their religious profession, to the newly baptized at the Mass following their baptism.

5. Council of Trent, sess. 21, *Doctrine on Communion under Both Species*, chap. 1– 3.

The first part of this next paragraph may sound strange to our ears. After fifty years of liturgical renewal, many people have not experienced a Mass in which few people receive Holy Communion. Prior to the Second Vatican Council, it was more common than not to receive Holy Communion outside of the celebration of Mass. With article 55, the Council Fathers are emphasizing that the "more complete form of participation in the Mass" includes receiving Holy Communion.[32] This is another of the liturgical reforms that most of the faithful have received with joy.

Article 51 also addresses receiving Holy Communion under both kinds—receiving the Precious Blood as well as the Sacred Body. The Council Fathers envisioned a rather limited use of this privilege. It should occur during occasions which happen only once to an individual: ordinations, religious professions, and Baptisms. The occasions for receiving the Precious Blood were to be "specified by the Apostolic See" and offered at the "discretion of the bishops." Soon, however, the United States Conference of Catholic Bishops requested other occasions for offering the Precious Blood to the faithful. It became common practice in many United States parishes to offer both species on Sundays and high feast days, for as the GIRM states, Communion is a response to the "Lord's command [that] his Body and Blood should be received as spiritual food"[33] and that this is a clearer sign of our "participation in the sacrifice actually being celebrated."[34]

Another line in this article begs comment. Before the comments permitting the faithful to receive the Precious Blood, SC states that the "dogmatic principles laid down by the Council of Trent remain intact." It is true that the decrees of the Council of Trent forbad offering the Precious Blood to the laity. But this decree must be understood in its historical context and intent. The theological principle that Trent was addressing is that one receives the whole Christ whether one receives only the Body or only the Precious Blood. So, the laity were henceforth permitted to receive *only* the Body of Christ as a way to make clear in their minds that they receive the *whole Christ*. In our time this is not a huge theological issue; the faithful understand that they receive the whole Christ. So, the Council Fathers opened the door for the fuller sign of receiving both Christ's Body and Blood to be implemented.

---

56. The two parts that, in a certain sense, go to make up the Mass, namely, the liturgy of the word and the liturgy of the eucharist, are so closely connected with each other that they form but one single act of worship. Accordingly this Council strongly urges pastors that in their catechesis they insistently teach the faithful to take part in the entire Mass, especially on Sundays and holy days of obligation.

The first part of this article is logically connected to article 50, which emphasizes the connection between the parts of the Mass. *Sacrosanctum Concilium* 56 develops this concept. This article suggests that the two most important parts of the Mass are the Liturgy of the Word and the Liturgy of the Eucharist. These two parts "are so closely connected with each other that they form but one single act of worship." *Sacrosanctum Concilium* 56 also references *Sacrosanctum Concilium* 35, which addresses the intimate connection between words and rites. None of these articles, however, help us understand exactly *how* they are related. The relationship between the Liturgy of the Word and the Liturgy of the Eucharist is an incredibly important theological point—one that still needs further exploration and catechesis.

The connection between Word and Sacrament is more deeply intertwined than simply Word instructs and Sacrament gives grace. If these two parts of the Mass are "but one single act of worship," what truly unites them is that we are nourished both on the Word proclaimed in Scripture and on the Word made present on the altar. In the Liturgy of the Word, especially with the proclamation of the Gospel, we hear about God's saving deeds and Jesus's life and ministry. Our hearing and open reception to God's inspired Word is itself one corporate act of worship. As members of the Body of Christ, we hear about *who* we should be and *how* we should live. We are challenged to become more perfectly who we profess to be: Christ's Body continuing his saving work in our day and time. This kind of living, too, is an act of worship. During the Liturgy of the Eucharist we are not mere "spectators,"[35] but instead unite ourselves with Christ's self-giving. As the bread and wine are placed on the altar, so are we. As the bread and wine are changed into the Body and Blood of Christ through the action of the Holy Spirit, so are we changed by that same Holy Spirit. We pray that "we, who are nourished / by the Body and Blood of your Son / and filled with his Holy Spirit, / may become one body, one spirit in Christ."[36] The Liturgy of the Eucharist fulfills the deepest longings of the Word we hear and appropriate during the Liturgy of the Word. In it we already do what our Baptism calls us as followers and disciples of Christ to do—give ourselves over for the good of others as he did. The self-giving of the Liturgy of the Eucharist is a ritual sacrifice of our own lives for the glory of God, informed and deepened by God's Word.

The last sentence of this article may now sound a bit odd to us: pastors are to catechize their people to take part in the entire Mass. Prior to the Second Vatican Council, fulfilling one's obligation to be at Mass on Sundays and Holydays of Obligation was spelled out in the great moments of the Mass to which, minimally, the faithful must be present: the proclamation of the Gospel, the consecration, and the priest's reception of Holy Communion. We celebrate Mass not to fulfill an obligation and be present for certain moments, but because during the Eucharistic celebration we participate in a great enactment of the whole mystery of Christ. While it is true that in most parishes there are a few people who come late and leave early (sometimes unavoidably, for example, a child is sick), for the most part, the faithful are there for the entire rite from the opening to closing hymns. No doubt much catechesis (and modeling) is still needed for the faithful to have a greater grasp of what is taking place at liturgy and how it unfolds as a single act of worship giving God praise and thanksgiving. This being said, the renewed liturgy has encouraged people to think of Mass as a whole and most happily take part in it from beginning to end.

---

57. § 1. Concelebration, which aptly expresses the unity of the priesthood, has continued to this day as a practice in the Church of both East and West. For this reason it has seemed good to the Council to extend permission for concelebration to the following cases:

1. a. on Holy Thursday, both the chrism Mass and the evening Mass;
   b. Masses during councils, bishops' conferences, and synods;
   c. the Mass at the blessing of an abbot.

2. Also, with permission of the Ordinary, who is the one to decide whether concelebration is opportune, to:
   a. the conventual Mass and the principal Mass in churches, when the needs of the faithful do not require that all the priests on hand celebrate individually;
   b. Masses celebrated at any kind of meeting of priests, whether secular or religious.

§ 2. 1. The regulation, however, of the discipline of concelebration in the diocese pertains to the bishop.

2. This, however, does not take away the option of every priest to celebrate Mass individually, not, however, at the same time and in the same church as a concelebrated Mass or on Holy Thursday.

The longest and most detailed of the articles in chapter II concerns concelebrated Masses—Mass with a main priest celebrant accompanied by other priest celebrants. The purpose for extending permission for more instances of concelebration "express as the unity of the priesthood." It is not often that concelebrations occur as noted in SC 57. Concelebration often happens during Holy Week when the priests of a diocese gather with the bishop for the Chrism Mass. This Mass is a favored time for the priests to renew publically their promises to their bishop. During the Sacred Paschal Triduum, concelebration may also occur if a parish or other liturgical community has more than one resident priest, since Triduum liturgies are not be repeated in a given locale. Concelebration may happen at other times when a number of priests are present—councils, conferences, and synods as well as the blessing of an abbot and in religious houses of clerics. In addition to what is articulated in SC 57, concelebration may take place during the dedication of a church, the jubilee Masses of priests, and of founding parishes. The local bishop regulates the occurrences of concelebration.

Sacrosanctum Concilium 57 cautions that concelebration may take place "when the needs of the faithful do not require that all of the priests on hand celebrate individually."[37] Concelebration should not interfere with normal priestly duties for the good of the faithful.

Sacrosanctum Concilium 57 also cautions that concelebration should not restrict the priest's option to celebrate Mass individually. This suggests that private Masses, that is, a Mass with perhaps only one server present, are permitted for the spiritual good of the priest. A private Mass may not take place at the same time as a concelebrated Mass, nor may a priest say a private Mass during the Sacred Paschal Triduum. *Sacrosanctum Concilium* 57 reminds us that it is preferable for Mass to take place with the faithful in attendance and Mass is not intended to be the private domain of those who are ordained. Jesus instituted the Eucharist at the Last Supper with his disciples—within a community. The purpose of Mass is to make present the Paschal sacrifice of Christ for the good of the whole Church. Privatizing the Mass diminishes this necessary communal aspect. It is the whole Body of Christ who celebrates liturgy.

58. A new rite for concelebration is to be drawn up and inserted into the Roman Pontifical and Roman Missal.

This brief, one-sentence article simply directs that a "new rite for concelebration" be "drawn up." This was done. The GIRM includes an entire section devoted to concelebrated Masses.[38] Additional rubrics for concelebration are provided in the third edition of *The Roman Missal*. These rubrics were adjusted and revised with more detail in recent publications of the Eucharistic Prayers for concelebration.[39]

Questions for Discussion and Reflection

1. What are ways we concretely show that Eucharist is central to the life of the parish? To the lives of individual parishioners?

2. What does it mean to say that Eucharist is a "sacred mystery" (SC, 17)? How might we live out in our everyday lives this sacred mystery?

3. According to the guidelines in chapter II of *Sacrosanctum Concilium*, what are we doing well in our Eucharistic celebrations?

What in our Eucharistic celebrations needs more attention and improvement?

4. In what ways do we understand and live Eucharist in a broader sense than just celebrating Mass? How might this broader understanding help us participate in Mass better?

5. What does it mean to say that the Eucharist is a "memorial" (SC, 47)? How does this relate to the fruits that the Mass promises?

6. How do we understand the relationship of the Liturgy of the Word and the Liturgy of the Eucharist?

NOTES

1. See *Catechism of the Catholic Church* (CCC), 1084.
2. See Luke 22:21.
3. See Matthew 28:19–20.
4. See SC, 47–48.
5. See ibid., 14.
6. See SC, 49–58.
7. This Sign of Peace was new to the faithful but not new to Mass. In the early Church, the Sign of Peace was exchanged by all present, but it eventually became a sign exchanged only among the clergy on more solemn occasions.
8. See CCC, 1328.
9. See the *Code of Canon Law*, canon 897; *Lumen gentium*, 11.
10. See SC, 6; CCC 1085, 1323.
11. See CCC 1330, 1357.
12. See ibid., 1363.
13. See ibid., 1359.
14. See ibid., 1341-1342.
15. See ibid., 1337.
16. See also ibid., 1325.
17. See 1 Corinthians 12:12–27; Matthew 25:40.
18. See CCC, 1340, 1362, 1391–1401.
19. See *Sacramentum caritatis*, 51.
20. John 20:1.
21. See CCC, 1343.

22. See SC, 21, which speaks about "immutable elements, divinely instituted" and "elements subject to change."

23. See *Fulfilled in Your Hearing: The Homily in the Sunday Assembly*, 52. This document is from the National Conference of Catholic Bishops (now United States Conference of Catholic Bishops) subcommittee, Priestly Life and Ministry. It was published in 1982.

24. See further commentary on SC 56 on page 91–92.

25. Here is an example from Eucharistic Prayer III: "May he make of us / an eternal offering to you, / so that we may obtain an inheritance with your elect, / especially with the most Blessed Virgin Mary, Mother of God, / with your blessed Apostles and glorious Martyrs / (with Saint N.: the Saint of the day or Patron Saint) / and with all the Saints, / on whose constant intercession in your presence / we rely for unfailing help."

26. Emphasis added.

27. SC specifically references 1 Timothy 2:1–12 which exhorts the faithful to include intercessory prayer at communal gatherings.

28. See GIRM, 70.

29. The GIRM leaves it open to parishes to determine what should be included in these "other circumstances."

30. See CCC, 1369.

31. This is quickly becoming the norm in the United States.

32. See also canon 918.

33. GIRM, 80.

34. Ibid., 85.

35. SC, 48.

36. Eucharistic Prayer III.

37. See canon 902.

38. See GIRM, chapter IV.

39. Ritual books for concelebration have been published by Liturgy Training Publications and Catholic Book Publishing.

✣CHAPTER III

The Other Sacraments and the Sacramentals

Sacrosanctum Concilium 59–82

Mark Francis, CSV

After having discussed "The Most Sacred Mystery of the Eucharist" in Chapter II, *Sacrosanctum Concilium* then moves to a description and discussion of the renewal of the other six sacraments. Its placement is both logical and significant since the Eucharist enjoys the central place in the life of the Church and the other sacraments are ordered to it. This relationship is described well in a later document of the Council, *Presbyterorum Ordinis* (*Decree on the Ministry and Life of Priests*): "But the other sacraments, and indeed all ecclesiastical ministries and works of the apostolate are bound up with the Eucharist and are directed towards it. For in the most blessed Eucharist is contained the entire spiritual wealth of the church, namely Christ himself our Pasch and our living bread. . . ."[1]

The chapter begins with broad descriptions of the purpose of the sacraments and sacramentals and their relationship to one another.[2] Echoing what was announced as the general purpose of the reform of the Sacred Liturgy set forth in SC 21, article 62 notes that the rites of the sacraments and sacramentals may need to be revised since their meaning may have become unclear with the passage of time. Principles of revision are then proposed in keeping with article 36 of SC: the "competent, territorial ecclesiastical authority" [3] (the National Bishops' Conferences) are invited to prepare vernacular rituals to meet the needs of particular regions provided that they are in harmony with the new Roman Ritual.

The chapter then gives specific directions regarding the revision of each of the sacraments. Seven articles are dedicated to Baptism: the restoration of the adult catechumenate[4]; a direct invitation to a suitable inculturation of the *Rite of Baptism*[5] ; the creation of both simple and solemn rites of adult Baptism as well as a ritual Mass "On the Occasion of a Baptism"[6]; a revised rite for the Baptism of infants[7]; the call for variants in the rite for baptizing a large number of children and a simple rite for Baptism when conferred by a lay person when the one to be baptized is in danger of death and when no priest or deacon is available[8]; the call for a new rite of the "Order of Supplying what was Omitted in the Baptism of an Infant" when the child was baptized using an abbreviated baptismal rite as well as a rite for receiving validly baptized converts into communion with the Church[9]; and finally the permission to bless baptismal water outside of Easter Time by using an approved shorter formula.[10]

Sacrosanctum Concilium 71 deals with the revision of the Sacrament of Confirmation, directing that the rite make its connection to the other Sacraments of Initiation more explicit. The Sacrament of Penance is to be revised in order to make its nature and effect more clear.[11] Several articles are dedicated to what was then called "extreme unction" which now is more fittingly called "anointing of the sick"[12]; that separate rites for Anointing of the Sick and Viaticum be prepared along with a continuous rite combining confession, anointing, and Viaticum[13]; the number of the anointings is to be adapted to circumstances and new prayers composed corresponding to the varying conditions of the person receiving the sacrament.[14] *Sacrosanctum Concilium* 76 calls for a revision of the *Rites of Ordination. Sacrosanctum Concilium* 77 and 78 deal with the revision of the *Rite of Marriage* (or Matrimony), encouraging the local Conferences of Bishops to adapt the rite to "usages of place and people" and stipulate that Matrimony should normally be celebrated in the context of the Mass.

The last section of chapter III deals with revision of the sacramentals, evoking the overall purpose of the liturgical reform itself found in SC 14: to enable the faithful to participate in a full, conscious, and active way. The possibility of the creation of new sacramentals in case of apparent need is also noted and the reservation of certain blessings to members of religious orders is done away with, retaining reserved blessings in favor of bishops or ordinaries.[15] Directions for revising religious profession[16] and funeral rites end the third chapter.[17]

Before moving to an article-by-article commentary of this chapter it is worth noting that while SC was especially careful regarding its authorization of changes in the Mass, its treatment of the celebration of the sacraments and the customs associated with sacramentals is less restrictive. These articles allow for much more leeway on the part of the Conferences of Bishops to propose changes based on local and cultural needs. The reason for this is because the Western Church has never had an absolutely obligatory ritual discipline regarding the sacraments or sacramentals. As opposed to the *Missale Romanum* of 1570 that had rigidly legislated the celebration of the rites of Mass, the Roman Ritual of 1614, containing the celebration of the sacraments and sacramentals, was never intended to suppress all local customs but to serve as a model for local rituals. Over the centuries the Roman Ritual came to supplant the local rituals in many regions, and local practices, if preserved at all, were relegated to the appendices of the local edition of the Roman Ritual. There was, however, significant variation in the celebration of many of the sacraments from one region to another up to the Second Vatican Council.

59. The purpose of the sacraments is to make people holy, to build up the Body of Christ, and, finally, to give worship to God; but being signs they also have a teaching function. They not only presuppose faith, but by words and objects they also nourish, strengthen, and express it; that is why they are called "sacraments of faith." They do indeed impart grace, but, in addition, the very act of celebrating them disposes the faithful most effectively to receive this grace in a fruitful manner, to worship God rightly, and to practice charity.

It is therefore of the highest importance that the faithful should readily understand the sacramental signs and should with great eagerness frequent those sacraments that were instituted to nourish the Christian life.

This first article of chapter III of SC seeks to explain the threefold purpose of the sacraments (sanctify human beings, build up the Church, and offer worship to God) and to distinguish *sacraments* from *sacramentals*. Unlike sacramentals that were instituted by the Church, the Council of Trent maintained that sacraments were divinely instituted and for that reason never fail to impart grace. *Sacrosanctum Concilium* does not make this dogmatic claim (nor is it denied) but reaffirms that grace is imparted by the sacraments whose very celebration "disposes" the faithful to receive that grace, to worship God, and to practice charity. While their fruitful reception depends on faith, *Sacrosanctum Concilium* maintains that they also are able to nourish, strengthen, and express faith.

For all of these reasons the Council underlines the importance that the faithful understand the signs used by the sacraments in order to profit from these important means of God's self-communication. The way these signs communicate has already been explained in SC 7: "In the liturgy, by means of signs perceptible to the senses, human sanctification is signified and brought about in ways proper to each of these signs . . ." For that reason, the signs used in the sacraments (washing with water, anointing, laying on of hands) need to be performed in such a way as they are understood by the faithful and ought not be minimalized or treated as a secondary consideration. The importance of intelligibility of the rites, already voiced in articles 11 and 21 is again emphasized specifically for the celebration of the sacraments.

---

60. The Church has, in addition, instituted sacramentals. These are sacred signs bearing a kind of resemblance to the sacraments: they signify effects, particularly of a spiritual kind, that are obtained through the Church's intercession. They dispose people to receive the chief effect of the sacraments and they make holy various occasions in human life.

Although related to sacraments, sacramentals are instituted by the Church and dispose those who celebrate the sacraments to receive sacramental grace. While this article does not give examples of sacramentals, later in chapter III, examples are offered: the rites surrounding funerals, religious profession, and special blessings. *Sacrosanctum Concilium* affirms that sacramentals, since they are sacred signs drawn from the material world, are able to make holy the various stages of human life.

---

61. Thus, for well-disposed members of the faithful, the effect of the liturgy of the sacraments and sacramentals is that almost every event in their lives is made holy by divine

grace that flows from the paschal mystery of Christ's passion, death, and resurrection, the fount from which all sacraments and sacramentals draw their power. The liturgy means also that there is hardly any proper use of material things that cannot thus be directed toward human sanctification and the praise of God.

Sacrosanctum Concilium 61 identifies the source of the grace derived from both the sacraments and the sacramentals as the Paschal Mystery of Jesus Christ, "the fount from which [they] draw their power." It also emphasizes that the material world, created by God, is capable of conveying God's grace and presence. In other words, SC is speaking here of what theologians have called the "sacramental imagination" of Catholics. This imagination is ultimately based on the Incarnation of Jesus Christ that made the Paschal Mystery possible. Just as Jesus entered wholly into our world as a human being, who suffered and died and rose again for sinful humanity, God in Jesus thus made the material world capable of imparting God's grace and presence.

---

62. With the passage of time, however, certain features have crept into the rites of the sacraments and sacramentals that have made their nature and purpose less clear to the people of today; hence some changes have become necessary as adaptations to the needs of our own times. For this reason the Council decrees what follows concerning the revision of these rites.

Echoing the reasons for the reform of the liturgy already expressed in SC 21, this paragraph explains the need for reforming both the sacraments and sacramentals. "With the passage of time . . . certain features have crept into the rites that have made their nature and purpose less clear to the people of today." The overarching concern motivating the revision, then, is the question of intelligibility. The particular norms that are consonant with the purpose for the reform of the Eucharist seek to clarify the meaning of the sacraments and sacramentals so that those in attendance might have "a good understanding of the rites and prayers . . . [and] take part in the sacred service conscious of what they are doing, with devotion and full involvement."[18]

63. Because the use of the mother tongue in the administration of the sacraments and sacramentals can often be of considerable help for the people, this use is to be extended according to the following norms:

a. With art. 36 as the norm, the vernacular may be used in administering the sacraments and sacramentals.

b. Particular rituals in harmony with the new edition of the Roman Ritual shall be prepared without delay by the competent, territorial ecclesiastical authority mentioned in art. 22, §2 of this Constitution. These rituals are to be adapted, even in regard to the language employed, to the needs of the different regions. Once they have been reviewed by the Apostolic See, they are to be used in the regions for which they have been prepared. But those who draw up these rituals or particular collections of rites must not leave out the prefatory instructions for the individual rites in the Roman Ritual, whether the instructions are pastoral and rubrical or have some special social bearing.

A key element in rendering the celebration of the sacraments and sacramentals more intelligible is the use of the vernacular languages. While supplements to *The Roman Ritual* in different countries provided for partial translations of the *Rites of Baptism, Matrimony,* and *Extreme Unction*, the Holy See approved a complete English translation of the *Rituale Romanum* for the United States as early as 1954. It was left up to the local ordinary, however, to determine its use in whole or in part. With article 36 of SC cited as the norm, blanket permission is given for the celebration of the sacraments and sacramentals in the vernacular language. Article 63.b mandates the preparation of new, pastorally adapted local editions of the Roman Ritual based on the new edition of *The Roman Ritual*. The stipulation that local versions of *The Roman Ritual* be used just in those regions for which they are prepared is easily understandable since adaptations for one region may not be useful or intelligible in other locales. Finally, the insistence that the new prefatory instructions (*praenotanda*), which provide theological and disciplinary norms regarding the sacraments prepared for *The Roman Ritual*, be included in the new local versions of the Ritual is important to maintain unity.

64. The catechumenate for adults, divided into several stages, is to be restored and put into use at the discretion of the local Ordinary. By this means the time of the catechume-

nate, which is intended as a period of well-suited instruction, may be sanctified by sacred rites to be celebrated at successive intervals of time.

The restoration of the catechumenate for adults, known in the early centuries of the Church, was a hope of many bishops and missionaries before the Council, especially those working in Africa where experiments had been underway since the late 1940s to provide this more holistic preparation for adult Baptism. It was also a concern for those living and working in de-Christianized parts of Europe where those who were not baptized as infants would present themselves for Baptism as adults. Significantly, the catechumenate is described with greater detail in *Ad gentes* (*Decree on the Church's Missionary Activity*): "Those who have received from God the gift of faith in Christ, through the church, should be admitted with liturgical rites to the catechumenate, which is not merely an exposition of dogmatic truths and norms of morality, but a period of formation in the entire christian life, an apprenticeship of suitable duration, during which the disciples will be joined to Christ their teacher."[19] Prayer, particular liturgical rites, and experience with other Christians in living the Christian life is an integral part of the formation received in the catechumenate which marks a real departure from the "convert classes" of the period before the Council that proved inadequate to the task of promoting a real conversion of both mind and heart.

Sacrosanctum Concilium 64 leaves it to the local ordinary to implement the catechumenate in his own diocese. In addition to the *Code of Canon Law* and the *Rite of Christian Initiation of Adults*, the *National Statutes on the Catechumenate*, passed by the United States Bishops in 1986 and approved by the Holy See in 1988, serve as a basic point of reference and regulation for the catechumenate in the United States.

---

65. With art. 37–40 of this Constitution as the norm, it is lawful in mission lands to allow, besides what is part of Christian tradition, those initiation elements in use among individual peoples, to the extent that such elements are compatible with the Christian rite of initiation.

Cultural adaptation, or what will later be termed "inculturation," of the faith was a real concern for the bishops at the Second Vatican Council. This article, referring to articles 37–40 of SC which are known as the *Magna Carta* of liturgical inculturation, expresses a remarkably concrete example of the openness of the Church to local cultures. It allows for the possibility of including in the Christian Rites of Initiation "elements in these peoples' way of life" that may aid in the celebration of initiation "provided the substantial unity of the Roman Rite is preserved."[20] These elements, of course, would need to be approved by local bishops and Conferences of Bishops and would not be definitively added to the rite without due deliberation and dialogue with the Holy See.[21]

66. Both of the rites for the baptism of adults are to be revised: not only the simpler rite, but also the more solemn one, with proper attention to the restored catechumenate. A special Mass "On the Occasion of a Baptism" is to be incorporated into the Roman Missal.

In light of the restoration of the catechumenate, both the simple and solemn *Rites of Baptism* for adults had to be revised since over the course of history elements of the separate liturgical celebrations of the catechumenate—anointings, exorcisms (scrutinies), *ephphetha*, and so on—had been telescoped into the one *Rite of Baptism*. In keeping with the centrality of the Eucharist for the Christian life, SC mandates the creation and incorporation of a ritual Mass, "On the Occasion of a Baptism," be inserted in *The Roman Missal*. This ritual Mass would be used in the event that an adult receives Baptism at a celebration apart from the usual time for initiation, at the Easter Vigil.

67. The rite for the baptism of infants is to be revised and it should be suited to the fact that those to be baptized are infants. The roles as well as the obligations of parents and godparents should be brought out more clearly in the rite itself.

Sacrosanctum Concilium then calls for a revision of the *Rite of Baptism* of infants because the rite used before the Council treated an infant to be baptized as if he/she were an adult. The previous rite required the presider to pose direct questions to the infant who could not possibly answer ("What do you ask of the Church?; Do you wish to be baptized?"). Moreover, since no attention was given in the previous rite to the role and duties of the parents and godparents SC indicates that the new rite should provide more explicit references.

68. The baptismal rite should contain alternatives, to be used at the discretion of the local Ordinary, for occasions when a very large number are to be baptized together. Moreover, a shorter rite is to be drawn up, especially in mission lands, for use by catechists, but also by the faithful in general, when there is danger of death and neither a priest nor a deacon is available.

One of the critiques of the pre-Conciliar baptismal rite was its lack of flexibility in special pastoral situations. This article allows the local ordinary to permit simplifications in the rite in the event there "a very large number" to be baptized. This simplification would be permitted for both adult and infant Baptism. The Council Fathers were also aware that in large parts of the Church—especially in those parts of the world where there is a shortage of the normal ministers of Baptism, that a simplified *Rite of Baptism* should be made available for catechists and others to use in emergency situations.

69. In place of the rite called the "Order of Supplying What Was Omitted in the Baptism of an Infant," a new rite is to be drawn up. This should manifest more clearly and fittingly that an infant who was baptized by the short rite has already been received into the Church. Similarly, a new rite is to be drawn up for converts who have already been validly baptized; it should express that they are being received into the commu-nion of the Church.

The "Order of Supplying What Was Omitted in the Baptism of an Infant" was eventually renamed in the revised rite to the "Rite of Bringing a Baptized Child to the Church." It was especially reformed to underscore that the baptized child is indeed a member of the Church, even though he or she was baptized because of an emergency situation: danger of death, religious persecution, or even a dispute within the family. An important focus for this rite—one that was presupposed by SC 69—is that the Christian community recognizes the child as one of her own and encourages parents and godparents, representing the Church, to accept the responsibilities that arise from having the child baptized.

The current "Rite of Reception of Baptized Christians into the Full Communion of the Catholic Church" was mentioned in this article since in the previous ritual it appeared just after the "Order of Supplying What Was Omitted in Baptism of an Infant." It is significant what this section of SC does not ask for—there is no demand for an abjuration of heresy that was part of the old rite. Rather, the rite should be more positive, emphasizing the Profession of Faith that is then celebrated in the reception of the Eucharist.

---

70. Except during the Easter season, baptismal water may be blessed within the rite of baptism itself by use of an approved, shorter formulary.

Sacrosanctum Concilium 70 changes a practice that had been in force since the Middle Ages of preserving the Easter water blessed on Holy Saturday in the baptismal font for Baptisms during the whole year. Many of the Council Fathers argued that this water, containing some sacred chrism that was poured into the water during the blessing, often appeared rather insalubrious after many months in the font. Hence, SC provides a new possibility of blessing the water of the font in a shorter prayer during the celebration of Baptism outside of Easter Time.

---

71. The rite of confirmation is also to be revised in order that the intimate connection of this sacrament with the whole of Christian initiation may stand out more clearly; for this reason it is fitting for candidates to renew their baptismal promises just before they are confirmed.

Confirmation may be conferred within Mass when convenient; as for the rite outside Mass, a formulary is to be composed for use as an introduction.

The Sacrament of Confirmation is treated by one article in SC that avoids the many debates that were raging around the meaning of the sacraments and discipline of when and in what order it ought to be conferred. *Sacrosanctum Concilium* calls for a clearer ritual connection of Confirmation with the two other Sacraments of Initiation, Baptism and Eucharist. Whenever the Sacrament of Confirmation is conferred, the *confirmandi* are to make a profession of their baptismal promises. Since it was the general practice to celebrate Confirmation without a Mass before the Council, the article seeks to make clear the connection of Confirmation with the Eucharist by authorizing that a ritual Mass for the conferral of Confirmation be prepared.

72. The rite and formularies for the sacrament of penance are to be revised so that they more clearly express both the nature and effect of the sacrament.

This rather laconic article simply calls for a reform of the *Rite of Penance* that before the Council was always a private celebration except for the removal of excommunication. Given the introductory paragraphs of chapter III of SC, however, it was presupposed that the relationship of this sacrament with the Christian community and with the Word of God would be addressed in the ritual revision. It was for this reason that communal options for the celebration were proposed in the revised rite.

73. "Extreme unction," which may also and more properly be called "anointing of the sick," is not a sacrament for those only who are at the point of death. Hence, as soon as any one of the faithful begins to be in danger of death from sickness or old age, the fitting time for that person to receive this sacrament has certainly already arrived.

Sacrosanctum Concilium now changes centuries of Church practice by redefining and renaming "Extreme Unction" (Last Anointing or the Last Rites) as "Anointing of the Sick." This sacrament is no longer to be viewed as only the sacrament of the dying, but as a sacrament for those in danger of death from both old age and sickness. This rather revolutionary revision of the sacrament that is based on both Jesus's ministry of healing the sick and the fifth chapter of the Letter of James that calls on the elders of the Church to pray over the sick person, restored a more ancient notion of its purpose as a sacrament of healing as well as simply of spiritual comfort at the time of death.

74. In addition to the separate rites for anointing of the sick and for viaticum, a continuous rite shall be drawn up, structured so that the sick person is anointed after confessing and before receiving viaticum.

Given the change in purpose of the sacrament and its recipients, SC is able to call for a more holistic approach to sacramental ministry to those who are seriously sick but conscious by mandating the creation of a continuous rite for the celebration Penance, Anointing, and Viaticum. The result of this article is *Pastoral Care of the Sick: Rites of Anointing and Viaticum.*

75. The number of the anointings is to be adapted to the circumstances; the prayers that belong to the rite of anointing are to be so revised that they correspond to the varying conditions of the sick who receive the sacrament.

The previous rite called for the Anointing of all of the senses (and the feet), asking for God's forgiveness for those sins committed by the senses and by "the power to walk." Many at the Council critiqued the content of the Anointing prayers since they emphasized forgiveness of sins rather than the care of the Church and a prayer for God's presence and healing. This article reflects the desire of the members of the Council that the sacrament be administered in a more flexible way that would be able to better deal with the varying conditions of the sick person.

76. Both the ceremonies and texts of the ordination rites are to be revised. The address given by the bishop at the beginning of each ordination or consecration may be in the vernacular.

When a bishop is consecrated, all the bishops present may take part in the laying on of hands.

Sacrosanctum Concilium 76 calls for the revision of the *Rites of Ordination*, without going into specific detail as to how the ceremonies and the prayers are to be changed. It is helpful to remember that prior to the

Second Vatican Council there were in effect seven "ordination" rites (the four minor and three major orders) as well as a ceremony for entry into the clerical state (tonsure). *Sacrosanctum Concilium* wisely avoids giving too much detail regarding these rites before the Council's discussion on ordained ministry except for two things: the *monitio* or address contained in the rite that preceded the conferral of the Consecration or Ordination may be in the vernacular and the bishops in attendance at the Ordination (Consecration) of a bishop, in addition to the co-consecrators, and the other bishops in attendance may lay on hands.

77. The marriage rite now found in the Roman Ritual is to be revised and enriched in such a way that it more clearly signifies the grace of the sacrament and imparts a knowledge of the obligations of spouses.

"If any regions follow other praiseworthy customs and ceremonies when celebrating the sacrament of marriage, the Council earnestly desires that by all means these be retained."[41]

Moreover, the competent, territorial ecclesiastical authority mentioned in art. 22, §2 of this Constitution is free to draw up, in accord with art. 63, its own rite, suited to the usages of place and people. But the rite must always conform to the law that the priest assisting at the marriage must ask for and obtain the consent of the contracting parties.

41. Council of Trent, sess. 24, *Decree on Reform,* chap. 1. See also RomR, title 8, chap. 2, n. 6.

Sacrosanctum Concilium's treatment of Marriage is perhaps the one article in this chapter that gives the most explicit mandate to the whole Church for an in-depth inculturation of this rite. Significantly, it quotes the Council of Trent: "If any regions follow other praiseworthy customs and ceremonies when celebrating the sacrament of marriage, the Council earnestly desires that by all means these be retained." The Second Vatican Council though goes beyond Trent by permitting bishops, even of non-missionary regions, the faculty of creating new Marriage rites proper to their own regions. The one constant is that these rites always have to ensure the exchange of consent—a consistent requirement of the Western Church for a valid marriage that was ultimately derived from the Roman law tradition.

78. Marriage is normally to be celebrated within Mass, after the reading of the gospel and the homily and before "the prayer of the faithful." The prayer for the bride, duly emended to remind both spouses of their equal obligation to remain faithful to each other, may be said in the vernacular.

But if the sacrament of marriage is celebrated apart from Mass, the epistle and gospel from the nuptial Mass are to be read at the beginning of the rite and the blessing is always to be given to the spouses.

Sacrosanctum Concilium 78, consistent with its treatment of the relationship of the sacraments to the Eucharist, encourages that Marriage be celebrated within a Mass. It also mandates that the nuptial blessing—originally prayed only over the bride—now be revised in the vernacular in order to bless both bride and groom and to call them to fidelity and to an awareness of their mutual obligations.

79. The sacramentals are to be reviewed in the light of the primary criterion that the faithful participate intelligently, actively, and easily; the conditions of our own days must also be considered. When rituals are revised, in accord with art. 63, new sacramentals may also be added as the need for them becomes apparent.

Reserved blessings shall be very few; reservations shall be in favor only of bishops and Ordinaries.

Let provision be made that some sacramentals, at least in special circumstances and at the discretion of the Ordinary, may be administered by qualified laypersons.

It is interesting to note that the sacramentals, as public acts of the Church, were to be revised following the overarching criteria for liturgical *aggiornamento* or updating established by the Council: that the faithful be able to participate intelligently, actively, and easily. Article 63, which speaks of the importance of the use of the vernacular for sacramentals, is referenced. This article essentially abrogates the reservation of certain blessings to members of religious institutes. For example, the Franciscans had a special indult to perform the rite of erecting the Stations of the Cross in a church and the Carmelites had the right to bless and impose the scapular of our Lady of Mount Carmel. Reserved blessings are now limited to those with official pastoral responsibility in the local Church. Finally, the possibility of laypeople administering certain sacramentals with the permission of the ordinary is provided by SC.

> 80. The rite for the consecration to a life of virginity as it exists in the Roman Pontifical is to be revised.
>
> A rite of religious profession and renewal of vows shall be drawn up with a view to achieving greater unity, simplicity, and dignity. Apart from exceptions in particular law, this rite should be adopted by those who make their profession or renewal of vows within Mass.
>
> Religious profession should preferably be made within Mass.

The two traditions for celebration of the consecrated life are covered by SC 80: the Consecration of virgins and that of religious profession. Both the "Rite of Consecration to a Life of Virginity" (by far the older rite, found in *The Roman Pontifical*, the ritual book reserved for the bishop) and the "Rite of Religious Profession," are to be revised, respecting the particular traditions of the religious institutes. Again, SC is concerned with making the relationship between this sacramental and the Eucharist clearer by encouraging that religious profession take place during Mass.

> 81. The rite of funerals should express more clearly the paschal character of Christian death and should correspond more closely to the circumstances and traditions of various regions. This applies also to the liturgical color to be used.

This article announces a decided shift in emphasis in the funeral rites of the Latin Rite of the Catholic Church. Rather than the medieval emphasis on sin, judgment, and God's wrath, epitomized by the sequence prescribed for every funeral, *Dies Irae* (Day of Wrath) and by the use of black vestments, SC mandates a funeral ritual more centered on the deceased Christian's participation in the Paschal Mystery of Jesus Christ. Funeral rituals also need to be in dialogue with local customs and cultural practices.

> 82. The rite for the burial of infants is to be revised and a special Mass for the occasion provided.

The old Roman Ritual provided prayers for the burial of children that largely centered on the theme of their purity. Moreover there was no ritual Mass provided for their burial. This article seeks to fill this pastoral need by mandating new prayers and a special ritual Mass that would better respond to the tragic situation of the death of a child.

Questions for Discussion and Reflection

1. How are both sacraments and sacramentals linked and directed to the Eucharist?

2. What is the difference between a sacrament and a sacramental?

3. How do the sacraments and sacramentals underscore the holiness of all creation and reflect the "Catholic imagination"?

4. Why is it more accurate to describe the catechumenate proposed by SC as real formation in the Christian life rather than just instruction in the truths of the faith?

5. In what ways does SC respond to different pastoral needs in mandating specific variations in the celebration of infant Baptism?

6. How did SC redefine the Sacrament of the Anointing of the Sick?

7. In what ways does this section of SC invite cultural adaptation of the sacraments?

8. What criteria are mentioned by SC for the revision of the sacramentals and how do these criteria parallel those for the revision of the sacraments?

NOTES

1. *Presbyterorum Ordinis* (PO), 5.
2. See SC, 59, 60, 61.
3. Ibid., 63 a, b.
4. See ibid., 64.
5. See ibid., 65.
6. Ibid., 66.

7. See ibid., 67.

8. See ibid., 68.

9. See ibid., 69.

10. See ibid., 70.

11. See ibid., 72.

12. Ibid., 73.

13. See ibid., 74.

14. See ibid., 75.

15. See ibid., 79.

16. See ibid., 80.

17. See ibid., 81, 82.

18. Ibid., 48.

19. *Ad gentes* (AG), 14.

20. Ibid., 37.

21. See ibid., 39, 40.

✣ CHAPTER IV

Divine Office

Sacrosanctum Concilium 83–101

Genevieve Glen, OSB

The daily round of psalms, readings, hymns, and prayers that came to be known as the Divine Office has recorded roots in the first Christian centuries. Impelled by the mandate to "pray without ceasing,"[1] early Christian communities, inspired by Jewish custom, seem to have taken a practical route to unceasing prayer by praying at fixed times of the day. They prayed together when they could, alone when they could not, at the beginning and end of the working day. The more fervent sometimes rose for prayer during the night. Groups of ascetics gradually began to meet for short prayer services at mid-morning, midday, and mid-afternoon. Psalmody was the staple content of these community prayers, but biblical readings, additional prayers, and eventually hymns came to be added to the repertoire as the practice spread throughout the early Christian world. Alternate forms sprang up among desert monastics from the third century on. In both contexts, scarcity of books and limited literacy gave rise to services led by those who could read but embraced by all who could listen, repeat, and slowly memorize the biblical texts. Form and text choice varied from place to place and time to time, but the tradition of communal as well as personal biblical prayer shows remarkable unity and great resilience.

Slowly, however, issues of language and literacy, as well as the gradual clericalization of liturgy in general, alienated many lay worshippers from the daily Offices. Those who could no longer understand or learn Latin turned to more accessible popular devotions. Benedictine monasticism, born in sixth-century Italy, created a form of the Latin Office that blended the traditions of town and city communities of worship, forerunners of our parishes, with those developed by desert monastics, male and female ascetics who lived alone or in small groups.[2] Where the Benedictine monasteries went, their form of prayer went with them, but, like the celebration of the Eucharist, continued to draw locals and visitors as observers and listeners rather than as active participants. Beginning in the twelfth century new religious orders such as the Franciscans and the Dominicans rejected the monastic fixity of place in favor of a freedom of movement that enabled them to serve as itinerant preachers, as their founders intended. Where the monastic Hours required different books for different ministers and participants—lectionaries, psalters, books of antiphons—the mendicants streamlined the Office to make it more portable as they traveled, but again they did not invite their often illiterate and vernacular-speaking audiences to join in because by that time, liturgy was largely perceived as the work of the clergy and the monastic religious orders.

The Church's pastoral wisdom has more than once preserved significant forms of liturgical worship from extinction by turning them into obligations solemnly imposed. So, fortunately, the Divine Office, as it came to be called, survived as a requirement imposed on clerics and religious in solemn vows. Even the name "Divine Office" means "holy duty." However, a simplistic summary of liturgical history sometimes gives the impression that it dried to dust on the spiritual shelves of all those bound to recite it. Better educated clerics, to be sure, understood Latin well enough to benefit from the power of the biblical texts. Monastics and students in monastic schools usually learned the language well enough to pray it with meaning. And even among those for whom Latin was unfamiliar, there was no doubt those who, remaining simply to the obligation, were made holy by their very fidelity to prayer without savor. To all of these men and women who kept faith with the Office in whatever spirit, we owe the fact that the Council still had an Office to be reformed.

By the early 1960s this Office had undergone a long history of abbreviation and expansion, of complication and simplification until a uniform rite was promulgated by Pope Pius V (1566–1572) and further reformed by Pope Pius X (1903–1914) and Pope Pius XII (1939–1958). While this Office retained the character of communal prayer in monasteries and among chapters of canons, it was reduced largely to a matter of individual and private obligation among most other clerics. You may remember seeing priests in movies pacing church grounds, book in hand, silently moving their lips as they read their Office. The book, called the Breviary, became the popular name for the prayer. Considered the priest's book, it nevertheless continued to trickle into parish life in places where pastors kept alive the custom of parish-sung Vespers (Evening Prayer), usually on Sunday evenings. European Catholic immigrants brought the custom with them, so even on the eve of the Council, there were communities who knew Vespers as community prayer.

In SC chapter IV, Council members laid the groundwork for serious renewal. The document takes tentative steps toward restoring the Office to its original character of communal liturgical prayer focused on time. As is evident in the texts below, SC mandates specific revisions to make the Hours accessible and formative for all worshipers, including clerics for whom it had become more obligation than prayer. *Sacrosanctum Concilium* prompted a massive reform of the Divine Office, retitled the Liturgy of the Hours and promulgated in Latin in 1971 and in English in 1976. The new rite, like all the other post-Conciliar reformed liturgies, was preceded by an exceptionally rich general instruction. The *General Instruction of the Liturgy of the Hours* (GILOH) is a significant source for the catechesis, formation, and the celebration of the Hours. In the United States, the Liturgy of the Hours, prefaced by the GILOH, is published in full in four volumes and in part in a single volume entitled *Christian Prayer* for those who do not regularly pray the Office of Readings.

The first *editio typica*[3] of the Hours was composed under serious time pressures, so an *editio typica altera*[4] appeared in 1985, containing further revisions and additional texts for some of the saints canonized after 1971. The United States Conference of Catholic Bishops announced in November, 2012, that work will begin on an English translation of the *editio typica altera* and is expected to be available for use in three to five years from this date. The project will be able to make use of a variety of revised liturgical texts already approved for use in the United States and will attend to further translations as needed. The currently approved texts include *The Revised Grail Psalms,* the 1986 translation of the New Testament of *The New American Bible*, and the prayers from *The Roman Missal* in use since November, 2011.[5]

Liturgia horarum, or the Liturgy of the Hours, the new title given to the Divine Office by the post-Conciliar reform is very significant. It makes clear first of all that together with the Eucharist and the other sacraments this form of prayer constitutes the Church's liturgy. All that is said in the first chapters of SC about the nature, meaning, and importance of the liturgy in general applies in full measure to the Hours. What is specific to the Hours is their relationship with time.

---

83. Christ Jesus, High Priest of the new and eternal covenant, taking human nature, introduced into this earthly exile the hymn that is sung throughout all ages in the halls of heaven. He joins the entire human community to himself, associating it with his own singing of this canticle of divine praise.

For he continues his priestly work through the agency of his Church, which is unceasingly engaged in praising the Lord and interceding for the salvation of the whole world. The Church does this not only by celebrating the eucharist, but also in other ways, especially by praying the divine office.

Article 83, together with articles 84 and 85 (see below), applies to the Hours what is said in SC 7 of all liturgy: "liturgy is considered as an exercise of the priestly office of Jesus Christ." Christ the High Priest is present and at work in the Church "praising God and interceding for the salvation of the whole world."[6] Christ's priestly work, carried out through the Church, is no mere matter of words or is rather a matter of the most powerful of words, the Word of God, "making the work of our redemption a present reality."[7]

While the Hours have often been described as a "canticle of divine praise," as they are here, the word "praise" can create false expectations for those who pick up the Hours for the first time. Every Office is certainly framed in praise and its usual companion, thanksgiving: the Introductory Rites always include the traditional Trinitarian doxology and the conclusion invites us to give praise and thanks to God. The major Hours—Morning (Lauds), Evening (Vespers), and Night Prayer (Compline)—include one of the three great Gospel canticles of praise: the Canticle of Zachary (Luke 1:68–79, sung in the morning and also known as the *Benedictus* from the first word of the Latin text); the Canticle of Mary (Luke 1:46–55, sung in the evening and also known as the *Magnificat*; and the Canticle of Simeon (Luke 2:29–32, sung at night and also known as the *Nunc Dimittis*).[8]

However, not all of the biblical texts in the Office praise God, or even address God. Some psalms and canticles are devoted almost entirely to praise, but other psalms and readings wrestle honestly with every aspect of human experience, from birth to death, from irrepressible joy to intense suffering, from deep guilt to profound gratitude for deliverance, from utter bewilderment to stark conviction. A large number of the psalms are categorized as individual or national laments, in which the psalmists protest ill treatment at the hands of enemies or even of God before turning to thanksgiving for deliverance. Praise is certainly found in the Hours, but it is often interwoven with much darker threads of guilt, contrition, anger, hatred, and despair.

Praise and intercession, the two dimensions of the Hours, actually work in tandem. As liturgy, the Hours are acts of worship. They express the faith that grounds the fundamental relationship between God and those who pray. This relationship is entirely defined by the conviction that "God is love,"[9] not in some empty sentimental way but as the ever-present, ever active, always powerful force who gives life, defends it, retrieves it from all manner of destruction, and transforms it into a reality more enduring than we know. Many of the morning psalms especially open with assertions that God has brought about and governs all of creation. From this faith perspective, those who pray acknowledge that in *all* and *every* human experience, no matter how baffling it may be, God is ultimately in charge and we, as human beings who are not God, in turn surrender ourselves into the divine hands in love and obedience, the two components of true worship. In that redemptive interchange, all of human experience resolves into praise because we are not alone, we are not abandoned to our own inadequate devices, we are not left purposeless: we are in the care of a love beyond our imagining. It may be pastorally important in times of severe personal, social, economic, or political distress to recognize that the Hours as "canticle of divine praise" do not require us to ignore or conceal the darker realities of human experience but rather give us tools for interpreting them in light of the reality of Christ's Resurrection and living them by that light.

Of course the Hours, like every liturgical celebration, affect not only those who pray but all others for whom we pray. We cannot doubt that the Hours, as the very prayer of Christ, could ever be ineffective in interceding with God for the salvation of the world, the ongoing transformation of the realm of evil into the reign of God by transforming human selfishness into love. The fruit of our intercession in Christ, and the intercession of the generations before and after us, is, though we do not see it, not only our own conversion and sanctification but this Paschal transformation of all humanity.

In addition to reiterating key points of SC 7, article 83 also reiterates SC 8 concerning the interchange between the earthly and heavenly liturgy. Liturgical celebrations—whether of the Eucharist, the other sacramental rites, or the Hours—join us with the One who lives in history but transcends this history. Liturgical celebrations have the character of memorial: past, present, and future are woven together in Christ's Death and Resurrection, which opens a door for us into eternity.[10] As GILOH 106–109 spells out more specifically, the texts of the Hours, especially the psalms, set before us and invite us into the past and present human experiences of joy and suffering, bewilderment and reassurance, desperation and hope, all taken up into the Paschal Mystery of Christ which bridges the mysterious chasm separating time and eternity. Both SC 83 and GILOH 16 remind us that "In the earthly liturgy we take part in a foretaste of that heavenly liturgy celebrated in the holy city of Jerusalem toward which we journey as pilgrims. . . ."

---

84. By tradition going back to early Christian times, the divine office is so arranged that the whole course of the day and night is made holy by the praises of God. Therefore, when this wonderful song of praise is rightly performed by priests and others who are deputed for this purpose by the Church's ordinance or by the faithful praying together with the priest in the approved form, then it is truly the voice of a bride addressing her bridegroom; it is the very prayer that Christ himself, together with his Body, addresses to the Father.

---

85. Hence all who render this service are not only fulfilling a duty of the Church, but also are sharing in the greatest honor of Christ's Bride, for by offering these praises to God they are standing before God's throne in the name of the Church, their Mother.

Two features distinguish the Liturgy of the Hours from all other liturgies. One is clearly expressed in SC chapter 4, the other only implied.

Every liturgical celebration has its own character and purpose. The particular purpose of the Liturgy of the Hours has from their beginning been the sanctification of time, particularly as it unfolds throughout the day. The development of the liturgical year impacted the content of the Hours but did not detract from their essential focus on daily time. As mentioned above, the change of name from Divine Office to Liturgy of the Hours in the post-Conciliar reform highlights this unique focus.

The Hours set forth in various ways the Paschal Mystery of Christ as it unfolds in the Paschal history of the world. Christ's Incarnation, Death, and Resurrection in all their fullness reoriented that history. Where before, death was an insurmountable wall against which every human story smashed and disintegrated in the end, Christ has opened a door in the wall through which we can all expect to pass if we so write our stories—in collaboration with their ultimate Author, of course—that they bring us to that doorway through which Christ is waiting to carry us. Because of Christ's Resurrection, the human story does not end at death's door but continues into the realm beyond time. In daily life, time is the medium in which we choose to live or to refuse the Paschal story of salvation.[11] In the hustle and bustle of the day, whether in a Roman marketplace or in today's streets and fields, it is easy to lose sight of the eternal orientation of human history transformed at its root by the Death and Resurrection of Jesus Christ. The many small purposes that eat up our attention and energy easily distract us from the fundamental choice that lies before us at every moment: self-centeredness or love? Death or life? The Hours faithfully embraced break in on our other pursuits to remind us throughout the day that every choice we make in the here and now of quotidian experience conditions our life in the there and then of God's Reign.

The shorthand expression describing the Hours' purpose as the sanctification of time is a bit misleading. Time itself has already been made holy by the fact that Christ has entered fully into human history and made it his own. However, time in the abstract is of very little interest. What is of interest is the way in which we human beings live out the time of our own lives as it unfolds day by day. It is we who cry out to be made holy in our journey through the hours of the day. The Hours are signals to "stop, look, and listen" and redirect our steps if they are not taking us to where God intends us to go.

The second unique feature of the Liturgy of the Hours is never mentioned but always assumed. *Sacrosanctum Concilium* 7 claims that "[i]n the liturgy, by means of signs perceptible to the sense, human sanctification is signified and brought about in ways proper to each of these signs. . . ." Every sacramental liturgy properly celebrated employs one or more tangible, material signs through which the grace of the sacrament is signified and activated in its recipients. The Hours, which are of course not sacraments but are liturgies, appear at first blush to offer no specific sign to participants. However, that may be simply because we take for granted the most profound and powerful of human signs: language. The Hours are made up entirely of words seen or said, spoken or sung, heard either by the mind alone or by the ears. Ceremonial may be employed but is secondary. In other words, the Hours give full play to the power of the divine force that first brought order out of chaos to set the stage for all forms of life, culminating in human life.[12] The Word of God not only creates but defines all reality, including especially human reality. The Word restores us to our truth, distorted since Eden. Furthermore, the Word calls for a return of words from us as human beings invited to enter into redemptive conversation with the God whose Word expresses creative love. The formality of the prescribed language of the Hours sometimes disguises that astonishing truth: we are sanctified most powerfully in the meeting between God's Word and ours. God has assured us, with regard to our own transformation and that of the world for whose re-creation we pray, "[My word] shall not return to me empty, / but it shall accomplish that which I purpose, / and succeed in the thing for which I sent it."[13]

Articles 84 and 85 of SC repeat not only the purpose of the Hours but also their ecclesial character, reiterating parts of article 83. Whether alone, as individual members of the "the entire human community,"[14] or as gatherings in which Christ has promised to be present,[15] we pray as Church in communion with Christ. Article 84 is quite inclusive in recognizing that the prayer of the Church includes priests but may also include others deputed for the task, meaning religious in solemn vows, and even "the faithful praying together with the priest in the approved form." We see here a flashback to the early Christian communities, who did in fact very often gather to pray the Hours with their clergy. The movement from an Office largely deputed to clergy and religious to an Office which belongs to all God's people has begun![16]

However, in a culture that has struggled to find the right relationship between men and women and to appreciate the power of marriage as a sign of Christ's communion with the Church in love, the imagery of the Church as Bride of Christ in articles 84 and 85 may have lost some of its impact, though none of the truth, as expressed in Ephesians 5:32: "This is a great mystery, but I speak in reference to Christ and the church."

---

86. Priests engaged in the sacred pastoral ministry will offer the praises of the hours with greater fervor the more vividly they realize that they must heed St. Paul's exhortation: "Pray without ceasing" (1 Thes 5:17). For the work in which they labor will effect nothing and bring forth no fruit except by the power of the Lord who said: "Without me you can do nothing" (Jn 15:5). That is why the apostles, instituting deacons, said: "We will devote ourselves to prayer and to the ministry of the word" (Acts 6:4).

Article 86 expressly sets out the ideal that animated the early Christian communities which chose to pray at fixed times in order to learn to "[p]ray without ceasing." It acknowledges further that work, even pastoral work, that is not saturated in and shaped by personal prayer must fail in its purpose, for prayer roots us in a living interchange with Christ, in, through, and for whom all pastoral work is done. Obviously prayer is at its fullest when it is both personal and liturgical, as are the Hours. This paragraph echoes the sentiments of the now famous identification of liturgy as the summit and source of all the Church's activity.[17] However, it is historically conditioned. Despite the best ideals of its authors, as seen in article 84, it continues to assume that the Hours are prayed primarily by priests.

---

87. In order that the divine office may be better and more completely carried out in existing circumstances, whether by priests or by other members of the Church, the Council, carrying further the restoration already so happily begun by the Apostolic See, has seen fit to decree what follows concerning the office of the Roman Rite.

Article 87 reiterates the concept that Church members other than priests may pray the Hours. It also acknowledges the pre-Conciliar Breviary reforms of Pope Pius X and Pope Pius XII. In that context, the text now turns our attention to the specific revisions mandated to put the theology of articles 83–87 into practice.

---

88. Because the purpose of the office is to sanctify the day, the traditional sequence of the hours is to be restored so that once again they may be genuinely related to the hour of the day when they are prayed, as far as it is possible. Moreover, it will be necessary to take into account the modern conditions in which daily life has to be lived, especially by those who are called to labor in apostolic works.

Here we see the primary consequence of restoring the understanding of the Hours as a liturgy of time.[18] Article 88 refers to what had become the common experience of priests and religious communities charged with praying the Divine Office. The pressures of ministry had over time eroded the link between the liturgical Hours and the time of day. It was not uncommon for busy priests to sit down at the end of a long workday to fit the entire daily Office into a single sitting. Under the same pressures, many religious communities had settled for such anomalies as praying Matins and Lauds for the next day at 6:00 PM of the previous day, and then praying Compline of the current day later in the evening. The three minor Hours of Terce, Sext, and None to indicate the appropriate times of day, were often crammed in among various devotional prayers offered before and after the morning Mass, while Vespers was quite frequently prayed in the interval between the noon meal and afternoon work. While mandating a return to the tradition of praying the Hours in proper sequence at the proper times of day, the authors acknowledge that the pressures which created the anomalies remain in force. Pastoral realism requires that they be taken into account in rearranging the daily liturgical or *horarium* schedule. In practice, obedience to this mandate has been facilitated by the shortening of the Hours (see Article 91 below). Still it calls for a certain amount of preparation and discipline so that a fruitful balance of work and prayer may be maintained. For busy priests this has sometimes meant taking advantage of the option for dispensation or commutation granted in SC 97 on page 135.

89. Therefore, when the office is revised, these norms are to be observed:

a. By the venerable tradition of the universal Church, lauds as morning prayer and vespers as evening prayer are the two hinges on which the daily office turns; hence they are to be considered as the chief hours and celebrated as such.

b. Compline is to be so composed that it will be a suitable prayer for the end of the day.

c. The hour known as matins, although it should retain the character of nocturnal praise when celebrated in choir, shall be adapted so that it may be recited at any hour of the day; it shall be made up of fewer psalms and longer readings.

d. The hour of prime is to be suppressed.

e. In choir the minor hours of terce, sext, and none are to be observed. But outside choir it will be lawful to choose whichever of the three best suits the hour of the day.

The cycles of light and darkness have held deep significance for human beings. Before the advent of electricity, sunrise and sunset defined alternating periods of safety and danger, of all the activities necessary for human life and of the exchange of activity for sleep. Many primitive religions gave religious significance to the forces of light and darkness and therefore to the succession of the times they dominated. Biblical texts like Psalm 104 reflect this mindset while attributing both light and darkness to the one divine life-giver. Not surprisingly, the early Christian communities to which we owe the Hours interpreted Christological significance to nightfall and daybreak. Sunset recalled the death and burial of Christ, but also the promise that forces of night have never extinguished the Light of the World.[19] Sunrise spoke of the work of creation and of the new creation achieved by Christ in his rising from the darkness of the tomb. The *General Instruction of the Liturgy of the Hours* 38–39 calls on key biblical and early Christian texts to offer an extensive reflection on this significance of Morning and Evening Prayer, as Lauds and Vespers are now retitled.

For practical as well as religious reasons, the early Christian communities of worship gathered most often at daybreak and sunset, the beginning and end of the usual working day in the Greco-Roman world, and therefore tended to develop those Hours most comprehensively. Today both parish and non-monastic religious communities tend also to choose these Hours as their primary forms of community prayer outside the Eucharist. Pragmatically speaking, the dangers of darkness in contemporary urban and suburban settings have made it more difficult for parishes to schedule regular Evening Prayer. That has led to the rather unfortunate practice of using Evening Prayer to open evening committee or educational meetings, thus relegating it to the status of a prayer for certain occasions rather than a prayer for this hinge time of day between light and darkness.

Compline, now called Night Prayer, has always been a form of bedtime prayer, quite often prayed by monastics in the privacy of the bedroom upon retiring. The current reform has placed an optional examination of conscience and short prayer of absolution at the beginning of the Hour as an opportunity to review one's day in the light of grace and sin. No form is prescribed. The use of one of the Penitential Acts provided for the Eucharist is recommended. The texts of the Hour tend to dwell on trust in the light of Christ as darkness approaches, as we see for example in the Canticle of Simeon. Night Prayer preserves the custom of marking the close of day with one of the traditional seasonal Marian antiphons.

The Office of Matins was traditionally prayed during the night or early morning hours. Detaching it from any given time seems an odd choice in light of SC's commitment to restoring the broken link between the Hours and the time of day. A free-floating Hour is an anomaly in a liturgy intentionally dedicated to the sanctification of time as it passes. The texts had in fact already lost much of their time-related content even before the Council. The reform has not restored it. Communities who wish to "retain the character of nocturnal praise" must do so largely through their musical choices.

When Matins had the character of a night vigil, the psalmody was quite lengthy. Pope Pius X had already reduced the long Sunday psalmody of Matins from eighteen psalms to nine every day. In this latest reform, the psalmody of Matins has been reduced from nine psalms to three. Quite often, the three "psalms" actually consist of one long psalm divided into three parts, each with its own antiphon and each concluding with the Trinitarian doxology. The readings, formerly divided into small portions marked off by blessings and responsories, have become two long readings, one from Scripture (but not from the Gospel) and one from an ecclesiastical writer.[20]

Prime was a short Office set between Lauds (Morning Prayer) and Terce (Mid-Morning Prayer). Added to the repertoire of Hours in the fourth century, it varied a great deal from place to place and community to community and often borrowed elements from the surrounding Hours, but in the Roman Office reformed by SC, it was similar in format to the three Little Hours, now known as Mid-Morning, Midday, and Mid-Afternoon Prayer. Over time it acquired a number of other prayers as a sort of tail, particularly prayers for the blessing of the day's work. It had the dubious advantage of bringing the total number of daily Hours to the seven mentioned in Psalm 119:164, with the night Office of Matins counted separately, but it was deemed an unnecessary accretion to be eliminated in the Conciliar process of simplifying the Hours in order to make them more practical pastorally.

The short Hours of Terce, Sext, and None are named for the third, sixth, and ninth hours of the day at which they were first prayed. Those were the ordinary break times in the Greco-Roman working day. They have been retitled Mid-Morning, Midday, and Mid-Afternoon Prayer to indicate in more contemporary English the appropriate times of day to pray them. The Liturgy of the Hours seems to presume that most users will pray only one of these short Hours. Different psalmody is provided for one hour only each day. The other two hours each repeat the same three psalms daily. This has created challenges for religious communities who pray all three Hours daily in choir.

---

90. The divine office, because it is the public prayer of the Church, is a source of devotion and nourishment also for personal prayer. Therefore priests and all others who take part in the divine office are earnestly exhorted in the Lord to attune their minds to their voices when praying it. The better to achieve this, let them take steps to improve their understanding of the liturgy and of the Bible, especially the psalms.

In revising the Roman office, its ancient and venerable treasures are to be so adapted that all those to whom they are handed on may more fully and readily draw profit from them.

The sixth-century *Rule of St. Benedict*, which greatly influenced the development of the Roman Office through its directives for praying the monastic Hours (chapters 8–20), urges: "let us stand to sing the psalms in such a way that our minds are in harmony with our voices."[22] Article 90 extends the reflection on the relationship of the Hours to personal prayer introduced in article 86 above. It further includes persons other than priests more specifically in the work of the Hours. The encouragement to deepen personal prayer through the Office by increasing one's understanding of the liturgy and its biblical content echoes SC 33 and 35 § 3 on the importance of liturgical and biblical catechesis. The GILOH currently provides a rich but compact sourcebook for gaining insight into the Hours and into the psalms as they have long been interpreted and prayed by the Church.

Tacitly reflecting the concern for prayer in article 86, this oddly placed sentence seems to set the tenor for the renewal of the Hours. The wealth of the long tradition that produced the pre-Conciliar Roman Office is to be mined and adapted in such a way that it can continue to speak to and inspire present and future generations. The revised Liturgy of the Hours has indeed been careful to preserve traditional texts and structures, adapting them as directed in the articles that follow in order better to meet the needs and suit the circumstances of those who pray them today.

---

91. So that it may really be possible in practice to observe the course of the hours proposed in art. 89, the psalms are no longer to be distributed over just one week, but over some longer period of time.

The work of revising the psalter, already happily begun, is to be finished as soon as possible and is to take into account the style of Christian Latin, the liturgical use of psalms, including their being sung, and the entire tradition of the Latin Church.

The *Rule of St. Benedict* prescribed that the entire Psalter be prayed in the Office each week. The result was lengthy Offices suited to the biblical and contemplative character of Benedictine monastic life. However, when the Roman Office imported the custom, these lengthy Offices began to be relegated to those corners of the day unoccupied by the pastoral duty of the clerics obligated to pray them, as noted under articles 88 and 90. Thus, the connection between the Hours and the time of day was weakened if not lost altogether in practice. The first paragraph of article 91 seems to be to recognize the impracticability of long Offices for those engaged in pastoral work, whether as clergy or as religious, and certainly for laypeople immersed in family life. Distributing the psalms over a period of time longer than a week made it possible to shorten the Hours. The artisans of the reformed Hours chose to distribute the psalms over four weeks, reducing the number of psalms in the principal Hours. New Testament canticles, other than the three Gospel canticles, were added to Evening Prayer. Nevertheless, the four-week cycle stretches the resources of the Psalter, so some of the psalms customarily used for the minor Hours are repeated in Morning or Evening Prayer. One contributing factor may have been the omission of two psalms, 58 and 109, composed almost entirely of vitriolic curses against the enemy. In a number of other psalms, the cursing verses are simply edited out, incidentally shortening those psalms too, but these two defy even the most skilled of editors. While Patristic commentaries on the psalms provide solid arguments for praying the cursing verses that appear in many psalms, the arguments assume relatively sophisticated participants comfortable with spiritual metaphor. The cursing verses usually do nothing but dismay ordinary participants.

The shorter Hours have proven practical and nourishing both for those obligated to pray them and for parish communities and apostolic religious communities wishing to pray the main Hours of the day at the beginning and end of what was the ordinary working day before the advent of institutions like flex time.

New Latin translations of the psalms from Hebrew texts began to appear during the pontificate of Pope Pius XII and gradually replaced the Vulgate in editions of *The Breviary* published after 1945. The most recent of these, published in 1969, is used in the *editio typica altera* of 1985. Article 91, paragraph 2, seems to intend to encourage this work in order to provide a style of Latin psalmody expressly suited to liturgical use. However, in the United States, the 1971 Liturgy of the Hours incorporated the 1963 *Grail Psalter*, an English translation of the French work of Joseph Gelineau, aimed at reproducing the rhythms of the Hebrew psalms in a text suitable for rhythmic communal chant. The English translation of the *editio typica altera* will make use of the most recent revision of the Grail translation, designed to preserve musicality while offering a more literally correct translation of the Hebrew.

92. As regards the readings, the following shall be observed:

a. Readings from sacred Scripture shall be arranged so that the riches of God's word may be easily accessible in more abundant measure.

b. Readings excerpted from the works of the Fathers, doctors, and ecclesiastical writers shall be better selected.

c. The accounts of the martyrdom or lives of the saints are to be made to accord with the historical facts.

Article 92a clearly echoes SC 35 §1. The Conciliar emphasis on providing biblical readings in greater abundance in all the rites has obviously played a significant part in the revival of Bible reading and study and consequently of the ancient tradition of *lectio divina* (prayerful personal reading of Scripture) so ardently promoted by Pope Benedict XVI. This movement represents a strong and happy shift from the pre-Conciliar era when suspicions generated by the Reformation and earlier suspect spiritualities led to official discouragement of vernacular translations and personal Bible reading by Catholics.

The biblical readings at the Hours other than the Office of Readings are generally somewhat longer than their counterparts in the pre-Conciliar Roman Office, but they remain quite short. However, the redistribution of the psalms over a four-week cycle has multiplied by four the number of all the Offices, thus making room for a far more expanded selection of biblical readings. The Lectionary for the Office of Readings makes generous use of the principle of semi-continuous reading of large portions of many biblical books, some of them fairly represented in the *Lectionary for Mass* but others not. The Book of Esther, for example, appears rarely in the *Lectionary for Mass* but is read in its entirety annually during the Office of Readings. Similarly, ample portions of the Books of Isaiah and Exodus, many of which are not employed in the *Lectionary for Mass*, are read during Advent and Lent respectively. Some Old Testament books, however, are difficult to divide coherently. The passages from the Book of Job containing the long theological exchanges between Job and his so-called friends, for example, are difficult passages in themselves and lose their clarity and impact when broken up over the course of several days.

Article 92b refers to the non-biblical readings at the Office of Readings. The Conciliar directive is remarkably vague. No definition or criteria are provided for creating a "better" selection from the rich storehouse of Patristic and later ecclesiastical literature. The members of the subcommittee charged with the responsibility of making the new selection were left to draw up criteria for themselves. Deciding to choose readings that would be of "spiritual help to the clergy, religious and laity of our day," they eschewed works that were too abstract or that represented outdated philosophical, scientific, or exegetical positions. The readings selected had to be in tune with the liturgical occasion or season, to encourage a love of Scripture, and to provide sound dogmatic, ascetical, and moral teaching. They also had to be texts that would lend themselves to vernacular translation. The result of this work was a wide compendium drawn from classical Patristic writers, later Doctors of the Church, Conciliar texts, and recent popes, as well as some classical works. The readings for Offices in honor of the saints were drawn as often as possible from the saints celebrated. The place of women in the development of the theological and spiritual tradition of the Church was not a pressing issue in the late 1960s, so women's writings appear only in the Sanctoral cycle. A declaration from the Congregation of the Doctrine of the Faith precluded texts by non-Catholic or living authors, so the readings are largely drawn from Christian antiquity and the Middle Ages, with some forays into the spiritual classics of later centuries. The English translations gave access to many Patristic and medieval texts not at that time available in modern English versions.[23]

In the pre-Conciliar Roman Office, readings for Matins were from either biblical or non-biblical sources that were broken up into several small portions interspersed with blessings and responsories. Many of the current, long, non-biblical readings, theologically profound as they are, make heavy demands on those who listen to them read at communal celebrations of the Hours. Though community members can follow the text in a book, if they have one, these readings really lend themselves much more readily to individual reading, where the reader can pause, reread, and reflect along the way. This raises a question as to whether the subcommittee really had community celebration in mind or thought primarily in terms of an Office recited privately by priests. The assumption that priests would be the primary audience for the Office of Readings certainly seems to have conditioned the choice of extensive selections from sources such as St. Gregory the Great's *Pastoral Rule* or St. Augustine's *Sermon on Pastors.*

Article 92c represents the Conciliar and post-Conciliar movement to omit legendary figures and stories from the post-Conciliar liturgy and its calendar of saints. While some of the legends were inspiring even as fiction, many were so exaggerated as to seem absurd, especially in an era when a critical scientific hermeneutics dominated biblical and other studies.

---

93. To whatever extent may seem advisable, the hymns are to be restored to their original form and any allusion to mythology or anything that conflicts with Christian piety is to be dropped or changed. Also, as occasion arises, let other selections from the treasury of hymns be incorporated.

Hymns were a somewhat later addition to the round of daily Hours. Many of the Latin hymns of the Roman Breviary were tentatively attributed to St. Ambrose; others were modeled on the style of hymnody credited to him, and underwent a number of revisions at the hands of post-Tridentine popes, most notably Pope Urban VIII. The pre-Urban revisions of Popes Pius V and Clement VIII have been restored in the 1985 *editio typica altera*. However, the English-language publishers of *The Liturgy of the Hours* and *Christian Prayer* currently in use have, for the most part, chosen English hymns dating from the nineteenth through the twentieth centuries rather than attempting contemporary translations of the Latin texts. Sadly, given the flux state of English hymnody in the 1960s, many of the selections printed without music have become largely unusable as fewer and fewer people remember the melodies for texts no longer used in Eucharistic celebrations. Many of these texts are free form rather than metrical, so they fit only the music originally composed for them. Those who use *The Liturgy of the Hours* or *Christian Prayer* do not always realize that the English-language publishers' choices of hymns are in no way binding. Those who prepare and pray the Hours are entirely free to replace them with "other selections from the treasury of hymns," which is not defined by any official regulation.

Although Article 93 deals only with the revision and selection of hymns, the artisans of the Conciliar reform in fact made an additional change by moving the hymns from their traditional place after the biblical readings to the beginning of each Hour, after the introductory versicle and response and the invitatory or doxology. The argument used was the value of ritual familiarity. All of the reformed rites that employ hymnody place it in the introductory rites, thus creating the expectation that this is the place where one should ordinarily find a hymn. Set at the beginning of the Hour, the hymn can enhance the awareness of the relationship of the liturgical Hour to the time of day by introducing the themes of morning or evening either as human experiences alone or as events charged with Christological meaning. They can play a similar role in introducing images appropriate to the season or the saint or event being celebrated. This change has been so readily accepted that it is now taken for granted.

---

94. That the day may be truly sanctified and the hours themselves recited with spiritual advantage, it is best that each of them be prayed at a time most closely corresponding to the true time of each canonical hour.

This directive regarding pastoral practice harks back to the principle set out in article 84 above regarding relationship of the Hours to the passing of time and also the specific directions given in SC 88–89 regarding the revisions of the Office required to honor that principle.

---

95. In addition to the conventual Mass, communities obliged to choral office are bound to celebrate the office in choir every day. In particular:

a. Orders of canons, of monks and of nuns, and of other regulars bound by law or constitutions to choral office must celebrate the entire office.

b. Cathedral or collegiate chapters are bound to recite those parts of the office imposed on them by general or particular law.

c. All members of the above communities who are in major orders or are solemnly professed, except for lay brothers, are bound individually to recite those canonical hours which they do not pray in choir.

---

96. Clerics not bound to office in choir, if they are in major orders, are bound to pray the entire office every day, either in common or individually, following the norms in art. 89.

Articles 95 and 96 return to the issue of obligation, which was so central to the perception and celebration of the pre-Conciliar Divine Office. Although commending the Hours to the use of Christian communities of worship which might or might not include clerics, the authors of SC were too wise pastorally to leave its celebration to chance. The post-Conciliar era, with its cultural and social demands for freedom, often undefined, taught the lesson once again that good intentions not reinforced or sustained by structure, including structures of obligation, tend to vanish in the wind under the pressures of other needs and interests. While the 1983 *Code of Canon Law*, promulgated nearly twenty years after SC, leaves a great deal to the particular law of various types of religious institutes, as presaged in article 96a, the general obligation of clerics and some types of religious institutes to pray the Office in full each day remains largely in place. Monastics and other religious in solemn vows are generally required by law or by the rules of their community to sing the full Liturgy of the Hours in common. This is what the term "choral Office" refers to. So serious is the responsibility of these members of the Church to carry out the ministry of liturgical prayer in this form that individual members of these groups are even obligated to pray the entire Office daily, whether or not it is possible to sing it in choir. The goal here is to preserve the centrality of this form of liturgical prayer in the overall life of the Church as well as in the lives of those committed to specific roles or to specific lifestyles by ordination or by vow or both. These articles appear at the end of chapter IV to indicate that obligation is not the primary reason for praying the Hours but is rather a tool for protecting this Church treasure from unintended loss.

This section does crystallize the ambivalence found elsewhere in the chapter about individual versus community celebration of the Hours. As liturgy, the Hours are indeed the public worship of the whole Body of Christ, Head and members.[23] Article 26 argues persuasively that the very nature of the liturgy gives preference to public over private celebration of the rites. The *General Instruction of the Liturgy of the Hours* (GILOH) 9 and 20 and following state very strongly that communal celebration of the Hours is preferable to private recitation. Chapter IV in SC recognizes in several places that even apart from religious communities, groups of clergy and faithful may very well pray the Hours together, but it is too strongly tied to the long memory of private clerical Offices to express any strong predilection for communal celebration.

---

97. Appropriate instances are to be defined by the rubrics in which a liturgical service may be substituted for the divine office.

In particular cases and for a just reason Ordinaries may dispense their subjects wholly or in part from the obligation of reciting the divine office or may commute it.

The pastoral wisdom of the Church includes the long-standing perception that rules of practice, other than those founded in unassailable moral law, sometimes impose an impossible burden even on those with the best of intentions. Therefore dispensation is a constant feature of Church law. Article 97 names two ways in which the obligation of the Liturgy of the Hours might be lifted in case of need. The mention of the Ordinary, usually the bishop of a diocese, recalls that the Hours are not simply a matter of personal whim but constitute theologically as well as structurally the prayer of the Church.

---

98. Members of any institute dedicated to acquiring perfection who, according to their constitutions, are to recite any parts of the divine office are thereby performing the public prayer of the Church.

They too perform the public prayer of the Church who, in virtue of their constitutions, recite any little office, provided this has been drawn up after the pattern of the divine office and duly approved.

Longstanding pre-Conciliar tradition recognized the Divine Office as the prayer of the Church par excellence. *Sacrosancum Concilium* and the *General Instruction of the Liturgy of the Hours* reaffirm that understanding. The first sentence of SC 98 is another of several openings in chapter IV to the notion that this prayer of the Church welcomes the participation of all Church members, not merely the ordained or solemnly vowed. Statements such as the one found in SC 84, "when this wonderful song of praise is rightly performed by priests and others who are deputed for this purpose by the Church's ordinance or by the faithful praying together with the priest in the approved form, then it is truly the voice of a bride addressing her bridegroom" both affirms and yet hesitates over the notion that the responsibility for the prayer of the Church really resides in the Church at large. *Sacrosanctum Concilium* continues to suggest that both the participation of a priest and the use of officially approved texts are necessary for any celebration of the Hours to qualify. The GILOH moves definitively away from considering the presence of an ordained minister essential to the Hours, and in fact explicitly encourages the laity to pray the Hours themselves, but it does not question the value of using approved texts. The underlying reason is the principle usually abbreviated as *lex orandi, lex credendi,* meaning basically that the law of prayer becomes the law of belief, though recognizing implicitly that the reverse is also true. If what we pray, and especially what we pray repeatedly, ultimately becomes what we believe—a bit of wisdom well understood by the advertising industry—then it is important the texts prayed offer us a genuine expression of the Church's full faith, not a narrow slice dictated by the preferences and prejudices of an individual, especially one with little theological knowledge. Religious communities who remember the "experimental Offices" used before the Liturgy of the Hours was promulgated readily recall endless repetitions of the comforting passages of the later parts of the Book of Isaiah or of Romans 8, to the exclusion of any texts that challenged or discomforted us, to say nothing of freely composed collects of very dubious theology.

The recognition that "little Offices" can also, under the right conditions, serve as "the public prayer of the Church" was and remains rather startling. "Little Offices" are abbreviated services modeled on the Liturgy of the Hours. They are usually relatively invariable and easy to memorize. They multiplied especially during the Middle Ages as supplements to or substitutes for the more difficult and daunting Divine Office and became especially popular among devout laypeople. The best known was the Little Office of the Blessed Virgin, adopted by or imposed on many apostolic religious communities whose heavy pastoral schedules simply did not allow for the recitation of the full Divine Office. They were usually described as devotional rather than liturgical Offices in community catechesis.

Many religious switched happily to the richer and more varied Liturgy of the Hours when it became available in the vernacular and they were permitted to recite only realistic portions of it, usually Morning and Evening Prayer.

The issue of simplified forms of the official Hours has taken on a new twist. *The Liturgy of the Hours* and even the one-volume *Christian Prayer* have proven expensive and cumbersome for those who wish to pray the Hours but are not obliged to use a particular form. The books are rather difficult to follow for those unaccustomed to the patterns governing text choice in the Office. The rubrics supplied in the GILOH do not appear within the rites themselves and so remain hidden from many praying communities unaware of the GILOH. As a consequence, many shortened and simplified versions of the Hours have appeared on the market without any official regulation at all and have become popular among those not obligated to the official Hours. Some have been endorsed by local ordinaries or clergy; others have gone unnoticed. Those who use them rarely seem to think they are not at some level praying in the name of the larger Church.

---

99. Since the divine office is the voice of the Church, that is, of the whole Mystical Body publicly praising God, those clerics who are not obliged to office in choir, especially priests who live together or who meet together for any purpose, are urged to pray at least some part of the divine office in common.

All who pray the divine office, whether in choir or in common, should fulfill the task entrusted to them as perfectly as possible: this refers not only to the internal devotion of their minds but also to their external manner of celebration.

It is advantageous, moreover, that the office in choir and in common be sung when there is an opportunity to do so.

The first paragraph of article 99 is curiously ambivalent. It reasserts that "the divine Office is the voice of the Church, that is, of the whole Mystical Body publicly praising God," but it then encourages only clerics not obligated to Office in choir and to priests gathered together for whatever purpose. Lay members of the "whole Mystical Body" remain invisible here, though they gain full visibility in the next article.

The value of singing the Hours is strongly emphasized and developed in GILOH 121–122.

100. Pastors should see to it that the chief hours, especially vespers, are celebrated in common in church on Sundays and the more solemn feasts. The laity, too, are encouraged to recite the divine office either with the priests, or among themselves, or even individually.

The parochial practice of singing the chief hours—usually Vespers—had already become quite strong in a number of western European countries before the Council and was imported into the United States by immigrants. In this context at last, the laity are encouraged to pray the Hours, either with priests, or in lay groups, or even individually. The reformed Hours underscore this encouragement by making provision for Hours led by lay ministers. The GILOH strongly encourages this practice, which has long been the reality for religious communities of women, and has now become the reality for many other groups. It is not exactly a return to the practice of the early Church, where Christians seem customarily to have gathered with various members of the clergy, but rather a step forward into what has now become the reality of worshipping communities totally deprived of clergy by the shortage of priests and even deacons but not thereby deprived of the Hours.

101. § 1. In accordance with the centuries-old tradition of the Latin rite, clerics are to retain the Latin language in the divine office. But in individual cases the Ordinary has the power of granting the use of a vernacular translation, prepared in accord with art. 36, to those clerics for whom the use of Latin constitutes a grave obstacle to their praying the office properly.

§ 2. The competent superior has the power to grant the use of the vernacular in the celebration of the divine office, even in choir, to nuns and to members of institutes dedicated to acquiring perfection, both men who are not clerics and women. The version, however, must be one that has been approved.

§ 3. Any cleric bound to the divine office fulfills his obligation if he prays the office in the vernacular together with a group of the faithful or with those mentioned in §2, provided the text of the translation has been approved.

The issue of vernacular translations of the rites of the Church recurs throughout SC. The largely European Liturgical Movement had already begun to promote vernacular liturgies seriously. They certainly met the need of many worshipers who followed in the footsteps of their medieval forebears who were also largely alienated from the Latin liturgy because they did not understand the language. Article 101 expresses the uneasy threshold upon which liturgical reformers were standing, here with regard to the Divine Office. Since that time, vernacular Hours have become commonplace, even among many of the clergy, though some clergy and religious and even laity have retained the use of Latin in their liturgical prayer.

Paragraph 3 of article 101 returns once again to the uneasy question of approved texts explored under Article 98 above.

Questions for Discussion and Reflection

1. What is your experience of praying the Liturgy of the Hours?

2. Have you prayed the Hours occasionally or regularly or not at all?

3. Have you prayed most often alone or in community?

4. Have you used the official books—*The Liturgy of the Hours* or *Christian Prayer?*

5. What have you found most valuable or useful about these books?

6. What have you found most challenging?

7. If you have chosen to use an unofficial version of the Hours, which one and why?

8. What does it mean for you as an individual and/or community to recognize that you are praying in and with Christ?

9. What does it mean for you as an individual and/or community to pray as Church?

10. Consider the various parts of the Hours as you pray them.

11. What elements of the Hours have you found most nourishing?

12. What elements of the Hours have you found most daunting, distracting, or annoying? Why?

13. Are you familiar with the *General Instruction of the Liturgy of the Hours*? If yes, what have you found most valuable and/or most challenging? If not, please consider taking it in hand.

14. What is the relationship between praying the Hours, whether in community or alone, and your personal prayer?

NOTES

1. See 1 Thessalonians 5:17; Luke 18:1; Romans 12:12; Colossians 4:2.

2. The style of the Office that developed in these early "parish" communities is often called "parish" or "cathedral," while the style developed by the desert monastics is called "monastic." Both forms contributed to the formation of the Roman Office through the medium of the blended Office crystallized in the *Rule of St. Benedict* for communities who chanted their complex Hours together in choir within their monastery churches.

3. The officially approved and promulgated Latin text of every liturgical rite is called the *editio typica*.

4. "*Editio typica altera*" basically means "another official edition." A new *editio typica* always replaces its predecessor once it is approved by the national Conference of Bishops and confirmed by the Holy See. The USCCB always announces the date on which the new version goes into effect and the older version may no longer be used. Obviously that will not happen for *The Liturgy of the Hours* until the *editio typica altera* is translated and the translation is duly approved.

5. The *Grail Psalms* used in the present *Liturgy of the Hours* are the 1963 edition. *The Revised Grail Psalms* are based on that text but have undergone extensive revisions to improve the accuracy of the translation without loss of its musicality. The revision was requested by the Committee on Divine Worship of the United States Conference of Catholic Bishops (USCCB) and was prepared by the Benedictine Monks of Conception Abbey in Conception, Missouri, under the editorship of Abbot Gregory Polan, OSB, and approved for liturgical use in the United States by the USCCB and confirmed by the Holy See in 2010. The 1986 translation of the New Testament of the *New American Bible* is used as the basis for the present *Lectionary for Mass*.

6. SC, 83.

7. Ibid., 2; quoting RomM, prayer over the gifts, Holy Thursday and 2d Sunday in Ordinary Time.

8. The canticles used in the Hours are poems that are structured like psalms but appear in biblical books other than the Book of Psalms. One Old Testament canticle is sung at Morning Prayer; one New Testament canticle, other than the three Gospel canticles, is sung at Evening Prayer. A morning canticle based on the Book of Daniel incorporates a Trinitarian doxology into the text and therefore does not end with the "Glory to the Father . . . ."

9. 1 John 4:8.

10. See SC, 10.

11. See GILOH, 10, 11.

12. See Genesis 1.

13. Isaiah 55:11.

14. SC, 83.

15. See Matthew 18:20; see also SC, 7.

16. The use of an "approved form" is discussed under article 98 on pages 135–137.

17. See SC, 10.

18. Refer to SC, 84.

19. See John 1:5.

20. See commentary below for SC, 92.

21. *Rule of St. Benedict* (RB), 19:7.

22. The information for this section was largely drawn from an account by Placid Murray, OSB, a member of the subcommittee. See "The Patristic Readings," in *Companion to the New Breviary*, ed. Austin Fleming, OP. Dublin: Costello Publishing Company, Inc., 1975, pp. 128–37.

23. See SC, 7; this article was inspired by Pope Pius XII's definition of the liturgy in his 1947 encyclical, *Mediator Dei*.

✣ CHAPTER V

The Liturgical Year

Sacrosanctum Concilium 102–111

Joseph DeGrocco

This chapter, dealing with the liturgical year, is comprised of ten articles that provide a foundation for understanding the meaning and rhythm of the liturgical year in the reformed liturgy. Consistent with the themes throughout the whole of *Sacrosanctum Concilium,* the Paschal Mystery is seen as the heart and theological center of the Church's celebration of the liturgy throughout the course of time each year. It is the Paschal Mystery in its fullness which is made present throughout the various celebrations of the year, and it is the Paschal Mystery which is unfolded throughout the course of the year. The follower of Christ cannot come to know him completely unless he or she travels the journey through liturgical time to encounter the fullness of the mystery in all its aspects. The different solemnities, feasts, memorials, and seasons of the liturgical year all help us to enter more deeply into that one central mystery; that of Christ's self-offering and his glorification, his passing over from death to new life. Each particular season and observance celebrates the Paschal Mystery through a different lens or focal point; all the different aspects of the liturgical year provide "points of contact," as it were, in different ways, to the one basic mystery.

Clearly the overall concern of this chapter is to reconnect the liturgical year to the life of the faithful. Having the faithful truly live a liturgical spirituality, such that the rhythms and ebbs and flows of liturgical time become part of the fabric of each individual's spiritual life, is to be seen as one of the goals of the reform launched by this document. Such a liturgical spirituality is to "duly nourish the devotion of the faithful who celebrate the mysteries of Christian redemption and above all the paschal mystery."[1] Therefore, customs and traditions are to be updated to fit modern times and conditions so that faithful can truly be nourished.

The first four articles, 102–105, are more general in nature and constitute the theological foundation for what follows. The remaining articles in the chapter, as they offer recommendations, more specifically seek to re-establish the connection between ecclesial spirituality centered in the liturgical year and each individual's spirituality. The recommendations exhort a return to the basics, so to speak, that is, returning foundational elements, which had become obscured by popular piety or by accretions over time, to their prominence as essentials at center stage: Sunday[2]; the prominence of the temporal cycle (sacred seasons) in general[3]; and the return to a baptismal and communal focus, in addition to the well-known penitential and individual focus, for Lent.[4] Finally, the sanctoral cycle is addressed and affirmed, but a re-prioritization is accomplished as it is clearly stated that the feasts of the saints do not take precedence over the feasts of the temporal cycle.

In the words of one of the bishops who participated in the Council, " . . . let us note that the whole of chapter V of the Constitution on the Sacred Liturgy, and especially the introduction, has the purpose of removing some deviations and bringing the faith of Christians more directly into the mainstream of the piety of the Church and illustrating it with the marvelous view of the history of salvation."[5]

---

102. The Church is conscious that it must celebrate the saving work of the divine Bridegroom by devoutly recalling it on certain days throughout the course of the year. Every week, on the day which the Church has called the Lord's Day, it keeps the memory of the Lord's resurrection, which it also celebrates once in the year, together with his blessed passion, in the most solemn festival of Easter.

Within the cycle of a year, moreover, the Church unfolds the whole mystery of Christ, from his incarnation and birth until his ascension, the day of Pentecost, and the expectation of blessed hope and of the Lord's return.

Recalling thus the mysteries of redemption, the Church opens to the faithful the riches of the Lord's powers and merits, so that these are in some way made present in every age in order that the faithful may lay hold on them and be filled with saving grace.

This first article sets the foundation for understanding the liturgical year by highlighting that it is of the very essence and nature of the Church to "celebrate the saving work of the divine Bridegroom." The "divine work" is, of course, the Paschal Mystery—the Passion, Death, and Resurrection of Jesus, the Passover of the Lord by which we are saved, and consequently the purpose of the liturgical year is to provide contact in our time and history with the saving mystery which has become trans-temporal and trans-historical. The celebration of this is achieved through *anamnesis,* by "recalling" the divine work, but this memorialization is done in concrete time in human history—thus, it must be recalled on specific and certain days throughout the course of the year. Yet, through the power of the Holy Spirit, the Church's act of recalling actually makes the mysteries present for all time; thus, enabling the faithful "may lay hold on them and be filled with saving grace." It is always the present actualization of the past saving event which is the focus of liturgical celebration. The liturgical year does not recall events from the past in the way a person recalls an anniversary or a country recalls a founding event; rather, liturgical celebration is always about the present actualization of the saving mystery, and our entrance into it in the here and now.

The whole liturgical year is presented in overview form in this article, since it is the whole cycle of a year that unfolds the fullness of the mystery of Christ, from Incarnation through Ascension, and even beyond, with his expected return. Thus, a transition from one liturgical cycle to another is hinted at, as the liturgical year both ends and begins with an eschatological focus looking to the Lord's Second Coming.

---

103. In celebrating this annual cycle of Christ's mysteries, the Church honors with special love Mary, the Mother of God, who is joined by an inseparable bond to the saving work of her Son. In her the Church holds up and admires the most excellent effect of the redemption and joyfully contemplates, as in a flawless image, that which the Church itself desires and hopes wholly to be.

Catholic spirituality gives a special place to the Blessed Virgin Mary, and this is no less true of liturgical spirituality. This next article notes how the Mother of God is honored within the celebration of the liturgical year because she "is joined by an inseparable bond to the saving work of her Son." Catholic Marian devotion, then, can rightly be seen as being centered in the Marian observances that are celebrated throughout the course of the year. Since the liturgy is the heart and source of Catholic spirituality, one need look no further than the Marian observances celebrated throughout the year to find an authentic Marian spirituality. The proper relationship between Christology and Mariology is maintained: Mary is celebrated in the liturgical year as she leads us to the saving work of her Son.

---

104. The Church has also included in the annual cycle days devoted to the memory of the martyrs and the other saints. Raised up to perfection by the manifold grace of God and already in possession of eternal salvation, they sing God's perfect praise in heaven and offer prayers for us. By celebrating their passage from earth to heaven the Church proclaims the paschal mystery achieved in the saints, who have suffered and been glorified with Christ; it proposes them to the faithful as examples drawing all to the Father through Christ and pleads through their merits for God's favors.

In addition to the Blessed Virgin Mary, however, the liturgical year also commemorates "martyrs and the other saints." These celebrations, too, are to be understood not in and of themselves, but as revelatory of and as drawing us more deeply into the Paschal Mystery of Christ. Insofar as we commemorate those who are "already in possession of eternal salvation," we recall that they have been "raised up to perfection by the manifold grace of God" only because of their own participation in the Paschal Mystery: they have "suffered and been glorified with Christ." Therefore, we commemorate the saints throughout the liturgical year precisely because they are examples of living the mystery, examples who can draw us to the Father through Christ.

---

105. Finally, in the various seasons of the year and according to its traditional discipline, the Church completes the formation of the faithful by means of devout practices for soul and body, by instruction, prayer, and works of penance and of mercy.

Accordingly the sacred Council has seen fit to decree what follows.

This article notes how the celebration of the liturgical year includes various "devout practices for soul and body." Such practices include instruction, prayer, and works of penance and mercy. What are being referred to here are the seasons of Advent, Lent, and ember days.[6] We can see in this article the important connection between the liturgical year and popular piety.

---

106. By a tradition handed down from the apostles and having its origin from the very day of Christ's resurrection, the Church celebrates the paschal mystery every eighth day, which, with good reason, bears the name of the Lord's Day or Sunday. For on this day Christ's faithful must gather together so that, by hearing the word of God and taking part in the eucharist, they may call to mind the passion, the resurrection, and the glorification of the Lord Jesus and may thank God, who "has begotten them again unto a living hope through the resurrection of Jesus Christ from the dead" (1 Pt 1:3). Hence the Lord's Day is the first holy day of all and should be proposed to the devotion of the faithful and taught to them in such a way that it may become in fact a day of joy and of freedom from work. Other celebrations, unless they be truly of greatest importance, shall not have precedence over the Sunday, the foundation and core of the whole liturgical year.

This key article underscores the place of prominence Sunday holds in liturgical theology. The origin of the meaning of Sunday is to be found in nothing less than the fact that it is the "very day of Christ's resurrection." The Paschal Mystery is celebrated every Sunday, and it is the day that gives the Church her identity, as it is the day the followers of Christ "must gather together." Jungmann notes how this article " . . . employs the language of primitive Christianity when it speaks of the 'eighth' day, which, even though itself again a new beginning, is the day of the New Creation, and therefore, goes beyond the seven days of earthly creation and of Jewish tradition."[7] The obligation for this gathering is not to be found in any mere legal observance, but rather because Sunday is the day to "call to mind the passion, the resurrection, and the glorification of the Lord Jesus" and to thank God for the new life the followers of Christ have received through their union with Jesus.

The centrality of Sunday cannot be overestimated. It is referred to as the original feast day. Notice what this means: it means that before there was ever an Easter Sunday, there was Sunday; the Church celebrated Sunday first, and then set one Sunday aside as Easter

Sunday. Easter Sunday gets its identity from Sunday, not vice versa; Sundays are not little Easters, but rather Easter Sunday is a big Sunday. Everything possible must be done to promote the prominence of Sunday as the day that gives the Christian faithful their identity as followers of Christ. Sunday is to be "proposed to the devotion of the faithful and taught to them in such a way that it may become in fact a day of joy and of freedom from work."

This article continues to have huge implications fifty years later. It is more challenging than ever in contemporary society to keep a sense of Sunday as a day of joy and freedom from work, a day to reconnect with spiritual values and to nurture relationships not only with family and friends, but also with fellow parishioners. Parishes would do well to examine what ways they might be able to nurture the vision of Sunday put forth in this article. Certainly, a critical review of the way the parish celebrates Sunday Eucharist would have to be a part of any examination undertaken by a parish staff or liturgy committee. For example, in large parishes that have many Masses on a weekend, it is not uncommon for the early Mass on a Sunday morning to be a so-called "quiet Mass," without any music. Does this really serve the vision of the centrality of the Sunday celebration? Is there really a noticeable distinction between this kind of Sunday celebration and a less solemn (and rightly so) weekday Mass, as there should be? Such an examination of the place of Sunday in the life of a parish would also lead to questions concerning the day as a whole: what other events or activities take place on that day in the parish? In what ways do other sacramental celebrations connect with the Sunday Eucharist?

Being sure that we are putting all our energies into making the Sunday Eucharist the primary celebration it is meant to be is a challenge issued in this article, as we are reminded that for the most part, other celebrations are not to take precedence over Sunday, "which is the foundation and core of the whole liturgical year."

---

107. The liturgical year is to be so revised that the traditional customs and usages of the sacred seasons are preserved or restored to suit the conditions of modern times; their specific character is to be retained, so that they duly nourish the devotion of the faithful who celebrate the mysteries of Christian redemption and above all the paschal mystery. If certain

adaptations are considered necessary on account of local conditions, they are to be made in accordance with the provisions of art. 39 and 40.

Article 107 calls for the revision of the liturgical year, a revision which is to modernize and adapt traditional customs and disciplines to modern times. The specific character of each of the different liturgical seasons is to be maintained, because each one in its own way nourishes the faith life of Christians. There is clearly openness to adaptation and change, however, as long as adaptations are made in accord with articles 39 and 40 of SC. Jungmann points out that included in the flexibility of this article is the question of the transfer of feast days to Sundays, or even to Saturdays, a question left to the competence of Conferences of Bishops.[8]

108. The minds of the faithful must be directed primarily toward those feasts of the Lord on which the mysteries of salvation are celebrated in the course of the year. Therefore, the Proper of Seasons shall be given the precedence due to it over the feasts of the saints, in order that the entire cycle of the mysteries of salvation may be celebrated in the measure due to them.

The prominence of the temporal cycle over the sanctoral cycle is made clear in this article. The proper of time is to be given preference over the feasts of saints, and therefore, by implication, the ecclesial spirituality of the liturgical year and the feasts of the Lord throughout the year are to be given preference over personal piety and devotion to the saints. It is vitally important that the Paschal Mystery not be obscured or hindered by the celebrations of the saints. At the time of the promulgation of SC, the liturgical calendar had been too heavily inundated with celebrations of the saints, and reform was necessary. This is not to, in any way, disparage such memorials or to imply that they should be avoided; rather, it is simply to keep such celebrations in the proper perspective as secondary to the centrality of the Paschal Mystery as it unfolds in the seasons of the liturgical year and in the Feasts of the Lord. Also of note is that the phrase, "mysteries of salvation," is given a certain emphasis, to highlight those feasts which commemorate the facts of the events of salvation, in distinction to the "idea feasts" such as the Holy Name of Jesus; the Holy Family of Jesus, Mary, and Joseph; and the Sacred Heart of Jesus. Feasts which celebrate the actual events of salvation are seen to be more central than feasts centered in abstract thinking.[9]

---

109. Lent is marked by two themes, the baptismal and the penitential. By recalling or preparing for baptism and by repentance, this season disposes the faithful, as they more diligently listen to the word of God and devote themselves to prayer, to celebrate the paschal mystery. The baptismal and penitential aspects of Lent are to be given greater prominence in both the liturgy and liturgical catechesis. Hence:

a. More use is to be made of the baptismal features proper to the Lenten liturgy; some of those from an earlier era are to be restored as may seem advisable.

b. The same is to apply to the penitential elements. As regards catechesis, it is important to impress on the minds of the faithful not only the social consequences of sin but also the essence of the virtue of penance, namely, detestation of sin as an offense against God; the role of the Church in penitential practices is not to be neglected and the people are to be exhorted to pray for sinners.

In this article, Lent is defined as having a two-fold character, which is made known both through the liturgy itself and through liturgical catechesis (this is the challenge implicitly given for parishes to make sure that liturgical catechesis is taking place in some form). The two aspects of Lent are, first and primarily, to recall or prepare for Baptism, and secondarily, to do penance. The penitential aspect is secondary not because it is to be minimized or considered second-class, but rather because it can be seen as flowing from the first aspect: penance is done not simply for the sake of doing penance or for the sake of the season, but as a means to prepare for or to prepare to renew one's Baptism at Easter. Lent is seen as leading toward the celebration of the Paschal Mystery at Easter. This renewed understanding of Lent is not surprising, since a reform of the Easter liturgy had been done in the years 1951–1955. Lent is also portrayed in this article of SC as a heightened time in the liturgical year for hearing the Word of God and for devoting oneself to prayer.

In order to more clearly bring out the two-fold character of Lent, the article calls for certain reforms to be made. First, the baptismal features inherent in the Lenten liturgy are to be given greater prominence. One can immediately think here of the connection with Lent as an immediate preparation for Baptism for the elect, and hence one of the baptismal features to be given greater importance is the Lenten component of adult initiation, that is, the Scrutinies." However, reforms are also to take place in the penitential elements of the season, reforms that are to move the faithful's focus away from an exaggerated personal and individual understanding of Lenten penance to a more ecclesial and communal one. Certainly the meaning of sin as an offense against God is upheld, but at the same time the social consequences of sin and the role of the Church in penitential practices are both given due accord, along with a mention of the role of the community of faith to pray for sinners.

---

110. During Lent penance should be not only inward and individual, but also outward and social. The practice of penance should be fostered, however, in ways that are possible in our own times and in different regions and according to the circumstances of the faithful; it should be encouraged by the authorities mentioned in art. 22.

Nevertheless, let the paschal fast be kept sacred. Let it be observed everywhere on Good Friday and, where possible, prolonged throughout Holy Saturday, as a way of coming to the joys of the Sunday of the resurrection with uplifted and welcoming heart.

This next article continues a renewed emphasis on the external and social aspect of Lenten penance. In particular, penitential practices are to be fostered according to modern sensibilities and different cultural regions, "according to the circumstances of the faithful," yet under the authority as described in article 22. Here is another area that would seem to be very open to adaptation.

However, one aspect is to be retained everywhere, regardless of region, because it is so central to the journey toward Easter, and that aspect is the Paschal fast. The fast on Good Friday is to be maintained universally and, in fact, where possible, continued throughout Holy Saturday. The purpose of this fast, however, is described not as penitential, but as preparatory "as a way of coming to the joys of the Sunday of the resurrection with [an] uplifted and welcoming heart." This article provides the roots for understanding the Sacred Paschal Triduum, not as a part of Lent, but as a portion of liturgical time unto itself.

111. The saints have been traditionally honored in the Church and their authentic relics and images held in veneration. For the feasts of the saints proclaim the wonderful works of Christ in his servants and display to the faithful fitting examples for their imitation.

Lest the feasts of the saints take precedence over the feasts commemorating the very mysteries of salvation, many of them should be left to be celebrated by a particular Church or nation or religious family; those only should be extended to the universal Church that commemorate saints of truly universal significance.

The last article of this section on the liturgical year, deals with the place of the celebration of the saints in the liturgical calendar. The foundation of these celebrations as resting in Christ, insofar as the saints, as servants of Christ, proclaim his works and provide examples to imitate in living the Christian life, is reiterated. Also reiterated, however, is the prominence of the temporal cycle, with feasts which commemorate "the very mysteries of salvation," over the sanctoral cycle. A restraint and moderation is called for in the calendar of saints so that these celebrations do not overwhelm the liturgical year. The article suggests that many of the feasts of the saints should be relegated to the calendars of particular churches or nations or religious communities, and that only the commemorations which are "truly [of] universal importance" should be included on the universal calendar. This is in keeping with the origin of the memorials of saints, which arose as local commemorations celebrated at the tomb of the martyr.

Questions for Discussion and Reflection

1. Do you personally experience a rhythm to the liturgical year, with different moods and emphases throughout the year?

2. In what ways does your parish attempt to highlight the differences between the liturgical seasons?

3. What does Sunday look like in your parish? In your own life? Is it truly a day set apart, a day that is the center of the week for you, your family, and your parish? Is Sunday liturgy perceived as an event central to the life of faith, or is it another thing to do on the weekend?

4. How does the understanding of Lent as a journey toward Baptism, or the renewal of Baptism, enrich your celebration of the season? How does your parish emphasize the character of Lent as preparation for Baptism (either in celebration or in renewal)?

5. In what ways is the communal nature of Lent emphasized in your parish? In what ways do you feel enriched by knowing that your Lenten penance is undertaken not as an individual, but as a member of a community?

6. How do you observe the Sacred Paschal Triduum as a time unto itself? How is this period of sacred time emphasized in your parish?

7. In what ways do you find the celebration of the saints helpful in drawing you more deeply into the Paschal Mystery?

NOTES

1. See SC, 107.
2. See ibid., 106.
3. See ibid., 107–108.
4. See ibid., 109–110.
5. Francis Zauner, in "Chapter V: The Liturgical Year," in *The Commentary on the Constitution and on the Instruction on the Sacred Liturgy,* eds. A. Bugnini and C. Braga. New York: Benziger Brothers, 1965, p. 232.
6. Josef Andreas Jungmann, "Constitution on the Sacred Liturgy," in *Commentary on the Documents of Vatican II, Volume One,* ed. Herbert Vorgrimler. New York: Herder and Herder, 1967, p. 72. Ember days are days set aside specifically for fasting. In the Latin Rite, these days are usually Wednesday, Friday, and Saturday; however, bishops may determine specific days. In the Diocese of the United States of America, January 22 is set aside as a day of prayer and penance for crimes against the unborn (see GIRM, 373). Although this is a fixed date, it constitutes an ember day.
7. Ibid.
8. Ibid., p. 73.
9. Ibid.

✣ CHAPTER VI

Sacred Music

Sacrosanctum Concilium 112–121

Steven R. Janco

Chapter VI of *Sacrosanctum Concilium* has had a profound and far-reaching impact on the reform of the liturgy. While today we may take its principles and provisions for granted and easily quote important sections from memory, early on there was confusion about how to interpret its principles and disagreement about how to implement its provisions. For some, the chapter was a source of encouragement and an inspiration to new musical creativity. Others saw it as questioning long-standing assumptions about the nature of sacred music and diminishing the importance of choirs. That there was (and still is) some confusion is not surprising, given that the chapter reflects the varied opinions and visions of liturgical music in play at the time it was written. Rather than choosing one vision over another and restricting options, chapter VI takes a "both/and" approach that recognizes established musical customs while at the same time presenting new priorities and making provision for new possibilities. Rather than viewing the chapter as a whole and interpreting it in light of principles articulated elsewhere in the document, some have chosen to focus only on those portions—even phrases—of the chapter that reinforce their existing convictions. The effects of this kind of selective interpretation were readily apparent when competition ensued in parishes between the "traditional choir" and the "folk group."

Some guidance for interpretation was provided in the 1967 instruction *Musicam sacram* (MS), which addresses "some problems about music and its ministerial function"[1] that were surfacing as the reform of the liturgy was getting underway. Clarification on other issues would come only when the first edition of the *General*

Instruction of the Roman Missal (GIRM) appeared in 1969 and the new English Order of Mass appeared in 1970.

In the United States, guidance was also provided by two subsequent documents issued by the Bishops' Committee on the Liturgy (now Divine Worship) of the National Conference of Catholic Bishops (now United States Conference of Catholic Bishops). *Music in Catholic Worship* (MCW) was published in 1972. As the reformed sacramental rites had not yet been issued, MCW established general principles and focused on music and the Order of Mass. *Liturgical Music Today*, issued in 1982 as a companion to MCW, addressed those rites published in the previous ten years and offers comment on a number of pastoral issues that had begun to surface, including the use of music of different cultures and the appropriate use of copyrighted materials.

These two documents were widely used as touchstones for classes, conferences, and workshops until 2007, when the United States Conference of Catholic Bishops issued its first conference document on liturgical music, *Sing to the Lord: Music in Divine Worship* (STL). The 2007 document is much more lengthy and comprehensive than its predecessors combined, incorporating introductory and rubrical notes about music from nearly every liturgical book in use.

Before we examine in some detail the ten articles of chapter VI, some clarification is warranted about the term "sacred music," which in earlier liturgical documents could have two distinct meanings—one broader, the other more specific. "Sacred music" was sometimes employed as an umbrella term that encompassed multiple categories of music, including Gregorian chant, polyphony, vernacular hymnody, instrumental music, and even music inspired by sacred themes performed in concert. The term was also used more narrowly to refer to music used in the celebration of liturgy. The term is used both ways in this chapter, though most articles focus on the Church's tradition of liturgical singing. In 1967, *Musicam sacram* (the first [and only] post-Conciliar instruction from the Sacred Congregation of Rites [now the Congregation for Divine Worship and the Discipline of the Saraments]) defined "sacred music" as including "Gregorian chant, the several styles of polyphony, both ancient and modern; sacred music for organ and for other permitted instruments, and the sacred, i.e., liturgical or religious, music of the people."[2] Today many use the term "liturgical music" when referring to music used in liturgical celebration.

112. The musical tradition of the universal Church is a treasure of inestimable value, greater even than that of any other art. The main reason for this preeminence is that, as sacred song closely bound to the text, it forms a necessary or integral part of the solemn liturgy.

Holy Scripture itself has bestowed praise upon sacred song[1] and the same may be said of the Fathers of the Church and of the Roman pontiffs, who in recent times, led by St. Pius X, have explained more precisely the ministerial function supplied by sacred music in the service of the Lord.

Therefore sacred music will be the more holy the more closely it is joined to the liturgical rite, whether by adding delight to prayer, fostering oneness of spirit, or investing the rites with greater solemnity. But the Church approves of all forms of genuine art possessing the qualities required and admits them into divine worship.

Accordingly, the Council, keeping the norms and precepts of ecclesiastical tradition and discipline and having regard to the purpose of sacred music, which is the glory of God and the sanctification of the faithful, decrees what follows.

1. See Eph 5:19; Col 3:16.

This opening and foundational article of chapter VI sets forth values and principles that would make music a key element of the liturgical reform and that continue to ground and guide pastoral musicians today. The nine paragraphs that follow provide direction as to how these principles can be upheld and put into practice.

Article 112 begins by identifying the musical tradition of the Church as a "treasure of inestimable value." Some focus on the word "treasure" and interpret this sentence as referring to a compendium or storehouse of inherited musical pieces—chant and polyphony in particular. However the following paragraph speaks of the Church's musical tradition more broadly as "sacred song," and then describes references clearly in the Scriptures and the writings of the Fathers of the Church, that predate the appearance of Gregorian chant. Article 112 makes clear at the outset of this chapter that the Church's musical tradition is a practice—a mode of worship, not a body of musical works. As "sacred song closely bound to the text" the Church's tradition of singing is a "necessary or integral part" of liturgical celebration.

This understanding is confirmed in the following paragraph, which presents a new definition of the "holiness" of sacred music. Earlier documents had defined holiness as a quality inherent in certain kinds of music, especially Gregorian chant. It was therefore possible to categorize some genres of music or modes of performance as sacred and others as profane or secular.[3] Article 112 makes a significant shift and instead claims that music is the more "holy" the more closely it is connected to the ritual action. Holiness becomes apparent when the music accomplishes its purpose or function in the liturgy. The article alludes to the many functions of music in the liturgy by pointing out three examples: it adds delight to prayer, fosters unity, and confers greater solemnity. The appropriateness of music for worship is determined by how well the music enables the ritual to unfold and the congregation to participate fully, consciously, and actively. That music in the reformed liturgy would not be limited to genres customary before the Second Vatican Council is stated plainly. The Church admits into worship "all forms of genuine art possessing the qualities required."

Article 112 ends by claiming that the ultimate purpose of sacred music is "the glory of God and the sanctification of the faithful." This same twofold purpose is ascribed to the liturgy itself in articles 7 and 10. *Sacrosanctum Concilium* could in no better way affirm that music is integral to worship. Music, more so than any other art, is necessary for liturgy to accomplish its fundamental purpose.

---

113. A liturgical service takes on a nobler aspect when the rites are celebrated with singing, the sacred ministers take their parts in them, and the faithful actively participate.

As regards the language to be used, the provisions of art. 36 are to be observed; for the Mass, those of art. 54; for the sacraments, those of art. 63; for the divine office, those of art. 101.

One of the goals of the reform of the Second Vatican Council was to reclaim the public and liturgical nature of rites that often had been celebrated without much attention to ritual detail. Article 113 affirms that music is a key aspect of this effort, as it gives "a nobler aspect" to liturgical worship. Liturgical books published since the Council embody this priority, discussing the role of music in their *praenotanda* (introductions to the ritual books) and pointing out in their rubrics moments when singing is appropriate. Many rites suggest antiphons and other particular texts for singing, while also allowing for other options.

Results have been mixed. While significant attention has been paid to the role of music in Sunday Mass, in many parishes little attention has yet to be given to music for rites celebrated at other times, usually with smaller congregations. For example, the *Rite of Baptism for Children* is still often celebrated as a quasi-private ceremony that is minimally "liturgical" and that includes little or no music. And very few parishes assign a cantor for the vigil for the deceased, as called for in the *Order of Christian Funerals*.

Article 113 references the celebration of the Liturgy of the Hours. While the celebration of the Hours has not become a regular and widespread phenomenon in many parishes, many Catholics today are familiar with the basic order of Morning Prayer and Evening Prayer, perhaps having experienced cathedral-style celebrations at conferences, or weekly Evening Prayer at their parishes during a particular season. Most Catholic hymnals and worship resources in use today include a simplified order of sung prayer for morning and evening, as well as a selection of corresponding hymns, psalms, and canticle settings. A number of resources for daily prayer, inspired by the pattern and order of the Liturgy of the Hours, are available from liturgical publishers as well.

The article concludes by citing other articles in the document that give permission for a more liberal use of the vernacular.

---

114. The treasure of sacred music is to be preserved and fostered with great care. Choirs must be diligently developed, especially in cathedral churches; but bishops and other pastors of souls must be at pains to ensure that whenever a liturgical service is to be celebrated with song, the whole assembly of the faithful is enabled, in keeping with art. 28 and 30, to contribute the active participation that rightly belongs to it.

Article 114 spells out how the Church's musical tradition is to be preserved and fostered: through the promotion of choral and congregational singing. Prior to the Council most Catholics had become accustomed to a Sunday Mass schedule that at best included one "high Mass" at which everything was sung by the priest and the choir and multiple "low Masses" at which little or nothing was sung. Though in 1955 Pope Pius XII had allowed for congregational singing of vernacular hymns during Mass,[4] and several vernacular hymnals were in print by this time, congregational singing during the Mass was still new and awkward for most English-speaking Catholics. Whether because of modesty or self-consciousness, many had a hard time embracing this recovered tradition.

Whereas choirs in cathedrals and many parishes had a well-defined and prominent, if limited, role prior to the Council, many wondered what kind of role the choir would have in a vernacular liturgy that would be "at pains" to make sure that the "whole assembly of the faithful" would be able "to contribute the active participation" which is rightly theirs. Some choir directors felt betrayed, fearing that liturgical reform would undercut their long-standing commitment to beauty and quality music making. In the early years of the reform there was a good deal of disagreement about the role of the choir and whether Latin Masses, motets, and antiphons that were the backbone of Catholic choral repertory at the time—and sung by the choir alone—would still be appropriate in the reformed liturgy.

This article says quite plainly that choirs are to be "diligently developed," especially in cathedrals. But it also indicates that the choir cannot replace the musical participation that rightly belongs to the faithful. The first edition of the GIRM in 1969 provided some clarification. One of the choir's principal roles in the Eucharistic liturgy is to lead congregational singing. While the GIRM describes a number of options where solo singing by the choir would be appropriate, including the Gloria and the Lamb of God, it also indicates that the Holy, Holy, Holy is to be sung by the entire congregation. That rubric alone meant that the choir could no longer sing a complete Mass setting on its own.

---

115. Great importance is to be attached to the teaching and practice of music in seminaries, in the novitiates and houses of study of religious of both sexes, and also in other Catholic institutions and schools. To impart this instruction, those in charge of teaching sacred music are to receive thorough training.

> It is recommended also that higher institutes of sacred music be established whenever possible.
>
> Musicians and singers, especially young boys, must also be given a genuine liturgical training.

This article says several important things. It is one of a number of articles in SC that promote education as essential for the effective implementation of liturgical reform.[5] But its focus extends beyond seminaries and formation in religious communities and calls for attention to music in "other Catholic institutions and schools." The reformed liturgy requires a broader-based and longer-term training in music. This kind of musical training for liturgy cannot be accomplished solely in the classroom, however. Educational and formational efforts must also include attention to the *practice* of music in liturgical celebration. Musical skills and appreciation aren't so much taught as they are "caught." Efforts must include good modeling, a steeping in well-celebrated liturgy, and opportunities for practice and growth in experience. Formation in liturgical music must be a comprehensive effort that leads all to become "thoroughly imbued with the spirit and power of the liturgy."[6] Making music a matter of great importance implies a high level of investment, an appropriate place in academic curricula, carefully trained teachers, and the resources and qualified personnel needed to celebrate liturgy well.

The article also calls for the establishment of "higher institutes of sacred music" when possible, implying that the educational programs in place at the time would not be sufficient to meet new expectations. Quite a few Catholic colleges and universities established or revised degree programs in liturgical music in the years following the Council. Some of these programs continue to flourish today, but, sadly, many have been shut down over the years.

While the article begins by calling for musical training for those who will be worshipers and liturgical leaders, it ends by calling for "genuine liturgical training" for "musicians and singers." Musical leadership for liturgical celebration requires more than musical ability. It requires an understanding of liturgy and a solid grounding in liturgical principles, values, and documents.

116. The Church acknowledges Gregorian chant as distinctive of the Roman liturgy; therefore, other things being equal, it should be given pride of place in liturgical services.

But other kinds of sacred music, especially polyphony, are by no means excluded from liturgical celebrations, provided they accord with the spirit of the liturgical service, in the way laid down in art. 30.

This article, like others in this chapter, recognizes long-standing custom while at the same time it leaves the door open for new options. It has also caused quite a bit of confusion over the years. Some have interpreted this article apart from the larger context of Chapter VI and the document as a whole, and have presumed that traditional Latin chant would be the favored musical genre in the reformed liturgy. There was enough disagreement and concern to warrant clarification in the 1967 instruction MS, which indicates that Gregorian chant is to be given pride of place in liturgies celebrated *in Latin*.[7] Pope John Paul II reasserted this narrower interpretation as late as 2003 in article 7 of his *Chirograph on Sacred Music*.

That being said, this article and the one that follows indicate an ongoing commitment to the Church's Gregorian chant tradition. The 2010 edition of the GIRM continues to call for congregations to be able to sing "at least some parts of the Ordinary of the Mass in Latin."[8] *Sing to the Lord* provides some practical guidance in this area.[9]

Consistent with the treatment of holiness in article 112, article 116 indicates that other kinds of sacred music may be used in liturgical celebrations, "provided they accord with the spirit of the liturgical service."

117. The *editio typica* of the books of Gregorian chant is to be completed and a more critical edition is to be prepared of those books already published since the reform of St. Pius X.

It is desirable also that an edition be prepared containing the simpler melodies for use in small churches.

Four separate volumes together comprise the Church's official texts and music for the celebration of Mass in Latin in the Roman Rite. They further serve as the *editiones typicae* (typical editions) from which vernacular translations are made: the *Missale Romanum (The Roman Missal)*, the *Ordo Lectionum Missae* (*Lectionary for Mass)*, the *Graduale Romanum (Roman Gradual)*, and the *Graduale Simplex (Simple Gradual)*. The last two are volumes of Gregorian chant. The *Graduale Romanum* is a complete volume of "propers" (entrance, gradual or tract, offertory, and Communion) and ritual music for every Sunday and feast of the liturgical year, taking into account the three-year cycle of readings in the Lectionary. The current edition is, in large part, a revision and adaptation of the edition used by choirs for celebration of "high Mass" prior to the Second Vatican Council. The *Graduale Simplex (Simple Gradual)*, a more compact volume, was created in response to this article's call for an edition with simpler melodies for use in smaller churches. The *Graduale Simplex* provides a smaller selection of "common" antiphons with psalm verses for use during particular seasons of the liturgical year, much as the Lectionary provides common Responsorial Psalms that may replace the proper psalm on any Sunday (or on all Sundays) during a particular season.

The Latin typical edition of the *Graduale Simplex* was completed in 1967, three years before the first English edition of the Order of Mass was issued. An English translation of the texts of the *Graduale Simplex* was issued in 1968. However, the Latin typical edition of the revised *Graduale Romanum*, a much more ambitious project, was not completed until 1974, four years *after* the original English edition of the Order of Mass came into use. The texts of the *Graduale Romanum* have never been issued in an English translation.

This background is helpful for understanding the pastoral impact (or lack thereof) of this article. Some suggest that the practice of singing antiphons was never given a chance after the Second Vatican Council—and that the practice is therefore worthy of recovery. By the time the *Graduale Romanum* was published in 1974, Mass had been "officially" celebrated in English for four years. Experimental texts had been in use for several years before that. Vernacular hymns, songs, and ritual music in various styles and with varying levels of difficulty were already receiving widespread use—and congregations were actually singing them. Repeated use of a smaller repertory—and not several new antiphons every week—was found to be an effective way to foster congregational singing.

Many forget—or are not aware—that in the mid-1960s, two collections of English Mass propers were published in the United States by well-established Catholic publishers.[10] These collections were available for a number of years before the 1970 Order of Mass was issued. They were used mainly in seminaries, religious communities, colleges, and perhaps in some larger parishes, where choirs were already used to preparing a different set of propers every week. (Congregations didn't sing the propers.) That the texts were in English did not reduce the time needed to learn the music. It was clear early on that the musical patterns in use before the Council could not readily be adapted to meet the needs of the reformed liturgy and the expectation of congregational singing.

It will be helpful to clarify one other matter. When the 2002 edition of the GIRM was published, some took notice that antiphons from the *Graduale Romanum* and *Graduale Simplex* were listed as first and second options for the Entrance and Communion Songs. Many who were not familiar with earlier editions of the GIRM assumed that this new edition was establishing a new preference for Latin antiphons during these ritual moments. In fact, the *Graduale Romanum* and *Graduale Simplex* have been listed as the first and second options in *every* edition of the GIRM, even though the volumes are used only in a very small number of communities. The reason for this is that, apart from adaptations approved for particular countries, the GIRM is an English translation of the Latin typical edition, which necessarily addresses the four official liturgical books approved for the celebration of Mass in Latin. Because the *Graduale Romanum* and the *Graduale Simplex* are listed first and second in the Latin edition, they are listed first and second in the English translation. Some composers and communities are finding creative ways to integrate the tradition of antiphon singing while maintaining congregational participation as a priority.

---

118. The people's own religious songs are to be encouraged with care so that in sacred devotions as well as during services of the liturgy itself, in keeping with rubrical norms and requirements, the faithful may raise their voices in song.

This article appears to draw inspiration from articles 62–66 of Pope Pius XII's 1955 encyclical, *Musicae sacrae disciplina* (MSD), which discuss the use of "popular religious hymns" that are "written in the language of the people" and which are "closely related to the individual mentality and temperament of individual national groups."[11] Pius XII spends several paragraphs extolling the blessing of popular religious song, noting, "these sacred canticles, born as they are from the most profound depths of the people's soul, deeply move the emotions and spirit and stir up pious sentiments."[12] This positive view of popular religious song was undoubtedly at the heart of Pius XII's decision to allow the singing of vernacular hymns during Mass.[13] He sums up this section by addressing the bishops and other local ordinaries to whom the encyclical is addressed: "We can do no less than urge you, venerable brethren, to foster and promote diligently popular religious singing of this kind in the dioceses entrusted to you."[14]

Even before SC appeared, the value of "the people's own religious song" was already being acknowledged, praised, and promoted by the pope himself—not just for devotions and pious exercises, but for Mass. Forty-eight years later, Pope John Paul II would stake out a similar position concerning contemporary worship music.[15]

119. In certain parts of the world, especially mission lands, people have their own musical traditions and these play a great part in their religious and social life. Thus, in keeping with art. 39 and 40, due importance is to be attached to their music and a suitable place given to it, not only in forming their attitude toward religion, but also in adapting worship to their native genius.

Therefore, when missionaries are being given training in music, every effort should be made to see that they become competent in promoting the traditional music of the people, both in schools and in sacred services, as far as may be practicable.

This article, perhaps more than any other in this chapter, lays bare the Eurocentric mindset of the framers of SC. Those trained in the western European musical tradition are the norm. Catholics in parts of the world with different kinds of musical traditions are grouped together as peoples of "mission lands." The article provides evidence of some significant progress as well, echoing SC's earlier call for "legitimate variations and adaptations to different groups, regions, and peoples . . . "[16] It embodies the scholarship of modern anthropology that understands music to be an important component of culture and identity. There is a "native genius" at work in each culture. Music imported from another culture cannot take the place of local musical traditions, even when it comes to Catholic worship. Rather than adapting local culture to meet pre-established or universal liturgical norms, this article speaks of adapting *worship* to reflect local musical gifts and traditions. Music is an important, concrete vehicle for liturgical inculturation.

While it seems to presume that each "land" has one particular cultural tradition, this article has also come to apply to countries whose populations include multiple cultural and linguistic traditions. The Catholic Church within a given region—and even within a particular language group—is often made up of smaller ethnic communities, each of which has its own musical traditions.

The article concludes by asserting once again that appropriate education and experience is necessary for the promotion of effective liturgical celebration.

---

120. In the Latin Church the pipe organ is to be held in high esteem, for it is the traditional musical instrument that adds a wonderful splendor to the Church's ceremonies and powerfully lifts up the spirit to God and to higher things.

But other instruments also may be admitted for use in divine worship, with the knowledge and consent of the competent territorial authority and in conformity with art. 22, §2, art. 37 and art. 40. This applies, however, only on condition that the instruments are suitable, or can be made suitable, for sacred use, are in accord with the dignity of the place of worship, and truly contribute to the uplifting of the faithful.

Once again SC repeats a permission granted eight years earlier by Pope Pius XII, who in MSD permitted the use of instruments other than the organ in liturgical celebration.[17] Pius highlighted stringed instruments as particularly suitable. Though it affirms the value of the pipe organ, this article cites no particular examples of other musical instruments that would be appropriate, leaving the door open to a wide variety possibilities—even guitar and percussion instruments.

What is perhaps most significant here is that decisions about the suitability of musical instruments for worship are entrusted to local authorities, an acknowledgement that customs and sensibilities vary from culture to culture and region to region—and that universal norms on an issue like this would be inappropriate.

---

121. Composers, filled with the Christian spirit, should feel that their vocation is to develop sacred music and to increase its store of treasures.

Let them produce compositions having the qualities proper to genuine sacred music, not confining themselves to works that can be sung only by large choirs, but providing also for the needs of small choirs and for the active participation of the entire assembly of the faithful.

The texts intended to be sung must always be consistent with Catholic teaching; indeed they should be drawn chiefly from holy Scripture and from liturgical sources.

Composing is here presented as a Christian vocation. Sacred music most appropriately comes from within the community of the faithful and reflects the Christian spirit at work in the composer.

The last article of this chapter hearkens back to the first. It summons composers to create "genuine sacred music" that serves the needs not just of large and sophisticated choirs, but of modest musical ensembles and musically untrained congregations. No genre of music is held up as a model. No particular composer is mentioned as worthy of emulation. Composing is presented not as a vehicle for artistic self-expression, but as a craft used to meet the needs of the Christian community in its many local expressions. Genuine liturgical music embodies the values established at the beginning of this chapter. It is integral to the liturgy. It serves a ministerial function. It is closely connected to the rite.

Also expressed is a concern for consistency "with Catholic teaching" in texts set to music, perhaps a reaction against the questionable theology and piety of some devotional music popular at the time. The chapter concludes by returning once again to the integral role of music in liturgical celebration as it invites composers to write musical settings for texts drawn from scriptural and liturgical sources.

Over the past fifty years, hundreds of writers and composers have taken up this challenge. Music employing many different styles and forms, written for congregations, varying vocal ensembles and a variety of instruments, has been made available to Catholic worshiping communities. Some of this music never caught on. Much proved useful only for a short time. Some is used only in particular kinds of communities. But some has achieved widespread acceptance and has become part of a developing core repertory that can be found in nearly every major hymnal and worship resource.

Having now briefly discussed the matters addressed in chapter VI, it is important to point out something that is not mentioned in any of its ten articles, something that many readers might expect to find in a discussion of sacred music in a document of such significant authority and import. The chapter nowhere mentions beauty. It might be argued that beauty in sacred music is simply taken for granted—and that may be true. But it can also be argued that the Council is establishing a new understanding of beauty that may be summed up in these two related principles:

1. Beauty cannot be determined by some kind of "objective" or universal set of standards.

2. New understandings and experiences of beauty will become apparent only after implementation of the reform, with time and experience, and as the sensibilities of dynamic cultures and communities continue to grow and evolve.

This new understanding undergirds this chapter's "both/and" approach, which recognizes established customs and sensibilities and opens the door to new possibilities. But it is also implied early in SC, for the document calls for liturgical commissions to be established by "the competent, territorial ecclesiastical" authorities (national or territorial conference of bishops)[18] and for the development of liturgical commissions in particular dioceses.[19] Certain decisions and judgments are best left to regional local authorities, who through consultative bodies can draw upon the expertise and experience of members of local churches.

MS also confirms an openness to new understandings of beauty when it says, "The real solemnity of a liturgical service, it should be kept in mind, depends not on a more ornate musical style or more ceremonial splendor but on a worthy and reverent celebration."[20] Later the document notes, "A liturgical celebration can have no more solemn or pleasing feature than the whole assembly's expressing its faith and devotion in song."[21] In the reformed liturgy, beauty is not so much a "what" as it is a "how." Beauty is experienced when liturgy is celebrated reverently and worthily, and when the voices of the entire assembly are joined in song.

It is difficult to make general statements or to draw broad conclusions about the practice of liturgical music in the United States today. Liturgy is celebrated in a great many languages, in a wide variety of ethnic and cultural groups, and in parishes large and small, urban and rural. One of the greatest contributions of chapter VI is its "both/and" approach. Healthy creativity is often best fostered not with limitless possibilities, but within parameters that become evident when multiple values are held in tension. Pastoral musicians would do well to keep this perspective in mind as they struggle to find the right balance between two sets of seemingly competing values that present an ongoing challenge: stability and variety; and diversity and unity.

While congregations more readily sing music that is used more frequently, music ministers who perform the same music more often tend to seek greater variety. How can parishes more diligently work to develop a relatively stable, familiar repertory for the congregation while at the same time providing variety for vocal and instrumental ensembles?

And how can parishes better balance the varying musical tastes of parishioners with the need to form disciples who are prepared to live and work in a multicultural society and to interact with people of differing perspectives? What do we say to the world when many of our parishes regularly divide into worshiping groups based upon—of all things—musical taste? How can we recognize varying styles and traditions while at the same time fostering a unity grounded in mutual respect and concern for the needs of others? How can musical choices and practices help the Church to form committed disciples who are ready to become bread broken and blood poured out for the life of the world?

Questions for Discussion and Reflection

1. Do you participate in the singing during Mass? Why or why not?

2. In your experience, what makes for good liturgical music? How do you experience music as integral to worship?

3. How can singing music in a variety of styles—and/or from a variety of cultures—help to form Christians for effective discipleship in a diverse society and world?

4. Does your parish community sing Gregorian chant? What aspect of Church is expressed when we sing music that was sung by generations before us—and that is sung by people of many cultures and language groups?

5. Does music in the liturgy—or do liturgical musicians—ever seem distracting? If so, how? How might this kind of distraction be avoided?

NOTES

1. *Musicam sacram* (MS), 2.

2. Ibid., 4b.

3. See *Tra le sollecitudini* (TLS), 2–6; *Musicae sacrae disciplina* (MSD), 41–43.

4. See MSD, 62–64.

5. See SC, 14. See also articles 16–18 on liturgical studies, and 129 on the history and development of sacred art.

6. SC, 14.

7. See MS, 50a.

8. GIRM, 41.

9. See STL, 75–76.

10. See *Complete English Propers for the High Mass for All Sundays and Principal Feasts*, ed. Paul Arbogast (Cincinnati, Ohio: World Library of Sacred Music, 1964). This volume used adapted Gregorian melodies for antiphons and psalm tones based on Anglican chant for verses. See also *Propers for Sundays and Principal Feasts, Volumes One and Two,* by Richard J. Wojcik and Joseph F. Mytych (Toledo, Ohio: Gregorian Institute of America, 1966). This later volume used adapted Gregorian melodies for antiphons and traditional Gregorian psalm tones for verses.

11. MSD, 62.

12. Ibid., 63.

13. See ibid., 64.

14. See ibid., 66.

15. See *Chirograph of the Supreme Pontiff John Paul II for the Centenary of the Motu Proprio "Tra le sollecitudini" on Sacred Music*, 7 and 11.

16. SC, 38.

17. See MSD, 59.

18. SC, 22 § 2.

19. See ibid., 44–46.

20. MS, 11.

21. Ibid., 16.

✣ CHAPTER VII

Sacred Art and Sacred Furnishings

Sacrosanctum Concilium 122–130

J. Philip Horrigan

The first nine paragraphs of chapter VII (articles 122–130) focus on sacred art and artists and their service to the Sacred Liturgy of the Church. The single sentence of article 130 refers to the appropriate use of papal insignia.

The Church has long been regarded as a great patron of the arts and the vast collection of masterpieces in the Vatican museums and galleries attest to the support the Church has given to artists and the care she has taken of her patrimony. There are also remarkable treasuries located in churches around the world, the result of a desire to preserve and foster the work of artists in a variety of media: painting, sculpture, metalwork, and music.

In addition to the finished work of art, the quality of the design and the integrity of the artists' craft have added to the beauty and worthiness of liturgical furnishings and appointments that have served the liturgical celebrations of the Church for generations.

This is the focus of this section of SC as the Council Fathers restate the role of the Church as the friend of the fine arts and offer their support and appreciation to all artists whose work contributes to the dignity of worship and the deepening of faith.

✣

122. The fine arts are deservedly ranked among the noblest activities of human genius and this applies especially to religious art and to its highest achievement, sacred art. These arts, by their very nature, are oriented toward the infinite beauty of God, which they attempt in

some way to portray by the work of human hands. They are dedicated to advancing God's praise and glory to the degree that they center on the single aim of turning the human spirit devoutly toward God.

The Church has therefore always been the friend of the fine arts, has ever sought their noble help, and has trained artists with the special aim that all things set apart for use in divine worship are truly worthy, becoming, and beautiful, signs and symbols of the supernatural world. The Church has always regarded itself as the rightful arbiter of the arts, deciding which of the works of artists are in accordance with faith, with reverence, and with honored traditional laws and are thereby suited for sacred use.

The Church has been particularly careful to see that sacred furnishings worthily and beautifully serve the dignity of worship and has admitted changes in materials, design, or ornamentation prompted by the progress of the technical arts with the passage of time.

Wherefore it has pleased the Fathers to issue the following decrees on these matters.

The use of the word "decrees" is somewhat ambiguous; the articles that follow outline more *considerations* than specific directives or detailed instructions. Nonetheless, the content of the articles in this section is to be seriously considered when churches are built, renovated, or redecorated.

Previous Church documents that have addressed some of these issues include the *Code of Canon Law* (1917) and the encyclical, *Mediator Dei* (1947) by Pope Pius XII. The *Code* devotes twelve canons to liturgical design and *Mediator Dei* a single paragraph (189). In June 1952, the Sacred Congregation of the Holy Office issued a pastoral instruction *De arte sacra* which indicated the role of the Church in determining what constituted art as sacred and worthy for worship and worship places. In 1955 Pope Pius XII issued the document *Musicae sacrae disciplina* which dealt with the use of sacred music in the liturgy.

Unlike the *Code of Canon Law*, which is a juridical document, and the encyclical which reflects the teaching of the Church, *De arte sacra* and *Musicae sacrae disciplina* are instructions and less authoritative; nonetheless they represent the ongoing concern and attention that the Church places on the importance of the liturgical arts. It should be noted here that the 1917 *Code of Canon Law* was replaced by the 1983 *Code of Canon Law* which devoted a number of canons to the design and care of churches.[1]

This first paragraph of chapter VII of SC sets forth general parameters for the construction, renovation, and ornamentation of churches—a concern that was not addressed in previous documents. Following the Council, bishops, pastors, contractors, and parish committees became more aware of the care that should be taken when choosing the architectural design and arrangement, as well as the arts, furnishings, and appointments that serve the liturgical work of the Church.

123. The Church has not adopted any particular style of art as its very own but has admitted styles from every period, according to the proper genius and circumstances of peoples and the requirements of the many different rites in the Church. Thus, in the course of the centuries, the Church has brought into being a treasury of art that must be very carefully preserved. The art of our own days, coming from every race and region, shall also be given free scope in the Church, on condition that it serves the places of worship and sacred rites with the reverence and honor due to them. In this way contemporary art can add its own voice to that wonderful chorus of praise sung by the great masters of past ages of Catholic faith.

A cursory study of the history of church architecture gives ample evidence that the Church has never espoused a single style of art or architecture as its own. The imagination of architects, designers, and artists has been a great gift to the Church for nearly two thousand years; and the Church has taken care to preserve that gift wherever possible. As the diversity of the Church becomes more apparent in contemporary times, the Church seeks to promote the hand of the artist in ways that would add to the treasury of art already created. Thus, the Church encourages new works of art in every media to be brought forth to enhance the ongoing "chorus of praise" initiated by the great masters of past ages.

This calls for artists to explore their own religious culture and spiritual imagination so that new works of art can be expressions of the faith and spirituality that reflect the breadth and creativity of the Church in the many regions of the world. Those who are engaged in church design projects—bishops, pastors, designers, and artists—are thus encouraged to take to heart the desire of the Church to support them in their efforts to bring to light ever new and refreshing expressions of faith.

124. In encouraging and favoring art that is truly sacred, Ordinaries should strive after noble beauty rather than mere sumptuous display. This principle is to apply also in the matter of sacred vestments and appointments.

Let bishops carefully remove from the house of God and from other places of worship those works of artists that are repugnant to faith and morals and to Christian devotion and that offend true religious sense either by their grotesqueness or by the deficiency, mediocrity, or sham in their artistic quality.

When churches are to be built, let great care be taken that they are well suited to celebrating liturgical services and to bringing about the active participation of the faithful.

The statements of this article have surely caused the most extensive and often divisive debates in recent times on the approach to the design and decoration of liturgical space. Although article 122 of this section indicated that "decrees" were to be followed in the matter of church design, article 124 allows for various interpretations. Words like "noble beauty," "sumptuous display," "deficiency," "mediocrity," or "sham" might be clear to one artist, observer, or patron; they may not mean the same to another artist, observer, or patron.

What is clear from these statements is that bishops, who are addressed as being the ones responsible for discernment and judgment in these matters, are to take seriously the connection between art—good or bad—and the fact that they can enhance or harm the religious sensibilities of the faithful. Underlying this issue of the relationship between art and faith is the understanding that the works of art that adorn places of worship have the capacity to affect the spiritual imagination and sense of divine presence in and of themselves. In a sense, no work of art that is placed in the context of sacred space is entirely innocent.

The direction to bishops to remove works of artists that are considered "repugnant" is surely good advice, though often those works of art had certain emotional attachments and their removal was sometimes seen as intrusive and ill advised. It could be said that this directive was sometimes used to simply remove any work of art that didn't suit the taste of a bishop, pastor, or parish. Beauty may be in the eye of the beholder, but sometimes one beholder has a sense of beauty not shared by others.

Later documents on this issue often use words like "quality" "appropriateness," or "able to bear the weight of mystery"[2] as criteria to assist in making decisions about removing or introducing works of art to liturgical places.

The last sentence of this article is especially significant. It refers to the larger issue of building new churches and the article clearly indicates that the building itself, and by inference its arrangement, should be suited to the active participation of the faithful in the liturgy of the Church. This represents a new approach to church design. No longer is the form, that is, the structure of wood, stone, glass, and steel the primary measure of the building's validity as a place of worship. Instead, it must be designed so as to serve well the function it houses; namely, the active participation of the gathered community of faith. Although no blueprint is set forth for church architecture, it is clear that the liturgical action within the building is the fundamental guide for design, arrangement, and ornamentation. This echoes the words of article 14 of SC where it states that the very nature of the liturgy is centered on the full, conscious, and active participation of all the faithful. Thus it follows that the liturgical space serves and enhances that vision.

---

125. The practice of placing sacred images in churches so that they may be venerated by the faithful is to be maintained. Nevertheless there is to be restraint regarding their number and prominence so that they do not create confusion among the Christian people or foster religious practices of doubtful orthodoxy.

The Church has a long standing and revered tradition of placing sacred images in churches. The most common images depict events in the life of Christ, paintings and sculptures of the Blessed Virgin under the many titles that have been ascribed to her, and images of the saints.

These images, in a variety of artistic expression, have sought to inspire and enrich the devotional life of the faithful. Although the council wishes to maintain the tradition of placing sacred images in churches, it expresses a twofold concern. First, that there can be too many images in a particular church and that they are often located in too prominent positions, thus distracting from the primary focus of the liturgy itself. Second, the number and prominence of sacred images can overshadow the "pride of place" that is reserved for the central objects of the Church's liturgy. The Council's concern is that some confusion could arise as to what is primary and what is secondary in the liturgical space and that religious practices might then develop that are not in keeping with approved devotional practices.

The Council does not give any direction as to the appropriate number of images to be considered, or where they might be suitably placed within the church.

The *General Instruction of the Roman Missal* (GIRM) is slightly more helpful in this matter.[3] It states that images of the Lord, the Blessed Virgin Mary, and the saints should be displayed since this is part of the tradition of the Church and allows for the veneration of the faithful. The GIRM does caution against the number of images, but makes no mention of how many would be too many. It does state, however, that there be only one image of any given saint.

In the *Directory on Popular Piety and the Liturgy* (2002) the Congregation for Divine Worship and Discipline of the Sacraments sets forth some guidelines that would be helpful in this matter. The Congregation makes a distinction between the primacy of the liturgical action of the Church and the secondary nature of devotions. It follows that this distinction should determine where devotional images, which are secondary, should be placed in relation to the more primary items used for the sacred liturgy. The primary consideration in both documents seems to be that all sacred images are of worthy design and materials and that they enrich the devotional life of the faithful.

When parishes renovate or build a new church the devotional life of the whole community needs to be understood and respected. Many parishes have a multicultural demographic and different ethnic communities have particular devotional traditions. Attempts to honor all those traditions, both with the respective image and a suitable site within the liturgical space can be a great challenge. But it can also be a catechetical opportunity for the whole parish to explore the universal identity of the Church through the prayers and practices of those from other cultures and faith traditions.

---

126. When deciding on works of art, local Ordinaries shall give hearing to the diocesan commission on sacred art, and if need be, to others who are especially expert, as well as to

> the commissions referred to in art. 44, 45, and 46. Ordinaries must be very careful to see that sacred furnishings and valuable works of art are not disposed of or damaged, for they are the adornment of the house of God.

The reference to articles 44, 45, and 46 sets the focus of this part of SC to Ordinaries who are to rely on the expertise of others to assist them in promoting the liturgical apostolate in their diocese. One of the forums for this consultation would be a commission on liturgy. A second commission is recommended in article 46, which would devote itself to the areas of liturgical music and the arts. There have been various results of this directive in dioceses. Many did initiate commissions with a broad agenda for considering liturgical matters in the diocese. Other dioceses set up an Office for Worship with a professional staff of consultants in various aspects of liturgy; others appointed ad hoc committees; others hired a director of liturgy who consulted with a volunteer committee on liturgical matters. In some cases neither a commission nor a director of liturgy was part of the diocesan personnel. This scenario is still the case today in many regions. What is clear is that the Council Fathers thought that the liturgical apostolate of the Church, especially in the diocesan Church, was important enough to urge the establishment of responsible forums that would assist the bishop, as the chief liturgist of the diocese, to see that the faithful would be informed and engaged in the liturgical reform and that the liturgical life of the local Church would be vibrant in every community.

The second part of this paragraph became a critical consideration in the years following the Council. As the Church had always been an eminent patron of new artistic expressions, she also had a concern for the preservation of worthy works of art from past generations. As many existing church buildings were renovated following the reform of the liturgy, there arose the issue of what to do with excess, unwanted, and sometimes unused works of art, as well as liturgical furnishings and appointments. Although many items might have been regarded as being of a poor or mediocre quality, or might not have *passed the test* of fine art,[4] there were reports that many objects of art were destroyed. Although the Council could not have foreseen this situation, article 126 has considerable relevance today as dioceses and parishes find themselves having to merge parish communities and close underused churches.

With this in mind, it would be wise for dioceses to have protocols in place that would assist parishes in the reallocation or suitable disposal of unwanted items no longer needed for liturgy or devotional practices. While it is commendable to preserve good works of art, sometimes a new church design does not easily accept artwork from another site, since matters of scale, color, materials, and different pieties need to be considered. Also, one parish community may have a different appreciation for works of art, especially if the cultural identity of the receiving parish is quite different than that of the donor parish. In some situations the community that builds a new church may decide to commission new art from reputable artists and thus contribute new beauty to the patrimony of the Church and encourage new expressions of faith and spirituality.

---

127. Bishops should have a special concern for artists, so as to imbue them with the spirit of sacred art and liturgy. This they may do in person or through competent priests who are gifted with a knowledge and love of art.

It is also recommended that schools or academies of sacred art to train artists be founded in those parts of the world where they seem useful.

All artists who, prompted by their talents, desire to serve God's glory in holy Church, should ever bear in mind that they are engaged in a kind of sacred imitation of God the Creator and are concerned with works intended to be used in Catholic worship, to uplift the faithful, and to foster their devotion and religious formation.

In article 127, the Council Fathers direct their attention to the artists. Bishops are charged with the ministry of supporting artists, to see themselves as teachers of the artist in the spirit of the liturgy and of sacred art itself. Although the Church has a historical reputation as patron and supporter of the arts, SC sees this role as extending to the establishment of institutions that would provide for the education and formation of artists whose work would in turn serve the Church and bring glory to God by its beauty and inspiration.

The bishops are challenged to do this in those parts of the world where such schools or academies might be useful. It is not clear what the word "useful" refers to, but perhaps schools for artists might be especially helpful in those parts of the world where new cultural expressions are being initiated and new artists are coming forth to place their creativity at the service of faith and religious imagination. In the contemporary world of sacred art, many artists have their own studios and are often self-taught or find resources in generic art academies when a school of sacred art is either too distant to access or simply not available. The artist guilds of the past might provide a model for a modern day response to the expectations of SC.

In addition to the study of art, its technique, and its complexity of form the artist is reminded that they have a great gift that lies within their spirit. The artist shares in the very act of creativity that echoes the work of the first artist, God the creator. Every artist is encouraged to be mindful of so great a gift in his or her spirit and to regard their work as sharing in the amazing spirit of God's own creative delight. The craft of the artist is seen as a vehicle that lifts up the faith of God's people and in turn gives praise to both the Creator and the work of creation.

In his *Letter to Artists* (1999), Pope John Paul II explored this wonderful relationship between the creative spirit of the artist and that of God the creator.

---

128. A long with the revision of the liturgical books, as laid down in art. 25, there is to be an early revision of the canons and ecclesiastical statutes regulating the supplying of material things involved in sacred worship. This applies in particular to the worthy and well-planned construction of places of worship, the design and construction of altars, the nobility, placement, and security of the eucharistic tabernacle, the practicality and dignity of the baptistry, the appropriate arrangement of sacred images and church decorations and appointments. Laws that seem less suited to the reformed liturgy are to be brought into harmony with it or else abolished; laws that are helpful are to be retained if already in use or introduced where they are lacking.

With art. 22 of this Constitution as the norm, the territorial bodies of bishops are empowered to make adaptations to the needs and customs of their different regions; this applies especially to the material and design of sacred furnishings and vestments.

This section of chapter VII offers the most encompassing direction for the renovation of existing churches and the building of new ones.

However, the directives are more generous than restrictive and there is much room for interpretation and a diversity of architectural design.

Although article 25 is noted as the beginning point for observing the directions in this paragraph, it is the articles that follow SC 25 that outline the reasons for the directives in this section. The norms in SC 26–31 outline the intent of the reform of the liturgy and the revision of the liturgical books. The reform of the liturgy and the necessary revision of the liturgical books were based on a twofold vision: the liturgy is by nature communal and the various ministers of the liturgy, including the assembly, are encouraged to fully and actively participate in the liturgy. The *Constitution* reiterates this vision in article 123.

The norms in article 128 are intended to further this vision and to give direction on how the design, arrangement, and furnishing of the liturgical space should complement the new understanding and practice of the liturgical action. The hope expressed in this article is that the places for worship should be worthy and well prepared. It is assumed that the preparation process for the modification or building of a new church would take into consideration the ritual needs of the liturgy as outlined in the revised liturgical books. The overriding requirement is that the new or renovated space would serve well the full and active participation of the whole liturgical assembly. The article doesn't specify what previous canons and norms are to be revised or abolished; this determination is left to those who are responsible for the oversight in church design and construction, namely bishops and those in positions of pastoral leadership. It would also mean that architects, consultants, and contractors should be familiar with the ritual expectations of the reformed liturgy.

The article offers a particular concern for altars, the place of Eucharistic reservation, and the baptistry.

The noble design and careful construction of altars is also of particular concern. One example that is addressed in later documents is the material for altars. The universal norm calls for the use of natural stone but allowance is made for other worthy materials.[5]

The place for Eucharistic reservation and the location of the tabernacle has often been a contentious issue in recent years and the interpretation of documents related to this has resulted in more than one specific arrangement. This article doesn't resolve the placement issue but rather underlines the importance of security and nobility. More prescriptive norms are found in later documents[6] and in diocesan guidelines issued under the prerogative of the local bishop.

The reference to the baptistry is a welcome note, if a somewhat incomplete treatment and has reinstated the importance of a specific place—the baptistry for the celebration of the Rites of Initiation. This also recovers the historical importance of the font as a primary liturgical furnishing for the waters of Baptism. The recent history of both the place and the vessel for the Sacrament of Baptism in many churches has not paid much attention to the importance of either in liturgical arrangements. Since the revision of the Rites of Initiation, especially the recovery of the Rite for Christian Initiation of Adults, the baptistry has been given a new visibility in the liturgical space. The introduction of immersion fonts has renewed the powerful symbolism associated with the sacrament as the action of dying and rising in Christ.

The last sentence of this article reminds the local Ordinary of his responsibility in this regard and suggests that he make whatever adaptations are needed within his particular jurisdiction. As a result of this directive many Conferences of Bishops eventually published norms and guidelines related to the renovation and building of new churches.[7] In addition to these national documents many dioceses published guidelines that regulated some aspects of liturgical design within their own dioceses. All of these documents have become valuable resources for parish committees when they engage in a renovation or new church construction project.

---

129. During their philosophical and theological studies, clerics are to be taught about the history and development of sacred art and about the sound principles on which the production of its works must be grounded. In consequence they will be able to appreciate and preserve the Church's treasured monuments and be in a position to offer good advice to artists who are engaged in producing works of art.

This article of SC makes it clear that those (clerics) who are engaged in academic preparation for Ordination are to be exposed to the history and development of sacred art and become familiar with the principles that govern the design and production of worthy art.

It seems that this directive would apply to the curriculum of seminaries, and that knowledgeable instructors, both those in the field of art history as well as practicing artists would be given a forum to instruct students of theology in the nature and role of art for the service of the Church.

As future liturgical leaders, the need for such an appreciation of the place of the arts in the liturgical life of the Church is paramount. The ministry of presiding is itself an art form, and so it stands to reason that presiders of liturgy should have a high regard for the quality of other art forms that sustain good liturgical celebrations for the faithful. This includes music that inspires; liturgical furnishings and appointments that are of worthy design and honest materials; images in different medium that assist the faithful to deepen their spiritual life and that reflect the best that the Church has to offer in the visual arts that adorn places of worship. All forms of art that are suitable in the service of the liturgy are created from the visible material of creation; through the hand of the artist they can inspire others to discover new ways to approach the invisible mystery of the transcendent.

130. It is fitting that the use of pontifical insignia be reserved to those ecclesiastical persons who have either episcopal rank or some definite jurisdiction.

The term "pontifical insignia" generally refers to those items of vesture or objects that belong exclusively to the person and office of the Roman Pontiff. These particular insignia are symbolic of the dignity and power associated with the pope as head of the Church. Examples of such insignia would be the vesture of the pope, for example, the pallium; or objects like the papal cross which the pope carries instead of the more commonly used crozier used by bishops; the papal coat of arms which includes two keys—one silver and one gold—signifying the kingdom of earth and the kingdom of heaven, respectively; and the Ring of the Fisherman which signifies the pope's connection with St. Peter.

The term pontifical insignia also refers to those items associated with the office and order of bishop, including particular vesture (for example, the mitre) and objects (such as the cathedra and the crozier) which are related to the dignity and position of bishops as pastoral leaders in the Church.

The article also mentions others with "some definite jurisdiction." This refers to those who, lacking Episcopal rank, are regarded as prelates of the Church in other offices and positions of authority and to whom is accorded some level of dignity and power.

In the *motu proprio* on *Pontifical Insignia* (June 21, 1968) by Pope Paul VI, one finds a list of those prelates, other than bishops, who are entitled to the use of certain pontifical insignia. The same document outlines the reasons associated with the use of pontifical insignia in the tradition of the Church and references this article from chapter VII of SC.

It is this reference that gives article 130 a context for inclusion in chapter VII. Pope Paul VI notes that there is a heightened awareness of the importance of signs both in the present age and in the understanding of how the true meaning of signs within the liturgy is a concern of the liturgical reform.

Questions for Discussion and Reflection

1. Are the works of art that adorn your church of good quality and honest materials?

2. Do the works of art in your church, especially the images of the Communion of Saints, reflect the cultural traditions of all the members of the community?

3. Is the baptismal font (baptistry) in a dedicated space that allows for all the Rites of Initiation to be celebrated in a suitable manner?

4. Does the baptismal font allow for the gesture of immersion which more fully expresses the theology of the Sacrament of Baptism?

5. Does the arrangement of the liturgical space, especially the place for the assembly, contribute to full and active participation in the liturgy?

6. Does the parish provide opportunities for local artists to study the liturgy and/or contribute of their gifts to the treasury of sacred art in the parish?

7. Consider developing various forums (for example, a parish retreat, mission, evening of reflection) based on this question: How does the sacred and liturgical art in your church enrich your personal spirituality and enhance the communal celebration of the liturgy?

NOTES

1. See canons 934–944 on the Reservation and Veneration of the Blessed Eucharist; and canons 1205–1239 in Part III: Sacred Times and Places.

2. See *Environment and Art in Catholic Worship* (EACW), 20 and 21, and *Built of Living Stones* (BLS), 147 and 148.

3. See GIRM, 318.

4. See SC, 124.

5. See GIRM, 310.

6. See ibid., 314–317.

7. The USCCB published two documents in this matter: *Environment and Art in Catholic Worship*, 1978; and *Built of Living Stones*, 2000—the latter supersedes the 1978 document.

❖ APPENDIX

Declaration of the Second Vatican Ecumenical Council on Revision of the Calendar

Sacrosanctum Concilium 131

Corinna Laughlin

The short appendix to Sacrosanctum Concilium offers a glimpse into a surprisingly lively debate at the time of the Second Vatican Council: the reform of the calendar.

Reform of the calendar is nothing new. Julius Caesar was a calendar reformer, introducing what we call the "Julian calendar" in 46 BC. The Julian calendar was a vast improvement on what came before, but it had its problems—most notably, the calendar year was about ten minutes longer than the solar year. This was not significant over a few years or even a few decades, but after a few hundred years it meant that the calendar and the equinoxes moved farther and farther apart—Easter was moving backward in the calendar year.

The Council of Trent called for a reform of the Julian calendar with Easter in mind. Thus Pope Gregory XIII introduced changes to the Julian system, and instituted a new and somewhat simpler way of calculating the date of Easter. He also moved the start of the year to January 1 (in the Julian calendar, the year began on March 1). Though it took some time, the Gregorian calendar eventually spread across Europe and then across the world. But many Orthodox Churches have continued to use the Julian calendar, which means that Easter and other important feasts are celebrated on different days in the Eastern and Western Churches.

The Gregorian calendar has its own weaknesses. It varies significantly from year to year, and there is no easy way to know on which day of the week the year will begin. In the past two centuries there have been many proposals for change to the Gregorian calendar. During the French Revolution, for example, France rejected the Gregorian calendar altogether, at least in part because of its deeply embedded religious meanings. The seven-day week was eliminated in favor of a ten-day system. In 1834, an Italian priest named Marco Mastrofini proposed a revision to the Gregorian calendar which would include a "non-hebdomadal day," that is, a day falling outside the week itself, which would be inserted in between December 31 and January 1.[1] This adjustment would allow for a perpetual calendar, that is, a calendar which would be the same year after year—if April 26 fell on a Wednesday, it would always fall on a Wednesday. Mastrofini felt that this would simplify both the liturgical calendar and the civil calendar. He also proposed that Easter always be celebrated on a designated Sunday in March or April, rather than moving the feast based on the moon and the vernal equinox—no more movable feasts!

Mastrofini's plan was taken up in the twentieth century by American Elisabeth Achelis, who began the "World Calendar" movement in the 1920s. The plan gained considerable momentum. It was discussed by the League of Nations in the 1930s, and then taken up again by the United Nations in the years following World War II.[2] The discussion was ultimately abandoned, largely because of protests from religious groups, especially in the United States: the Jewish, Christian, and Muslim calendars are all based on the seven-day week, and all of these traditions consider the rhythm of the week to be sacred.

Given the importance of time in the liturgy, it is little wonder that the calendar debate came up at the Council. This brief appendix to SC reveals the openness of the Council Fathers to continuing discussion on reform of the calendar.

While we do not hear much about a perpetual calendar today, questions of the calendar have continued to come up with some regularity as the Church deals with the changing patterns of modern life. One example is the transfer of weekday solemnities (the Ascension of the Lord and the Most Holy Body and Blood of Christ [*Corpus Christi*]) to the nearest Sunday, which has been embraced in some areas, rejected in others. And there are threats to Sunday as well. In his apostolic letter *Dies Domini*, Pope John Paul II acknowledged that "changes in socioeconomic conditions have often led to profound modifications of social behavior and hence of the character of Sunday. The custom of the 'weekend' has become more widespread."[3] And when Sunday becomes part of a weekend, it makes it more challenging for Christians to preserve its meaning and to set it apart as a sacred day. Since the sanctification of time is at the heart of our worship, we can anticipate that debate on this subject is not yet concluded.

---

131. The Second Vatican Ecumenical Council recognizes the importance of the wishes expressed by many on assigning the feast of Easter to a fixed Sunday and on an unchanging calendar and has considered the effects that could result from the introduction of a new calendar. Accordingly the Council issues the following declaration:

1. The Council is not opposed to the assignment of the feast of Easter to a particular Sunday of the Gregorian Calendar, provided those whom it may concern, especially other Christians who are not in communion with the Apostolic See, give their assent.

2. The Council likewise declares that it does not oppose measures designed to introduce a perpetual calendar into civil society.

Among the various systems being suggested to establish a perpetual calendar and to introduce it into civil life, only those systems are acceptable to the Church that retain and safeguard a seven-day week with Sunday and introduce no days outside the week, so that the present sequence of weeks is left intact, unless the most serious reasons arise. Concerning these the Apostolic See will make its own judgment.

The Fathers of the Council have given assent to all and to each part of the matters set forth in this Constitution. And together with the venerable Fathers, we, by the apostolic power given to us by Christ, approve, enact, and establish in the Holy Spirit each and all the decrees in this Constitution and command that what has been thus established in the Council be promulgated for the glory of God.

The Council Fathers express a certain openness to the introduction of a perpetual calendar and a fixed Sunday for Easter. But the language is tentative. The Council "is not opposed" to changing the date of Easter, and "does not oppose" the idea of a perpetual calendar. Certainly we do not hear in this passage the enthusiasm and urgency we sense elsewhere in SC and throughout the documents of the Second Vatican Council. Changes to the calendar must give way before the greater value of ecumenism. The Church will entertain the idea only if other Christian denominations support it as well.

The Council Fathers offer a significant caveat. They are open to the concept a perpetual calendar, but they reject the "days outside the week" which were the key to the World Calendar, the plan which had the most widespread support at the time. The value of the "seven-day week with Sunday" is far greater than the uniformity and simplicity of a perpetual calendar. Only in the case of "the most serious reasons" would such a scheme be acceptable, and then the final decision would be referred to Rome. It is easy to guess at what those "serious reasons" might be—if such a calendar were to be implemented in civil life around the world, the Church would need to decide whether to stick with the Gregorian calendar, or adapt to the times. As Pierre Jounel observes in quoting this passage, "The rhythm of the week and the celebration of this day that was both the first and the eighth were always considered to be the fundamental points of reference in relation to which time was organized within Christianity. The *Declaration* . . . makes all this explicitly clear."[4]

Sacrosanctum Concilium ends with the words by which Pope Paul VI formally promulgated the document on December 4, 1963, after the final vote had been taken. This formula, which would be repeated for the other documents produced by the Council, emphasizes the unity both of SC itself—"all and to each part"—and of the Council Fathers, who approved it so overwhelmingly.

The formula is itself the fruit of the Council. During the second session, including the weeks immediately preceding the vote on SC, there had been a vigorous and sometimes bitter debate around the *schema* on the Church, which would become the document *Lumen gentium*. A particularly thorny issue was collegiality, that is, the sharing of the body or "college" of bishops with the Holy Father in the leadership of the Church.[5] Pope Paul VI expressed his support for collegiality in the way he promulgated SC. In the Council of Trent, for example, the formula was quite different: the pope acknowledged the advice and consent of the Council Fathers, but he promulgated the teachings on his own authority. Here, Pope Paul VI not only acknowledges the support of the bishops for the teachings contained in SC, but, he "approve[s], enact[s], and establish[es]" those teachings, not alone, but "together with the venerable Fathers" and in the Holy Spirit.

When he heard these words, Yves Congar, OP—the theologian whose work had such a profound impact on the teachings of the Council, particularly on *Lumen gentium*—wrote: "I breathed a sigh of relief. The formula is good."[6]

Sacrosanctum Concilium guided the liturgical reforms and thus brought the reforms of the Council to every parish and to every Catholic. But this document did even more: in many ways it prepared the way for the other great teachings of the Second Vatican Council.

Questions for Discussion and Reflection

1. How do you react to the concept of "non-hebdomadal" days, days outside the seven-day week? Why?

2. Why is the seven-day week so important in our liturgy and theology?

3. Where do you experience friction between the civil calendar and the liturgical calendar, between secular and sacred understandings of time?

NOTES

1. Adolf Adam, trans. Matthew J. O'Connell, *The Liturgical Year: Its History and Meaning after the Reform of the Liturgy*, New York: Pueblo, 1981, p. 293.

2. Molly E. K. McGrath, "The Elisabeth Achelis Story." Available from: www.theworldcalendar.org/TWCA-Then.htm; accessed on April 24, 2013.

3. *Dies Domini*, 4.

4. Pierre Jounel, *The Liturgy and Time*, Volume IV of *The Church at Prayer*, ed. A. G. Martimort, trans. Matthew J. O'Connell. Collegeville, Minnesota: The Liturgical Press, 1986, p. 3.

5. See *Lumen gentium*, 22-25.

6. Yves Congar, OP, *My Journal of the Council*. Collegeville, Minnesota: The Liturgical Press, 2012, p. 466.

Additional Questions for Discussion and Reflection

After having read the entire text of Sacrosanctum Concilium *(SC) and the corresponding commentaries, please reflect as a diocesan or parish staffs, diocesan or parish teams, small faith communities, or as individuals on the following questions.*

1. Why have you chosen to take this opportunity to study SC? What are you hoping to get out of this experience?

2. What understanding did you have about the origins of the Second Vatican Council prior to now? How would you have summed up the impact of the Second Vatican Council prior to beginning this course of study?

3. Do you have any personal memories, or have you heard stories from family members, about what it was like to experience this period of liturgical reform in the Church?

4. How do you feel that the Church continues to sustain her tradition and reach a contemporary audience today?

5. Why is it important to study SC today—fifty years past the Council?

6. How does SC continue to form and shape our liturgical preparations and our understanding of the liturgy?

7. What in SC did you surprising? Inspiring? Formational?

8. What have been the successes in implementing SC in your parish, in your diocese, and in the universal Church?

9. What parts of SC do you think still need to be received?

10. What areas of liturgical implementation, catechesis, and formation are needed in your parish, your diocese, or in the universal Church?

11. Is there an article of SC that you particularly favor?

12. Fifty years after the Council, what kind of catechesis should be done to help people connect active participation in the liturgy and participation in social responsibility?

13. Do you think that a fifty-year distance from the Council provides some perspective to understanding the Council? What do you think is in store for the next fifty years?

14. After reading SC, what are you now inspired to do with your liturgical preparations and ministry?

15. What is SC asking of us when it states in article 14, "In the reform and promotion of the liturgy, this full and active participation by all the people is the aim to be considered before all else"? What does this mean for your liturgical preparation? For the future?

16. SC calls liturgy the "summit and fount" of our life of faith (SC, 10). To what degree does this describe your experience? Does it correspond with the attitude of people in your parish? Why or why not?

About the Authors

ARCHBISHOP GREGORY MICHAEL AYMOND, as the fourteenth Archbishop of New Orleans, holds the unique distinction of being the first New Orleans native to serve as Archbishop of New Orleans in the 216-year history of the local Church. He was born in Gentilly, Louisiana, on November 12, 1949. He graduated from St. Joseph Seminary College in St. Benedict, Louisiana, in 1971 and earned a master's degree in divinity from Notre Dame Seminary in New Orleans in 1975. Aymond was ordained a priest that same year.

From 1973 to 1981, he was professor, business administrator, and then rector of St. John Vianney Prepartory Seminary in New Orleans. From 1981 to 1986, he was professor of pastoral theology and homiletics and director of pastoral education at Notre Dame Seminary. The bishop served as president-rector of Notre Dame Seminary from 1986 until the end of the 1999–2000 academic year, longer than any rector in the seminary's history. He also was a member of the seminary faculty for eighteen years. During his tenure, Notre Dame Seminary grew to become the third-largest seminary in the country. Bishop Aymond also served as the executive director of the archdiocesan Department of Christian Formation, with responsibility for Catholic schools and religious education, and as the archdiocesan director of the Society for the Propagation of the Faith.

He made mission work a strong emphasis of his ministry. In the 1980s, Bishop Aymond and groups of Notre Dame seminarians began to visit Sotuto, Mexico, where they built housing and offered religious training. In 1994, he began a medical mission program in Nicaragua called "Christ the Healer," taking volunteer teams of health care professionals to the town of Granada to offer medical help at San Juan de Dios Hospital.

Archbishop Aymond was ordained an auxiliary bishop of New Orleans in 1997 and became coadjutor bishop of Austin in 2000, succeeding to head the diocese. Archbishop Aymond has served as chairman of the United States Bishops' Committee on the Protection of Children and Young People. He was also the chairman of the Board of Directors of the National Catholic Education Association from 2000 to 2004. He currently serves as a member of the United States Bishops'

Committee on Laity, Marriage, Family Life and Youth and the Committee on Clergy, Consecrated Life and Vocations and is the chairman of the United States Bishops' Committee on Divine Worship.

JOSHUA R. BROMMER, STB, STL, is a native of Lancaster county Pennsylvania and a priest of the Diocese of Harrisburg. He is a 2002 graduate of the Pontifical College Josephinum College of Liberal Arts where he earned a BA in philosophy and English literature. His graduate studies, within the seminary formation of the Pontifical North American College, Rome, took place at the Pontifical Gregorian University, Rome, where he earned a STB (2005) and STL (2007) with a specialization in dogmatic (systematic) theology. His licentiate studies focused on sacramental theology and the doctrine of grace. In the Diocese of Harrisburg, he has served as parochial vicar in Gettysburg, Hershey, and Mechanicsburg, and, most recently, served as the administrative assistant to Bishop Joseph McFadden. Presently, he is the administrator of Saint John the Baptist parish, New Freedom, Pennsylvania, and the liturgical coordinator of the Diocese of Harrisburg. Fr. Brommer teaches regularly in the catechetical Diocesan Institute, has taught in the formation program for permanent deacons, and regularly offers presentations on theological, sacramental, and liturgical matters in the Diocese of Harrisburg and throughout the region. Brommer is a regular contributor to *The Catholic Witness*, the Harrisburg diocesan newspaper, offering during the Year of Faith his insights on the documents of the Second Vatican Council. He is a member of the Federation of Diocesan Liturgical Commissions, Region III, serves as the chairman of the Harrisburg Diocesan Commission on the Sacred Liturgy, and is the author of LTP's *Imbued with the Spirit of the Liturgy: Ten Insights from Vatican II's "Constitution on the Sacred Liturgy."* Rev. Brommer provided commentary on SC 5–13.

JOSEPH DEGROCCO, DMIN, pastor of Our Lady of Perpetual Help Church, Lindenhurst, New York, and former professor of liturgy and director of liturgical formation at the Seminary of the Immaculate Conception in Huntington, New York, holds an MA in theology (liturgical studies) from the University of Notre Dame and a doctor of ministry degree from the Seminary of the Immaculate Conception. He is the author of *A Pastoral Commentary on the General Instruction of the Roman Missal*, the *Dictionary of Liturgical Terms*, *The Church at Worship: Theology, Spirituality and Practice of Parish Liturgy*, the "Q & A" column in *Pastoral Liturgy* (all from LTP), and is a member of his diocese's Liturgical Commission.

MICHAEL S. DRISCOLL, PHD, STD, is a presbyter of the Diocese of Helena and an associate professor of sacramental theology and liturgy at the University of Notre Dame. Besides having a theoretical appreciation of the liturgy, he is actively involved in pastoral practice: he has worked as choir director of the Cathedral of St. Helena and as a liturgical consultant across the country. He is the founding director of the graduate program in sacred music and the undergraduate minor in liturgical music ministry at the University of Notre Dame. He is the current president of the Catholic Academy of Liturgy and is past president of the North American Academy of Liturgy. Rev. Driscoll provided commentary on SC 14–20.

DAVID W. FAGERBERG, STM, PHD is associate professor in the Department of Theology at the University of Notre Dame. He holds an MDiv from Luther Northwestern Seminary; an MA from St. John's University, Collegeville; an STM from Yale Divinity School; and the PHD from Yale University. His work explores how the Church's *lex credendi* (law of belief) is founded upon the Church's *lex orandi* (law of prayer). He is the author of *The Size of Chesterton's Catholicism* (Notre Dame Press, 1998); *Theologia Prima* (Liturgy Training Publications, 2003); and *On Liturgical Asceticism* (Catholic University Press, 2013). Dr. Fagerberg provided the introductory commentary for Chapter I.

MARK FRANCIS, CSV, SLD, is a native of Chicago and holds an MDiv and an MA in theology from the Catholic Theological Union. Ordained in 1982 and having served for three years in Bogotá, Colombia, Mark studied in Rome and obtained a doctorate in sacred liturgy (SLD) from the Pontifical Liturgical Institute of Sant'Anselmo in 1988. For twelve years he taught liturgy at CTU and was a regular lecturer at the Liturgy Institute of Chicago (a program of liturgical formation for lay pastoral ministers run by the Archdiocese) and its Spanish language counterpart. Mark also served on the revision/translation subcommittee of ICEL (the International Commission on English in the Liturgy). He has written numerous articles on liturgical topics and is especially interested in the relationship between liturgy and culture. Among his many articles and several books, he is the author of *Shape A Circle Ever Wider: Inculturating the Liturgy in the United States* (LTP). In July of 2000 Mark was elected superior general of his religious community, the Viatorians, and currently resides in Rome. Although principally responsible for his religious community in sixteen countries around the world, he is a regular lecturer at the Pontifical Liturgical Institute of St. Anselm and was elected by the Union of Superiors General to be a participant at the recent Bishops' Synod on the Eucharist, held at the Vatican in October of 2005.

GENEVIEVE GLEN, OSB, MA, is a Benedictine nun of the contemplative Abbey of St. Walburga in Virginia Dale, Colorado. She holds master's degrees in systematic theology from St. John's University, Collegeville, Minnesota, and in spirituality from the Catholic University of America in Washington, DC, where she also did extensive doctoral studies in liturgy. She has lectured and written extensively on the Church's rites for the sick and dying. She is coauthor of the *Handbook for Ministers of Care, Second Edition* (Liturgy Training Publications) and contributing editor of *Recovering the Riches of Anointing: A Study of the Sacrament of the Sick* (Liturgical Press).

J. PHILIP HORRIGAN, STB, MED, MTH, DMIN, is a presbyter of the Archdiocese of Kingston, Ontario, Canada. As a pastor he was responsible for starting a new parish and leading a parish through a new church building project. He served as the director of the Department of Art and Architecture, Office for Divine Worship, Archdiocese of Chicago (1997–2009). He acted as a resource/consultant for those parishes involved in building or renovation projects. He is an independent liturgical design consultant on several projects in Canada and the United States. He is a frequent speaker at conferences and workshops on topics related to the building and renovation of liturgical spaces; the liturgical environment; and the history, documents, and components of liturgical design. His particular interest is understanding and exploring the relationship between ritual space and ritual event. In addition to chapter VII, Rev. Horrigan provided the commentary for SC 41–42.

STEVEN R. JANCO, MCM, STL, DMIN, is director of the Rensselaer Program of Church Music and Liturgy at Saint Joseph's College in Rensselaer, Indiana, which offers summer study leading to master's degrees in church music and pastoral liturgy, as well as a number of three-day intensives—including its long-standing Gregorian Chant Institute. A composer of liturgical music, his published works include three Mass settings written for the texts of third edition of *The Roman Missal*. He has had articles and reviews published in a number of liturgy and liturgical music journals. He is a member of the North American Academy of Liturgy, the Catholic Academy of Liturgy, the National Association of Pastoral Musicians, and the National Association for Lay Ministry. He is also a life member of the Hymn Society in the United States and Canada and has served on the society's executive committee.

CORINNA LAUGHLIN, PHD, is the director of liturgy for St. James Cathedral in Seattle. She also serves on the Liturgical Commission for the Archdiocese of Seattle. She coauthored *The Liturgical Ministry Series: Guide for Sacristans* and *The Liturgical Ministry Series: Guide for Servers* (both LTP), and is a frequent contributor to *Sourcebook for Sundays, Seasons, and Weekdays: The Almanac for Parish Liturgy.* Corinna has also written articles for *Pastoral Liturgy*, *Today's Liturgy*, *Ministry & Liturgy*, and *AIM: Liturgy Resources*. She holds a doctorate in English from the University of Washington and a bachelor's degree in English from Mount Holyoke College. In addition to the pastoral notes and appendix, Dr. Laughlin provided commentary on SC 43–46.

PAUL TURNER, STD, is pastor of St. Anthony Parish in Kansas City, Missouri. A priest of the Diocese of Kansas City–St. Joseph, he holds a doctorate in sacred theology from Sant'Anselmo in Rome. His publications include *At the Supper of the Lamb* (Chicago: Liturgy Training Publications, 2011); *Glory in the Cross* (Collegeville: Liturgical Press,

2011); *ML Bulletin Inserts* (San Jose: Resource Publications, 2012); and *Celebrating Initiation: A Guide for Priests* (Chicago: World Library Publications, 2008). He is a former president of the North American Academy of Liturgy and a team member for the North American Forum on the Catechumenate. He is a member of *Societas Liturgica* and the Catholic Academy of Liturgy. He serves as a facilitator for the International Commission on English in the Liturgy.

MARK E. WEDIG, OP, PHD is a Dominican friar of the Province of St. Martin de Porres, the associate dean for graduate studies, professor, and chair of the Department of Theology and Philosophy, College of Arts and Sciences, Barry University in Miami Shores, Florida. He holds a PHD in liturgical studies from the Catholic University of America. His scholarly interests lie at the intersection of liturgy, the hermeneutics of visual Christianity, and culture studies. He is an active member of the North American Academy of Liturgy, the Catholic Academy of Liturgy, the American Academy of Religion, and the Catholic Theological Society of America. Wedig contributed to *A Commentary on the Order of Mass of The Roman Missal* (Liturgical Press, 2011) and *A Commentary on the General Instruction of the Roman Missal 2002* (Liturgical Press, 2007). Rev. Wedig provided commentary for SC 21–40.

JOYCE ANN ZIMMERMAN, CPPS, PHD, STD, is the director of the Institute for Liturgical Ministry in Dayton, Ohio; adjunct professor of liturgy at the Athenaeum of Ohio; a liturgical consultant; frequent speaker and facilitator of workshops on liturgy, spirituality, and other related topics; and an award-winning author of numerous books and articles on liturgy and spirituality. She is the recipient of the Notre Dame Center for Liturgy 2008 Michael Mathis Award and the 2010 Georgetown Center for Liturgy National Award for Outstanding Contributions to the Liturgical Life of the American Church. She is a theological consultant to the United States Conference of Catholic Bishops' Committee on Divine Worship.

Index

acclamations: SC 30

acolytes: SC 29

adaptations: SC 24, 37–40, 44, 62, 107, 119, 128

altar: SC 128

Anointing of the Sick, Sacrament of: SC 73–75;

art, liturgical/sacred artists: SC 122, 124, 127, 129
- criteria for: SC 125, 129
- fine art: SC 122
- general: SC 44, 46, 112, 122–130
- role of in liturgies: SC 127
- sacred art: SC 122-130
- types of: SC 46, 122–28

Ascension: SC 102

assembly: SC 33, 114, 121

Baptism, Sacrament of
- adaptations of: SC 30–33
- catechumenate: SC 64, 66
- connection to other sacraments/ Christian life: SC 10, 14
- danger of death: SC 68
- font: SC 128
- godparents/sponsors: SC 67
- meaning of: SC 6, 10
- parents: SC 67
- renewal of baptismal promises: SC 71
- requirements for (matter and form): SC 64–70
- revision of baptismal rites: SC 66–70
- rights of the baptized: SC 14, 54
- Sunday observances: SC: 14
- water/blessed or holy water/ baptismal water/blessing of water/ sprinkling: SC 70

blessings: SC 57, 78, 79

Bible services: SC 35

bishops
- as diocesan leaders: SC 22, 44–45
- liturgical adaptations by: SC 36, 39, 77, 120
- role in liturgies: SC 41–42

calendar, Church: SC 131

catechesis: SC 14, 16, 18, 24, 35, 56, 109

catechist(s): SC 68

charity: SC, 9, 47, 59

Christ
- nature of liturgy: SC 5–7
- prayer of: SC 83–84
- presence of: SC 7
- priesthood of: SC 7

Christian death
- children: SC 82
- Christ's Death: SC 5, 6, 47, 61
- music for funerals: SC 81–82
- paschal character: SC, 81
- revision of funeral rites: SC 48–56

churches
- building and renovation of: SC 124, 128
- decoration of: SC 125, 128
- furnishings for: SC 122–28
- role of cathedrals: SC 41

clergy
- bishops: SC 13, 20, 22, 25, 26, 35, 36, 41, 42, 45, 55, 57, 76, 79, 114, 124, 127
- deacons: SC 35.4, 68, 86
- pastors: SC 11, 14, 19, 42, 56, 100, 114
- training: SC 14–18, 115, 129

collaboration: SC 46

commentators: SC 29

commission (international, diocesan, liturgical): SC 44–46, 126 concelebration: SC 57, 58

conference(s) of bishops: SC 57, 128

Confirmation, Sacrament of: SC 71

Council of Trent: SC 55

devotions/sacramentals
- Connection to the Liturgy: SC 7, 13
- encouragement for: SC 13, 118
- revision of: SC 13, 7

Divine Office/Liturgy of the Hours
- component hours: SC 88, 94
- elements of: SC 83–85, 90
- importance of: SC 84, 88
- miscellaneous celebrations: SC 100
- music for: SC 93
- revision of: SC 89–101

Eucharist, Sacrament of:
- bread: SC 6
- communion under both forms: SC 55
- meaning of: SC 2, 6, 7, 10, 41, 47–56
- nature of: SC 5–9, 48–56, 106
- Paschal Mystery: SC 5–9, 106
- reception of Holy Communion: SC 30, 55
- revision of rites: SC 58–56

formation: SC 14, 17, 105, 127

fount: SC 10, 61

Funerals, Order of Christian: SC 81–82

gestures: SC 30

Holy Orders, Sacrament of: SC 76

homilies
- character and purpose of: SC 52
- connection to Scripture: SC 24
- place in liturgy: SC 53, 78
- preparation for: SC 35, 52

imbued with the spirit: SC 14, 17, 29

inculturation
- general principles: SC 37–40, 65, 68, 119
- use of vernacular language: SC 36, 54, 63, 101

lay faithful/laity
- formation/catechesis: SC 3, 14, 16, 18, 35, 56, 105, 109
- ministers: SC 28–29, 79

liturgical books: SC 25, 31, 38–39, 128

liturgical year
- Advent: SC 35.4
- Easter (Time): SC 70, 102, 131
- feasts of the saints: SC 108, 111
- Good Friday: SC 110;
- Holy Thursday: SC 57
- Lent: SC 34.4, 109, 110
- meaning of: SC 102
- Pentecost: SC 102
- revision of: SC 107–11
- Sunday: SC 42, 49, 106 131
- seasons: SC 107–10

Liturgy of the Eucharist
- relationship to Liturgy of the Word: SC 56

Liturgy of the Hours: SC 83–85, 89–101

Liturgy of the Word
- elements and nature of: SC 24
- relationship to Liturgy of the Eucharist: SC 56

Marriage, Sacrament of: SC 77–78

Mary (Blessed Virgin Mary): SC 103
- ritual Masses: SC 67

Missal: SC 58, 66

mission: SC 6, 38, 40.3, 65, 68, 119

music, liturgical/sacred
- chants: SC 116–17
- choir(s): SC 29, 89, 95–96, 99, 101, 114, 121
- composers: SC 121

general principles: SC 112–14, 118–19, 121
Gregorian chant: SC 116, 117
instrumentalists: SC 120
mucisians: SC 115
organ: SC 120
singing: SC 7, 8, 33, 54, 83, 104, 113, 115

mystery, experience of: SC 115

noble simplicity: SC 34

participation, liturgical: SC 12, 14, 19, 26, 27, 30, 41, 50, 55, 113-114, 121, 124

Paschal Mystery: SC 5–6, 61, 104, 106, 107, 109

pastoral care of the sick
Anointing of the Sick: SC 73–75
danger of death: SC 73; PCS 174, 175
Extreme Unction: SC 73
presence, Christ's (Four-Fold presence): SC 7, 35
Viaticum: SC 74

psalms: SC 90–91

radio and television: SC 20

readers: SC 29

Reconciliation (Penance), Sacrament of: SC 72, 110

redemption: SC 2, 5, 102–103, 107; IO 55

responses: SC 30

rites, liturgical
character of: SC 3–4, 21, 34, 50, 62
sacraments, nature of: SC 7, 27, 36, 59, 63

sacrifice: SC 2, 6, 7, 10, 12, 47, 49, 55

saints: SC 8, 92, 104, 108, 111
relics of: SC 111

Scripture: SC 6, 7, 16, 24, 35, 51, 52, 90, 92, 112, 121,

Second Vatican Council: SC 1, 3, 4, 14, 21, 43, 49, 56, 57, 62, 77, 87, 105, 112, 131

server: SC 29

silence: SC 30

source and summit: SC 10, 14, 35, 90

statues and images: SC 125

study: SC 15–16, 115

symbols: SC 122

tabernacle: SC 128

texts, liturgical: SC 25, 31, 38

Universal Prayer: SC 12, 53–54

vestments: SC 124, 128

women: SC 101; IO 18